More Praise for *Late Bloomers*:

"*Late Bloomers* is a profoundly important book. It will immeasurably and happily improve the lives of millions of kids, parents, baby boomers—just about all of us."
—Steve Forbes, chairman and editor in chief of Forbes Media

"A gem. A remarkable quality of humankind is our 'contagion' to the emotions, thoughts, and behaviors of those around us. At times, this quality can be destructive, as with the absurd overvaluing of early achievement in our culture. Karlgaard tackles this head on. He calls 'the emperor has no clothes' on this preoccupation, while making an articulate and elegant argument that developmentally informed parenting and education should value patience, experience, and wisdom."
—Dr. Bruce Perry, M.D., Ph.D., senior fellow at the ChildTrauma Academy; professor of psychiatry and behavioral sciences at the Feinberg School of Medicine, Northwestern University; author of *The Boy Who Was Raised as a Dog*

"Rich Karlgaard's *Late Bloomers* shines a much-needed light on an essential human truth—that each one of us can realize our gifts and unlock our full potential, whether we're an early achiever or a late bloomer. As he shows, life is not a race, it's a journey."
—Arianna Huffington, founder and CEO of Thrive Global

"In *Late Bloomers*, Rich Karlgaard makes the important case that our society and our communities suffer when we don't embrace different pathways for unique individuals."
—Diane Tavenner, cofounder and CEO of Summit Public Schools

"Karlgaard captures the truth about human development. We are all wonderfully gifted, and with patience and the right circumstances, we can all bloom in amazing ways."
—Todd Rose, director of the Mind, Brain, and Education Program at Harvard University and author of *The End of Average* and *Dark Horse*

"*Late Bloomers* is absolutely on target. Our capacity to succeed does not expire—it is never 'too late' to discover our potential. In the military, young officers often seek advice from the battle-scarred sergeants whom they technically outrank. Leveraging the wisdom of experience is often the difference between victory and defeat."
—General Stanley McChrystal, retired commander of the U.S. Joint Special Operations Command and author of *Team of Teams*

"We need a national conversation about the insane levels of performance pressure and anxiety our young people carry. We need inspiration about the power of patience in lives that can flourish at their own pace. Rich Karlgaard's *Late Bloomers* is brilliant, wonderfully readable, and urgently needed. I hope it is read and digested by millions."

—John Ortberg, senior pastor of Menlo Church and author of
Eternity Is Now in Session

"*Late Bloomers* reads like a message of hope. It encourages us all to deconstruct who we were before the world imposed upon us what they thought we should be."

—Erik Wahl, performance artist, motivational speaker, and author
of *The Spark and The Grind*

"Rich Karlgaard destroys myths that hold us back. If you're aspiring to greatness in any field at any age, read this book."

—Robert C. Wolcott, chairman and cofounder of TWIN Global
and clinical professor of innovation at the Kellogg School of
Management, Northwestern University

"In our hyper-competitive society that pushes every child to be a Nobel Prize winner, Olympic athlete, and concert cellist by age eighteen, this book lets readers breathe a big, relaxing sigh of relief. *Late Bloomers* reminds us that life is a long, wonderful journey, and that people need a healthy exploration period as they find their lane. Filled with inspiring anecdotes, hard science, cautionary tales, and the author's own meandering path to spectacular success, this is a book you won't put down."

—Ted Dintersmith, venture capitalist, education change agent,
author of *What School Could Be*, and producer of the award-winning
documentary *Most Likely to Succeed*

"While popular culture loves the remarkable success stories of youthful 'wunderkinds,' Karlgaard makes a compelling case for the potential of those who apply their accumulated powers of resilience, insight, and wisdom to achieve greatness later in life. Karlgaard transforms the term 'late bloomer' from mere faint praise to a badge of honor, freeing you to find a personal path to success at your own pace. He makes one proud to be a late bloomer."

—Tom Kelley, coauthor of *Creative Confidence*

"Rich Karlgaard shows that late bloomers are really not late at all, but rather individuals who are out of step with our society's fascination with, and overemphasis on, early exceptional achievement. *Late Bloomers* is an important book—not only for late bloomers or those who think they may be, but also for their parents and their teachers, their spouses and their employers."

—Dr. Jeffrey Prater, clinical psychologist of family systems therapy

"Thank you, Rich Karlgaard, for exposing the American obsession with early achievement. Thank you for defending all of us late bloomers, and for reminding everyone that we all have incredible potential, journeys, and destinations."

—Daniel Struppa, president of Chapman University

Late Bloomers

The Power of Patience
in a World Obsessed
with Early Achievement

Rich Karlgaard

CURRENCY
NEW YORK

CURRENCY and its colophon are trademarks of Penguin Random
House LLC.

Currency books are available at special discounts for bulk purchases
for sales promotions or corporate use. Special editions, including
personalized covers, excerpts of existing books, or books with
corporate logos, can be created in large quantities for special needs.
For more information, contact Premium Sales at (212) 572-2232 or
e-mail specialmarkets@penguinrandomhouse.com.

Library of Congress Cataloging-in-Publication Data
Names: Karlgaard, Rich.
Title: Late bloomers : the power of patience in a world obsessed with
    early achievement / By Rich Karlgaard.
Description: First edition | Currency : New York, [2019] | Includes
    bibliographical references and index.
Identifiers: LCCN 2018044360 | ISBN 9781524759759 |
    ISBN 9781524759766 (Ebook)
Subjects: LCSH: Success. | Self-realization. | Older people. |
    Middle-aged persons.
Classification: LCC BF637.S8 K365 2019 | DDC 158.1—dc23
    LC record available at https://lccn.loc.gov/2018044360

ISBN 978-1-5247-5975-9
Ebook ISBN 978-1-5247-5976-6

Printed in the United States of America

*Charts on page 178 by Human Kinetics, Inc.; all other charts
by Mapping Specialists
Jacket design by Lucas Heinrich*

10 9 8 7 6 5 4 3 2 1

First Edition

For late bloomers of all ages,
Destiny has called our names

Contents

It's not our fault.

It's not our fault that we failed to earn straight A's, make perfect College Board scores, and get into our first choice of college. Or that we were distracted by life at age twenty-one and missed our first on ramp to an enchanted career that matched perfectly our talents and passions. It's not our fault that we failed to earn millions of dollars by twenty-two and billions by thirty—thus getting ourselves on the cover of *Forbes*—or to end malaria, solve tensions in the Middle East, advise a president, or win our third Academy Award by thirty-five.

It's not our fault, and we're not a failure in any sense just because our star didn't glow white hot from the start. And yet early twenty-first-century society has conspired to make us feel shame for exactly that, for not exploding out of the starting blocks like an Olympic sprinter—for not blooming early. By using the word *conspired* here, I'm not suggesting a conspiracy of shady characters who've decided in a secret room to rig the economy and its financial and social rewards for early bloomers. The conspiracy I speak of is real, but it is not evil. It consists of us. What I suggest is that parents, schools, employers, the media, and consumers of media are now crazily overcelebrating early achievement as the best kind of achievement or even the only kind. We do so at the cost of shaming the late bloomer and thus shortchanging people and society.

It wasn't always so.

. . .

Joanne, fifty-three, is a late bloomer. Her teenage years were unstable and unhappy. Her mother suffered from multiple sclerosis. Her father earned enough money to support the household, but he was too emotionally frozen to deal with his wife's illness. Joanne and her father barely spoke to each other.

In school, Joanne blended into the background. She earned above-average grades but hardly good enough to earn high honors and distinction. A teacher recalls Joanne as bright but unexceptional. An introvert, Joanne passed through high school with few remembering her. She was rejected by the elite college of her dreams. At her fallback college, she kept up her practice of acceptable mediocrity. She was good enough to get by but little more. According to one professor, she showed passion not for academic work but for alternative rock music, to which she dreamily listened for hours a day.

Typical of many reasonably bright, unfocused college grads, Joanne entertained thoughts of grad school, perhaps in teaching English. But her first swing at full-time employment was more humbling, a low-level administrative job. For a while, she was a secretary at the local chamber of commerce office.

Bored, Joanne impulsively married a man from a different country she'd met on a lark. They had a baby girl. But theirs was a marriage of opposites—she was dreamy and passive; he was volatile with an implied streak of violence. The marriage didn't survive two years despite the child. They divorced amid hints of domestic abuse.

At nearly thirty, Joanne saw herself at a dead end, with no job and a dependent child. Perhaps not surprisingly, she began to spiral down. She was diagnosed with clinical depression and occasionally thought about suicide. Her depression prevented her from working much and earning money. She hit an economic bottom: "I was as poor as possible without being homeless," she says. Making matters worse, her ex-husband began stalking her and her daughter, forcing her to seek a restraining order.

But Joanne had something going for her, a unique talent that no one else knew she possessed. Her formal education hadn't unearthed it. No teacher had seen it. Her classmates had no idea. But it was there all along, her very own awesome, waiting to be discovered. In the months after Joanne hit economic bottom and went on welfare to feed her daughter, she let her imagination drift to her childhood fantasies. It was an act of escapism that society said was irresponsible. But oddly enough, it took her closer to her gift. Only when Joanne let go and let her imagination run loose did her talent begin to surface in spectacular fashion.

Ken, sixty-eight, is another late bloomer. The youngest of three, his family nickname, Poco, is Spanish for "little." Ken's oldest brother—a star athlete, teacher's pet, popular, handsome, articulate—won a Rockefeller Scholarship and got into Stanford. Ken, however, was no early bloomer, and his school years just slipped by. He began to believe that Poco meant "of little significance."

After graduating from high school in California, Ken went to the local junior college and promptly flunked out. "I had no particular direction," he said, shrugging. Then he applied himself, retook the courses he'd failed, graduated, and transferred to Humboldt State, where he majored in forestry. But actual jobs in forestry, he discovered, were more about pushing paper than adventurous hikes in the woods. He became disillusioned.

Ken then went into business with his father, a financial adviser of national renown. But the two didn't get along. "My father," he says, "suffered from a condition that today would be recognized as Asperger's Syndrome," a form of near-autism. "He was physically twitchy, he would pace the floor, he couldn't keep his hands from tapping. He had no ability to fathom what others were feeling. He could say the cruelest things, yet he wasn't cruel."

After nine months, Ken left his father's business and hung out his own shingle as a financial adviser. But with few clients, most of whom he would lose after a few years, he spent long hours with nothing to do. To bring in money, he took construction jobs. He even played slide guitar in a bar. But mostly he read. "Books about management and business—and maybe thirty trade magazines a month for years. During this decade, I developed a theory about valuing companies that was a bit unconventional."

With an Asperger's Syndrome father, Ken had no role model for leadership. His first part-time secretary left after nine months, claiming Ken was a lousy and imperious boss. "I probably was that," he admits today.

Throughout his twenties, Ken's financial advisory service struggled. But his theories landed him a few minor deals in venture capital. One led him to serve as a temp CEO. He felt his ambition stirring and worked it hard.

> There were about thirty employees. I'd never managed anyone. Now I had to. And I did okay—much, much better than expected. Do you know what I learned? I learned the most important part of leadership is showing up. Could have fooled me. That wasn't in the books I'd read. I sure didn't learn it from my father. Turns out eagerness is infectious. I moved the CEO's office to an open-glass conference room where everyone could see it and me. I made it a point to be the first there every day and the last to leave. I took employees to lunch every day and to dinner every night—at cheap diners but I gave them my time and interest. I wandered around endlessly talking to them, focusing on every single one and what they thought.
>
> The effect amazed me. And them. That I cared made them care. Suddenly I felt what it was like to lead.

Ken was thirty years old before he began to touch his potential.

Have you identified these two late bloomers? Here's a hint: Joanne and Ken are both self-made billionaires who regularly appear on the *Forbes* list of the wealthiest people in the world. Joanne Kathleen (J. K.) Rowling is author of the *Harry Potter* series. Ken Fisher is the founder of Fisher Investments, which manages $100 billion in stocks and bonds for more than 50,000 clients worldwide.

"Where have you gone, Joe DiMaggio?" asked Simon and Garfunkel in "Mrs. Robinson," a pop song from the 1960s. Songwriter Paul Simon knew the turbulent 1960s had overthrown the quiet unassuming hero of the 1940s and 1950s as a cultural icon. The new hero was young, hip, and brash.

In our own disruptive and turbulent economic age, we might ask: *Where have you gone, late bloomer?*

I ask this question because successful late bloomers like Rowling and Fisher, with their bashful young years, slow starts, and unhurried journeys, have appealing stories. But their stories are also curiously out of step with today's hip social media culture. Rowling is in her fifties, and Fisher in his sixties. Which might lead us to ask: *Where are today's inspiring late bloomers?* Are rich societies such as the United States, Britain, western Europe, and rising Asia not creating as many late bloomer success stories as they once did? Or is there another reason? Is the late bloomers' slower walk of discovery out of step with today's hypercompetitive, data-analytical, real-time pressures?

The belief that late bloomers do not get their due recognition, and that both people and society suffer for it, led me to investigate the subject and write this book. I believe the story of those who bloom later in life is more necessary and urgent than ever.

• • •

At the opposite end of the success spectrum is the early bloomer, the fast starter. Five-foot-one-inch Riley Weston was spectacular; at age nineteen, she landed a $300,000 contract with Touchstone, a division of Walt Disney, to write scripts for the television show *Felicity*—the coming-of-age story of a UCLA freshman. Weston's fast start in major league television landed her on *Entertainment Weekly*'s list of Hollywood's most creative people.

There was only one problem. Riley Weston was not nineteen. She was thirty-two, and her real identity, until this profitable ruse, was Kimberly Kramer from Poughkeepsie, New York. "People wouldn't accept me if they knew I was thirty-two," she said in her defense. She was probably right.

Never before, it seems, has precocity been such an advantage as it is now. In 2014 seventeen-year-old Malala Yousafzai became the youngest person ever to win the Nobel Prize, which goes along nicely with her Sakharov Prize and her Simone de Beauvoir Prize. In technology, whiz kid Palmer Luckey, the twenty-year-old founder of Oculus VR (acquired by Facebook for $2 billion), became a face of virtual reality, while fourteen-year-old Robert Nay cleared over $2 million in just two weeks with his mobile game Bubble Ball. At twenty-six, Evan Spiegel was worth $5.4 billion when Snapchat issued public stock in 2017. But Spiegel has miles to go to catch up with Facebook's Mark Zuckerberg, now an elder statesman at thirty-four, who with $60 billion is one of the five richest people in the world.

Even in the stodgy world of chess, Norwegian Magnus Carlsen was a three-time world champion by twenty-five. This after earning the title of grandmaster at thirteen; at twenty-one, he'd become the youngest person ever to be ranked number one, and at twenty-three, he was named one of the "100 Most Influential People in the World" by *Time* magazine.

Today's celebration of early bloomers is a staple of magazine lists. Every year *Forbes* celebrates young superachievers in a "30 Under 30" issue, featuring today's disruptors and tomorrow's brightest stars. Nor is *Forbes* the only publication to celebrate the precocious among us. *The New Yorker*'s "20 Under 40," *Fortune*'s "40 Under 40," *Inc.*'s "35 Under 35," and *Time*'s "30 Under 30" issues likewise tip to those who succeed spectacularly at an early age.

Please don't misunderstand me. There is nothing wrong with applauding or encouraging early success. Achievements of all types deserve recognition and admiration. But today's powerful zeitgeist goes far beyond simple recognition. Excessively promoting the primacy of early measurable achievement—grades, test scores, glamour job, money, celebrity—conceals a dark flipside: If we or our kids don't knock our SATs out of the park, gain admittance to a top-ten university, reinvent an industry, or land our first job at a cool company that's changing the world, we've somehow failed and are destined to be also-rans for the rest of our lives.

This message, I believe, creates a trickle-down societal madness for early achievement. This has led to very costly mistakes on the part of educators and parents in how we evaluate children, inflict pressure on them, and place senseless emotional psychological burdens on families.

Consider how, in high-pressure cities, some elite *preschools* play on the fears of affluent parents of three- and four-year-olds. The Atlanta International School in Atlanta offers a "full immersion second language program"—for three-year-olds. Just pony up $20,000 for a year's tuition. But that's a bargain compared to the fees at Columbia Grammar School in New York, which will set you back $37,000 a year. Your three- and four-year-olds will get a "rigorous academic curriculum" dished out in three libraries, six music rooms, and seven art studios. Writes *Parenting* magazine, "Columbia Grammar School's program is all about preparing kids for their futures—attending prestigious colleges."

Ah, the truth spills out. For what else would motivate parents to spend $40,000 to give their three-year-old a head start? According to these luxe preschools, there is one goal that justifies the cost: Get your toddler into a prestigious college fifteen years later. The message could hardly be more direct—or more threatening. If your kid doesn't ultimately get into a "prestigious college," his or her life will be needlessly hard.

The pressure doesn't stop with gaining admission to a proper preschool. "I'm contacted by a lot of parents who are completely freaking out that their 14-year-old is not spending the summer productively," Irena Smith, a former Stanford University admissions officer, told the *Atlantic*. Smith now runs a college admissions consultancy in Palo Alto, California, where clients typically spend $10,000 more.

The prize itself—an elite college admission—comes at a steep price. The cost of a four-year college degree from any of the top-twenty private colleges in the United States now exceeds a quarter of a million dollars, including room, board, books, and fees. The top-twenty public universities cost less, but even they average between $100,000 and $200,000 for a four-year degree, including room, board, books, and fees, depending on one's state resident status.

Society's desire for early-blooming validation has led to—let's be honest—price gouging by those official scorekeepers of early achievement, colleges and universities. The rest of us are stuck with big bills and massive debt. Since 1970, college tuition costs have risen three times faster than the rate of inflation. College debt in the United States is now $1.3 trillion, with an 11.5 percent default rate. By all measures, the rush to bloom early has helped create a potential bust bigger than the 2008 housing bubble.

Is it worth it? Let's pause and think about this. Let's question the basic premise that early blooming is necessary for lifelong success and fulfillment. Frankly, I don't see the evidence. In fact, I see plenty of evidence going the other way.

A recent sports story makes the point. In the 2018 Super Bowl, neither the Philadelphia Eagles nor the New England Patriots had many five-star recruits in their starting lineups. Translation: Only six of the forty-four starters were top-rated prospects in high school.

Now look at the quarterbacks. New England's Tom Brady didn't merit even a humble two or one ranking in high school. His ranking was NR—"no ranking." The victorious Eagles quarterback, Nick Foles, winner of the 2018 Super Bowl's most valuable player award, had a three ranking in high school. But for most of the season, Foles was actually the Eagles backup. He got to play only after starting quarterback Carson Wentz hurt his knee toward the end of the season. Wentz, like Brady, had an NR ranking in high school. No surprise: As a high school junior, Wentz wasn't primarily a quarterback. His school's football program listed him as a wide receiver.

With his lowly NR rank from high school, no major college football program had recruited Wentz. He went to North Dakota State, a small-college powerhouse. But while he was there, he grew to six-five and 230 pounds. Wentz literally blossomed in college, which is late by football standards. Now let's ask ourselves. How many of us are potential Carson Wentzes in our own way? How many of us were tagged with "no ranking" in high school, or dismissed early in our careers, or are dismissed even now? What gifts and passions might we possess that haven't yet been discovered but that could give us wings to fly?

Google once believed in early bloomer supremacy, and it's easy to see why. The company was started by two Stanford graduate students who had scored blazing math SATs. For the first few years, Google hired young computer scientists and math whizzes in the image of its brilliant founders. Then Google discovered its workforce was lopsided; it had too much analytical IQ and not enough artistic sensibility and common sense. This disparity led to costly mistakes in the Google homepage design. More recently Google has discovered that having high SAT scores and an elite college degree are insufficient predictors of an employee's career success at the company.

Early bloomers are the current rage, but late bloomers more than hold their own. Bestselling novelist Janet Evanovich, born in 1943, grew up in a New Jersey blue-collar family. As a married housewife, she didn't discover her true passion and gift for writing until her thirties. Then for another ten years she had only false starts and rejections: "I sent my weird stories out to editors and agents and collected rejection letters in a big cardboard box. When the box was full I burned the whole damn thing, crammed myself into pantyhose and went to work for a temp agency."

Evanovich didn't learn to write thrillers until her forties: "I spent two years . . . drinking beer with law enforcement types, learning to shoot, and practicing cussing. At the end of those years I created Stephanie Plum."

Billionaire Diane Hendricks, daughter of dairy farmers, sold houses in Wisconsin, married, divorced, then ten years later met her next husband, Ken, a roofer. The two maxed out their credit cards to start ABC Supply, a source for windows, gutters, and roofing material. Today Hendricks presides over a company worth $5 billion. She also produces Hollywood movies. Speaking of movies, actor Tom Hanks, the son of a hospital worker and part-time cook, was a slow starter with no obvious prospects who attended his local community college. Record-setting astronaut Scott Kelly, who has spent more than five hundred days in space, the most of any American, said he was so bored in high school that "I finished in the half of class that made the top half possible." General Motors CEO Mary Barra had a job inspecting fenders and hoods at a GM plant so she could pay for college. Former Xerox CEO Ursula Burns grew up in public housing and worked as an executive assistant early in her career. Jeannie Courtney was fifty when she started a globally respected therapeutic boarding school for troubled teenage girls. She had no formal training in the field but rather a typical hodgepodge background that sounds, well, quite average. She had taught eighth grade, run a video rental store, and sold property.

"There are no second acts in American lives," wrongly observed the *Great Gatsby* author F. Scott Fitzgerald. But Fitzgerald was an early-blooming snob: He attended Princeton and was already a famous literary success in his mid-twenties. But that was his peak. By his thirties, Fitzgerald was spiraling downward. He must have met all kinds of late bloomers and second acts who were on their way up. He died a bitter man at forty-four, the same age that Raymond Chandler began to write detective stories. Chandler was fifty-one in 1939, the year his first book, *The Big Sleep*, was published.

• • •

Are things now different? Early bloomers are in the headlines, but are they succeeding as much as the media lead us to believe? In fact, many early bloomers are suffering terribly. The pressure to achieve early success led to three student suicides in the 2014–15 school year at Gunn High School, a public school in Palo Alto, California, three miles from the elite Stanford University campus. All were good students striving for early achievement. By March in the same school year, forty-two Gunn students had been hospitalized or treated for suicidal thoughts.

Theirs is hardly an isolated story. Rates of depression and anxiety among young people in the United States have been increasing for the fifty years. Today five to eight times as many high school and college students meet the diagnostic criteria for major depression and/or anxiety disorder as in the 1960s. The Centers for Disease Control recently found that among high school students in the United States, "16 percent reported seriously considering suicide, 13 percent reported creating a plan for suicide, and 8 percent reported trying to take their own life in the 12 months preceding the survey."

These numbers are grim. As with many cultural trends in America, we seem to have exported our anxiety as well. A 2014 survey released by the World Health Organization found depression to be the number one cause of illness and disability in adolescents worldwide.

And if you think getting into the right college eases that anxiety, think again. In the past fifteen years, depression has doubled and suicide rates have tripled among American college students. A study by the University of California found that incoming freshmen showed the lowest rates of self-reported emotional health that had been seen in five decades of tracking. In fact, nearly all the campus mental health directors surveyed in 2013 by the American College Counseling Association reported that the number of students with severe psychological problems was rising at their schools.

Students themselves report high rates of emotional distress—and they too are rising. A 2014 survey by the American College Health Association found that 54 percent of college students said they had "felt overwhelming anxiety" in the previous twelve months.

These rising rates of mental illness in young adults is nothing short of alarming. Some part of the increase is likely due to better diagnosis, increased access to care, and greater willingness to seek help. But most experts agree that a significant portion of the trend is due to our changing cultural expectations. And these expectations—based on intensified measurement and evaluation—seem to have made even the most successful students more fragile than ever before.

Brittleness and fragility should not be the prizes of early academic achievement.

• • •

Being seen as a potential late bloomer was once a mark of vitality, patience, and pluck. Nowadays, more and more, it is seen as a defect (there must be a reason you started slowly, after all) and a consolation prize. This is an awful trend, since it diminishes the very things that make us human—our experiences, our resilience, and our lifelong capacity to grow.

Even early bloomers are not exempt from the suspicion that they are somehow flawed if, God forbid, their life takes a complicated turn. Women especially feel society's scorn for not living up to their early-blooming potential. Carol Fishman Cohen was an early bloomer: She was the student body president at Pomona College, then a Harvard Business School graduate, and finally a star performer at a Los Angeles investment bank, all before thirty. Then life intervened, as it does: Cohen stepped off the fast track to have four children and raise them. When she tried to step back into a career of investment banking, she found the doors locked. As weeks of frustration piled up, she began to doubt her own capabilities. "I felt a shattering loss of confidence. So much had changed while I was out, from the way financial deals were done to small things like email, text messaging, and PowerPoint presentations."

Cohen had a suspicion she wasn't the only person who felt like this. She started a company in Cambridge, Massachusetts, called iReLaunch. Its focus is the professional who wants to reenter the workforce after a hiatus and bloom once more. Her company bills itself as the "return to work" experts and consults both to reentering professionals and to the companies that hire them. Cohen writes frequently for *Harvard Business Review* on these topics. Once an early bloomer, she is now a stellar example of a second-act late bloomer

. . .

The fact is, many of us are late bloomers (or potential ones) of some kind. At some point, we got stuck. I did, for many years. At twenty-five, despite a four-year degree from a good university, I failed to hold a job beyond dishwasher, night watchman, and temporary typist. I was ragingly immature. Not surprisingly, my deep inferiority feelings grew worse as I remained glued to life's launching pad. As I look back, I'm more forgiving of my early-twenties self, since my brain's prefrontal cortex, the location of what brain researchers call executive functioning, was not fully developed. My brain, literally, was not ready to bloom.

Does that sound like you? Are your kids like that? Given the intense pressure on us to succeed—in school, in sports, in our early careers—we panic. But neuroscience makes it clear that we should go easier on ourselves. The median age for the full maturation of executive functioning is around twenty-five. I was closer to twenty-seven or twenty-eight before I became conscious that I could think rationally, plan ahead, and comport myself like an adult. This was a full decade after I took the SAT (to middling results) and a half-decade after I graduated from a good university (with mediocre grades). I shudder to think what would have happened if those two failures had been my ultimate sorting criteria. (I'm grateful that society's early bloomer sorting machine wasn't as brutally efficient as it is today.) Record-setting American astronaut Scott Kelly, a late bloomer himself, was even less of a standout. "I spent most days looking out the classroom window," he told me. "You could have held a gun to my head, and it wouldn't have made a difference." Kelly's brain wasn't ready to bloom.

Many of us see more of ourselves in Scott Kelly than in Mark Zuckerberg. We too have stories of fumbling starts, confusion, career or educational gaps, bad habits, bad luck, or lack of confidence. For the fortunate majority of us, however, some kind of intellectual or spiritual awakening happened, and we stepped onto a new, improved road. We found our way. But others become so steeped in shame or see themselves as so far removed from opportunity that they never develop their ability to bloom. And I would argue that failure to bloom during one's lifetime is catastrophic for people—and for societies.

You would think, therefore, that society would be encouraging of potential late bloomers, especially as we live longer, reach adulthood later, and explore new employment possibilities with greater frequency. People need to know they can bloom and excel and come into their own at any age or stage.

So what exactly does it mean to be a late bloomer? Simply put, a late bloomer is a person who fulfils their potential later than expected; they often have talents that aren't visible to others initially. The key word here is *expected*. And they fulfill their potential frequently in novel and unexpected ways, surprising even those closest to them. They are not attempting to satisfy, with gritted teeth, the expectations of their parents or society, a false path that leads to burnout and brittleness, or even to depression and illness. As Oprah Winfrey says, "Everyone has a supreme destiny." Late bloomers are those who find their supreme destiny on their own schedule, in their own way.

In researching this book, I asked academics, psychologists, and other social scientists how they define and view late bloomers. *Is there a rigorous, extensive research base out there to tap for latent clues or familiar guideposts?* I wondered.

The simple answer is no. Up to now, little formal research has been done on late bloomers. Much of academia seems to have ignored this particular aspect of human development, except in rare cases in which it is connected to a developmental disorder. In other words, late blooming is usually explored through the lens of dysfunction or as an abnormality. Even in academic research, the late bloomer gets little respect.

Recently, scholars have begun to explore aspects of the late bloomer concept, debunking the "myth of average" and studying the intricacies of individual development. L. Todd Rose, the director of the Mind, Brain, and Education Program at Harvard University, and Scott Barry Kaufman, scientific director of the Imagination Institute in the Positive Psychology Center at the University of Pennsylvania, are spectacular late bloomers themselves who nearly flunked out of high school, as they recount in their books. Still, a specific, all-purpose definition of a late bloomer or any type of helpful taxonomy of late bloomers eludes us.

To help fill this gap, I began researching people, both in history and living today, whose paths toward destiny and fulfillment could be called late blooming. In addition, I interviewed hundreds of people who had bloomed late or were on a quest to do so. How did they define the arcs of their success, including false starts along the way? How did they overcome cultural and self-confidence challenges that often afflict late bloomers?

• • •

As I started my research, my thesis was that a society that excessively focuses on early achievement colors perceptions about individuals' potential for later success in a way that disregards far more people than it rewards. And I assumed that potential late bloomers—that is, the majority of us sorted by society's efficient early bloomer conveyor belt into "less than" bins—just needed to jump back onto the same conveyor belt with new skills, new habits, and new techniques. I was confident that all they had to do was shake it off and get back in the game.

But that's not what I discovered. Most of the late bloomers I interviewed didn't bloom by belatedly copying the habits, skills, and career paths of early bloomers. In fact, trying to do so was almost always a recipe for failure and heartbreak.

Think about the starting point of a late bloomer. In all probability, his or her talents and passions were overlooked by a culture and educational system that measures for a cruelly narrow range of skills. It closed off the person's paths of discovery and encouragement and potential. It did not open the doors to a successful future for them because it didn't even see them. So it makes little sense for the late bloomer to climb back aboard the early bloomer conveyor belt with renewed determination, hardened resolve, and more training and college debt. The conveyor belt is going in only one direction.

What potential late bloomers have to do is to get *off* the conveyor belt and find a new path of discovery. My fondest hope is that this book will inspire you—or your children—to do just that.

• • •

Late Bloomers is structured in the following order. The first two chapters examine how we arrived at this moment of early-blooming madness, and the shockingly high price we pay for it, both as individuals and as a society. Chapter 3 reveals how the latest neuroscience and cognition research supports the concept of blooming—not just in our teens and young adult years but throughout our lives. That means our current obsession with early blooming is a human construct, not supported by science. I believe you'll be surprised, relieved, and happy as you read Chapter 4 and its explanation of six unique and powerful late-blooming gifts. The book's second half dives deeper into additional late bloomer advantages that are not obvious; in fact, they may seem like barriers at first. But with insight, practice, and patience, we can harness them toward a lifetime of blooming.

Enjoy the journey, and when you're finished, let's keep the discussion going.

. . . .

CHAPTER 1

Our Early Bloomer Obsession

Pop-neuroscience writer Jonah Lehrer was the very definition of an early bloomer. Born and raised in Los Angeles, at fifteen the precocious teenager won a thousand-dollar prize for a NASDAQ-sponsored essay contest. Lehrer attended Columbia University, the Ivy League's New York anchor, where he majored in neuroscience and coauthored a paper that delved into the genetic origins of Down Syndrome. But young Lehrer was no mere science whiz. He also bestrode Columbia's political and literary world, first as a writer for the *Columbia Review*, then for two years as the esteemed journal's editor.

It surprised no one that Lehrer's next move was to win a Rhodes scholarship. At Oxford University's Wolfson College, he walked in the steps of Wolfson's founder, the legendary Sir Isaiah Berlin, and studied philosophy. It could be rightly said that young Lehrer was a polymath, that rarest of people who, like Thomas Jefferson, are expert across many different disciplines. Lehrer, like Jefferson, could also write cogently. In 2007, at twenty-six, he published his first book, the well-reviewed *Proust Was a Neuroscientist*. Two other books quickly followed: *How We Decide* in 2009 and *Imagine: How Creativity Works* in 2012, which made the *New York Times* bestseller list.

If Lehrer was a polymath in his grasp of varying intellectual topics, he was also a paragon of multimedia. Not only could he write in different formats—books, essays, columns, and blogs—he proved to be a gifted radio host on National Public Radio's *Radiolab*. On television he was a witty guest on the *Colbert Report* and other shows.

Money soon followed. Lehrer was said to have earned a million-dollar book advance for *Imagine*. He began a lucrative side career as a paid speaker. While he was not in the $80,000-per-speech fee range of his *New Yorker* colleague and writer Malcolm Gladwell, he was earning up to $40,000 for an hour's talk. With money pouring in, Lehrer, only twenty-nine, bought an architecturally famous home, the Shulman House, in California's Hollywood Hills, for $2.2 million.

Lehrer achieved big and early, and he did it with his own radiant intellect.

• • •

Lehrer's astonishing rise in the intertwined worlds of publishing and journalism parallels the rise of what, with a nod to *Quiet* author Susan Cain, we might call the Wunderkind Ideal. Translated, *wunderkind* literally means "wonder child." Throughout the early 2000s, Lehrer's flashing rise from talented student to bestselling author to media phenomenon embodied a new cultural hero, the early bloomer, whose emergence reached a tipping point just as we were finding our footing in a new millennium. The archetypical wunderkind, like Lehrer, blooms early, becomes rich and famous—and makes sure we all know it. He or she may be precociously talented or technologically gifted, possessed of an otherworldly attractiveness or the beneficiary of great family connections. Regardless, wunderkinds not only reach the pinnacle of their chosen field faster than anyone else, they likely become wealthy in the process.

The media is a powerful lens through which to observe and track the rise of wunderkinds. Use of the term in various media platforms has skyrocketed in the last several decades. According to Google, the appearance of the word *wunderkind* in books, articles, newspapers, and other media has increased by more than 1,000 percent since 1960. And it's no wonder—these have been great times for precocious bloomers. Singers like Taylor Swift, Adele, Rihanna, Selena Gomez, and Justin Bieber; rappers like The Weeknd and Chance the Rapper;

actors like Jennifer Lawrence, Margot Robbie, Adam Driver, and Donald Glover; and models like Kendall and Kylie Jenner and Gigi and Bella Hadid are cross-platform celebrities who wield culture-defining influence. And at the time of their rise, they were all in their twenties or younger.

Our newest mass media platform, the Internet, is dominated by a slew of young "Web celebs." YouTubers and Instagrammers like Lilly Singh (IISuperwomanII), Jake Paul (jakepaul), Mark Fischbach (Markiplier), Zoe Sugg (Zoella), and Lele Pons (lelepons) have turned their millions—or tens of millions—of followers into media mini-empires that include major corporate sponsorship, merchandising deals, and paid public appearances. All the cited Web celebs did this while in their teens and early twenties.

In sports, it's to the athlete's advantage to bloom young. Early achievement on the field or in the gym wins a spot on the best teams, garners the best coaching, and makes available the greatest resources. This has always been the case. What's changed is how much earlier these athletes get picked out for being exceptional. At fourteen, Owen Pappoe already had thirty scholarship offers from collegiate football powerhouses like Florida State, Notre Dame, Louisiana State, Ohio State, and Alabama. Other young football stars considering scholarship offers include Kaden Martin, thirteen; Titan Lacaden, eleven; and Bunchie Young, ten. But they all seem on the mature side compared to Havon Finney, Jr., who was offered a football scholarship to the University of Nevada as a nine-year-old. It's not just in football, though, that young, hopeful superstars are plucked from the masses. Nearly 30 percent of all recruits in lacrosse, soccer, and volleyball are offered scholarships while they're still too young to officially commit to a school.

But these days it's not just athletes who seem to get younger every year. P. J. Fleck of the Minnesota Gophers became the youngest head football coach in Big Ten history at thirty-six. Lincoln Riley became head football coach of the Oklahoma Sooners—a perennial top-twenty team—at thirty-three, with an annual paycheck of $3.1 million. And at thirty, Sean McVay of the Los Angeles Rams became the youngest head coach in modern NFL history.

What about general managers, those cigar-chomping, backroom dealmakers who control rosters and hire (and fire) coaches? As I write, no fewer than ten Major League Baseball general managers are under forty, with David Stearns, of the Milwaukee Brewers, the youngest at thirty-one. Stearns is downright old, though, compared to twenty-six-year-old John Chayka, the general manager of the National Hockey League's Phoenix Coyotes. Chayka is the youngest general manager in major professional sports history.

It's well known that technology is a young person's game, but it's surprising to see just how young. In 2016 PayScale, an online compensation information company based in Seattle, surveyed the median age of workers at thirty-two of the most successful companies in the technology industry. Just six of the companies had a median employee age greater than thirty-five years old. Eight had a median age of thirty or younger. While these results may affirm a widely held hunch, they're nonetheless striking. Just to put it in context, according to the Bureau of Labor Statistics, the overall median age of American workers is 42.3 years. Some of the companies with the youngest workers in the PayScale survey included Facebook, with a median age of twenty-eight (and median salary package of $240,000), and Google, with a median age of twenty-nine (and median salary package of $195,000).

What about the owners, executives, and CEOs? Currently, *Forbes* lists ten billionaires in business under thirty, including Evan Spiegel, the CEO of Snap, and Bobby Murphy, Snap cofounder. The two started Snap when they were both twenty-two.

And what about politics, our country's control center? National political operatives under thirty-five include Lorella Praeli, Jenna Lowenstein, Symone Sanders, and Ben Wessel. In the White House, Stephen Miller became the president's senior adviser for policy at thirty-one, and Hope Hicks became White House communications director at twenty-eight. Hicks subsequently resigned.

Media have latched onto this rise of the Wunderkind Ideal. My own magazine, *Forbes*, has turned its "30 Under 30" issue into an entire industry, with separate lists broken down by country and multiple conferences worldwide. At this point, nearly every major magazine has a yearly issue based on a list of early achievers. There are "40 Under 40" and "30 Under 30" lists in business, fashion, advertising, entertainment, professional cooking, poetry, and even meatpacking.

But forget these "30 Under 30" lists: When it comes to achievement, thirty is becoming the new fifty. In 2014 *Time* started an annual list of "Most Influential Teens." That's right, teens. This fetish for youth and early blooming has reached such a fever pitch that fashion commentator Simon Doonan pronounced, "Youth is the new global currency."

Let's pause. We're not wrong to recognize and congratulate early bloomers. Their achievements deserve acknowledgement. But our culture's obsession with early achievement has become detrimental to the majority of the population—to the multitudes of us who develop in different ways and at different paces. It pushes the message that if you haven't become famous, reinvented an industry, or banked seven figures while you're still young enough to get carded, you've somehow made a wrong turn in life.

This message, I believe, is far more dangerous than most people realize.

• • •

Around the middle of the twentieth century, meritocracy began to trump aristocracy (see Chapter 2). That trend accelerated throughout the second half of the twentieth century. Today it's widely accepted that meritocracy and aristocracy have become one and the same. The lords of the universe are not sitting on trust funds. Rather, they possess wealth of a more modern kind. Like Jonah Lehrer, most of the new lords achieved perfect or near-perfect scores on their SATs at age sixteen or seventeen, setting them up for admission to a top-ranked university.

In response to the new meritocracy, we have become obsessed with test scores and college rankings. Teenagers take college preparatory tests—either the SAT (Scholastic Aptitude Test) or the ACT (originally an abbreviation for American College Testing) or both—at a higher rate now than ever before. More than 1.6 million students took the SAT in 2017. And for the first time, the number of students who took the ACT surpassed the SAT takers by about two thousand. Many students take both tests, take them multiple times during their junior and senior years, and also take the PSAT, the SAT II subject tests, and Advanced Placement tests. In fact, over 6.7 million test takers completed the SAT or a PSAT-related assessment during the 2016–17 school year.

With all the concern over higher education costs and the growing burden of student debt, it's easy to overlook the significant cost of preparing to apply to college. The expenses start adding up well before students ever apply for college, in the form of commercial test preparation classes and tutoring for the SAT and the ACT. The tests are an industry unto themselves, with hundreds of millions of dollars spent on test fees, administration, and preparation. The test prep industry generates nearly $1 billion every year and provides income for more than 115,000 people.

Raising the stakes even higher, some of the most select in-person or one-on-one online tutoring packages, aimed at rich parents, can cost many thousands of dollars. The high cost is in part because of the demand for individual tutoring. The rich can and do pay big bucks. Parents in Silicon Valley casually talk of spending $50,000 on tutors over their child's four years of high school. Group classes, offered by companies like Princeton Review and Kaplan Test Prep, are still popular and relatively affordable. Thirty hours of group preparation with Princeton Review, for example, costs $1,000 to $1,600, depending on the size of the class. Individual tutoring, however, is all the rage, and it usually comes at a steep price. One New York–based tutor, Anthony-James Green, recently gained attention with his $1,000-an-hour fee. The prices clearly indicate that students and families are engaged in a college admissions "arms race," in the words of Robert A. Schaeffer, public education director of FairTest, an equity-in-testing advocacy group. But for most people, paying to get an edge on standardized test scores is not only worth it—it's necessary. As long as high-stakes tests remain an important aspect of competitive college admissions, there'll be no shortage of people looking for an advantage.

We see the same pressure cooker for early measurable achievement outside academics. Consider sports. According to a recent *Washington Post* story, 70 percent of kids quit sports by age thirteen. Why? The kids have a ready explanation: "It's not fun anymore." But why exactly would that be so? Sports have become highly specialized and brutally competitive at earlier and earlier ages, for two distinct reasons.

One reason is an acceleration of the traditional one: Some kids just want to be as good as they can in sports. They want to run in the district track meet, start on the high school basketball team, or win a football letter jacket. The talented and ambitious ones keep going, to see if they can compete at the highest college levels, on full scholarships, then perhaps play in the pros or make the Olympic team. Kids in every era have aspired to be on the Wheaties box. But increased affluence has accelerated this trend, providing young athletes with opportunities to go to summer sports camps at age eight, buy the best equipment at ten, and get excellent coaching and perhaps even a personal trainer at fourteen. In short, the table stakes—time and money—for achieving sports excellence are far higher today.

The second reason driving early sports achievement is subtler and more corrosive. As the *Post* reported, "Our culture no longer supports older kids playing for the fun of it. The pressure to raise 'successful' kids means that we expect them to be the best. If they are not, they're encouraged to cut their losses and focus on areas where they can excel. We see it in middle school orchestra, where a kid who doesn't make first chair wonders if it's worth continuing to play."

Playing for the simple love of the sport or the music? How twentieth century! Sports for many students is simply a way to prove their merit early. Again, the culprit appears to be the race to get into the right college—and on the right track for early success.

This idea of sports as a résumé enhancer is validated by Judi Robinovitz, a certified educational planner at Score at the Top Learning Center and Schools. Robinovitz earns her living by getting kids into the best colleges possible and has published a guide called *The 10 Most Important Factors in College Admissions*. She advises her clients to focus on "continually improving grades in a challenging curriculum" and on gaining "solid SAT scores." No surprise there. She also emphasizes extracurricular activities, advising her clients how to frame their participation in them to maximum advantage in the college admissions process. Pay attention to the language in her suggestions four and six:

4. Passionate involvement in a few activities, demonstrating leadership, initiative, impact. Depth, not breadth, of experience is most important. Colleges seek "angled" students with a passion, not "well-rounded" students.

6. Special talents or experiences that will contribute to an interesting, well-rounded student body. A student who goes the extra mile to develop a special talent in sports, research, writing, the arts, or anything else will gain an edge.

Again, the sword of college admissions hangs over kids today. Did you note the absence of the words *passion* and *fun*? Fun is beside the point. A kid must excel in a sport (or in music, drama, debate, or even volunteering). Loving the activity is beside the point. College admissions demand that the student demonstrates excellence. He or she has to find the right activity in which to excel, then drop the others into the frivolity waste bin, in order to "gain an edge" and "stand out."

And why not? It's now harder than ever to gain admittance to college—even to many of the schools that used to be considered failsafe "backups." The following table shows just how much harder it's become since 2001 to be accepted by ten of the most prestigious universities in the United States.

School	2015	2014	2013	2012	2011	2010	2009	2008	2007	2006	2005	2004	2003	2002	2001
Columbia University	7	7	7	7	10	10	11	11	12	12	13	13	14	14	N/A
Duke University	11	11	13	14	16	19	22	23	23	24	22	21	23	26	N/A
Harvard University	6	6	6	6	6	7	7	8	9	9	9	10	10	10	11
Johns Hopkins University	14	16	18	18	19	22	28	26	26	28	35	31	31	35	34
Massachusetts Inst. of Tech.	8	8	8	9	10	10	11	12	12	13	14	16	16	16	17
Princeton University	7	7	7	8	8	9	10	10	10	10	11	13	10	12	12
Stanford University	5	5	6	7	7	7	8	9	10	11	12	13	13	13	13
University of Chicago	8	9	9	13	16	19	27	28	38	40	40	40	40	42	44
University of Pennsylvania	10	10	12	13	12	14	18	17	16	18	21	21	20	21	22
Yale University	7	6	7	8	8	8	9	10	9	10	10	11	13	14	16

Percentages of Admitted Applicants

In 2001 the University of Chicago accepted 44 percent of applicants. By 2015, it offered incoming spots to just 8 percent. Similarly, Johns Hopkins accepted 34 percent in 2001, but by 2015, that number had dropped to 14 percent. Some 22 percent of applicants were admitted to the University of Pennsylvania in 2001, but in 2015, that number was less than half. In fact, the acceptance rates in eight out of the ten schools on the list have been cut by half or two-thirds in just fifteen years. That's an extraordinary increase in competition—and exclusivity—in a single generation. For historical context, consider that Stanford University's acceptance rate in 1950 was nearly 85 percent. In 1990, it was 22 percent. Today, it's just 4.6 percent, the lowest in the nation.

But it's not just the elite schools that have become significantly harder to get into. In the last decade, the acceptance rates for a broad group of universities and colleges has plummeted. At Northeastern University, the acceptance rate has dropped from 62 percent to 32 percent; at the University of Tulsa, from 76 percent to 40 percent; at Tulane from 55 percent to 26 percent; at Colorado College, from 58 percent to 22 percent; and at Vanderbilt, from 46 percent to 13 percent. What about those "backup" schools? Even former party schools like San Diego State and Cal State Long Beach now admit only one-third of all applicants. Spanning all accredited universities and colleges, the nationwide acceptance rate dropped by 10 percent in the last ten years. The simple fact is, there are very few "automatics" anymore in the world of higher education.

This intense pressure has spawned entire industries based on squeezing the best performance out of kids and young adults, no matter the cost. A quick search on Amazon turns up a seemingly endless list of books with titles like *Grit for Kids*, *The Grit Guide for Teens*, *How Children Succeed*, *Positive Pushing*, *How I Turned My Daughter into a Prodigy*, *Top of the Class*, and *Battle Hymn of the Tiger Mother*. Even the "For Dummies" series is in on the act with *Raising Smart Kids for Dummies*. And make no mistake, intelligence-boosting products are big business: Toys, DVDs, software, games, and educational programs are designed and marketed to make a child into an intellectual prodigy. Baby Einstein, a $400 million-a-year company formerly owned by Disney, makes multimedia toys intended to enhance the cognitive abilities of infants and toddlers. Guaranteed to "enrich baby's young mind," these toys are available at Walmart, Target, and Amazon. This is but one of many companies and products that make up a child-enhancement industry that sells Smarty Pants Vitamins, STEM toys (STEM stands for "science, technology, engineering, and mathematics"), and other tech toys—all products that promise to give your child a leg up on the competition. We certainly can't have toddlers deficient in STEM skills.

Every summer break, according to an American Express survey, parents spend $16 billion on software coding camps, tech academies, music and dance lessons, additional academic coursework, and private tutoring. Youth athletics has become a $15 billion-a-year industry, where parents can now hire $100-per-hour strength and conditioning coaches, private hitting or passing coaches, and all-star traveling teams. According to *Time*:

> Local leagues have been nudged aside by private club teams, a loosely governed constellation that includes everything from development academies affiliated with professional sports franchises to regional squads run by moonlighting coaches with little experience. The most competitive teams vie for talent and travel to national tournaments.

Some families spend up to 10 percent of their income on registration fees, travel, camps, and equipment to keep their kids practicing for success on the field or in the gym.

But today it's not enough that kids practice. They have to practice *the right way*—in a way that conforms to research psychologist Anders Ericsson's concept of "deliberate practice." As described by Ericsson, famous for his ten-thousand-hour concept discussed in Malcolm Gladwell's 2008 bestselling *Outliers*, deliberate practice involves the systematic pursuit of personal improvement by focusing on well-defined, specific goals and areas of expertise. Parents who want their child to practice deliberately must hire a teacher or coach who has a demonstrated ability to help others improve the desired area—say chess, ballet, or music—and who can also give continuous feedback. It also requires your child to constantly practice outside his or her comfort zone.

Writing about her eleven-year-old son, author and entrepreneur Penelope Trunk perfectly described the rigor—and madness—of deliberate practice. Her son, auditioning as a cellist for Juilliard's pre-college program, spent three hours every day for six months learning to play one four-minute song. "He learned to practice by changing the rhythm of the piece. He learned to play one note at a time with a tuner. He learned to play each measure with a different metronome timing, and then he played the piece so slowly it took twenty minutes instead of just four." At one point, her son and his private cello teacher spent one hour practicing five notes. And yes, he made the cut at Juilliard.

With concentration, it seems, any child can be taught to be a prima ballerina or chess champion, a mathematics prodigy or a Michelin-star chef. According to the prevailing theories on grit, focus, and practice, any child with enough deliberate practice—and parents with a lot of money—can become a concert-level cellist or an Olympic equestrian. The experience of trying to reach that level can help them get into college and later, land the perfect job.

So what could possibly be the downside to these trends?

• • •

For too many children, this intense pressure for early achievement is damaging to their physical and mental health. Millions of American children are on prescribed drugs for attention deficit disorder (ADD), primarily because their ADD hurts their ability to sit still and pay attention in school, thus hurting their grades, their standardized test scores, and ultimately their college prospects. Dr. Leonard Sax, a medical doctor and psychologist who wrote about troubled teenagers in *Boys at Risk* (2007) and *Girls on the Edge* (2010), told me:

> A kid in the United States is now fourteen times more likely to be on medication for ADD compared to a kid in the U.K. A kid in the United States is forty times more likely to be diagnosed and treated for bipolar disorder compared to a kid in Germany. A kid in the United States is ninety-three times more likely to be on medications like Risperdal and Zyprexa used to control behavior compared to a kid in Italy. So in this country and really in no other country, we now use medication as a first resort for any kid who's not getting straight A's or not sitting still in class. No other country does this. This is a uniquely American phenomenon, and it's quite new.

One might say that twenty-first-century society has turned a college rejection into a clinical disease. Now, more than ever, it views a college degree as a prerequisite for a good life. But since the number of openings at colleges has barely increased, parents are essentially trying to push an ever-growing number of kids through an ever-narrowing funnel.

Let's stop and ask: Is the sacrificial expenditure of money, wrecked family dinners, and kids exhausted from organized activities producing better, more productive, or happier people? Is it helping people bloom? For the majority of kids, it's doing the exact opposite. This pressure for early achievement has an unwitting dark side: It demoralizes young people. By forcing adolescents to practice like professionals, to strive for perfection, and to make life choices in their teens (or earlier), we're actually harming them. We're stunting their development, closing their pathways to discovery, and making them more fragile. Just when we should be encouraging kids to dream big, take risks, and learn from life's inevitable failures, we're teaching them to live in terror of making the slightest mistake. Forging kids into wunderkinds is making them brittle. Journalist Megan McArdle has written extensively about the fear of failure that plagues today's young adults. In 2014 she recounted the following exchange with an ambitious high schooler:

> The other day, after one of my talks, a 10th-grade girl came up and shyly asked if I had a minute. I always have a minute to talk to shy high school sophomores, having been one myself. And this is what she asked me: "I understand what you're saying about trying new things, and hard things, but I'm in an International Baccalaureate program and only about five percent of us will get 4.0, so how can I try a subject where I might not get an A?'

To paraphrase McArdle's response: If you can't try something new in tenth grade, when can you?

This topic is of particular importance to Stanford psychology professor Carol Dweck, author of the bestselling 2006 book *Mindset: The New Psychology of Success*. On a late summer day, I sat down with Dweck to discuss the changes she's seen in her years of teaching college freshmen. "I think society is in a crisis," she told me. "Kids seem more exhausted and brittle today. I'm getting much more fear of failure, fear of evaluation, than I've gotten before. I see it in a lot of kids; a desire to play it safe. They don't want to get into a place of being judged, of having to produce." And these are the kids who were admitted to Stanford—these are the early "winners" in life. The optimism of youth, it seems, has been warped into a crippling fear of failure.

But it gets worse.

Rates of teen depression and suicide have climbed sharply since 2011. This is especially tragic, because on most counts young people's habits are improving. Drinking, smoking, and drug-taking are down in the United States, as in other developed countries, and teen pregnancies are at a record low. Yet it's clear that teens are in the midst of a mental health emergency.

Rates of depression and anxiety among teenagers have jumped by 70 percent in the past twenty years. The number of young people turning up at mental health clinics or counselors' offices with a psychiatric condition has more than doubled since 2009, and in the past three years, hospital admissions for teenagers with eating disorders have almost doubled. In the United States, high school and college students are five to eight times as likely to suffer from depressive symptoms as were young adults fifty years ago.

This isn't just a problem in the United States. Adolescents around the world are experiencing depressive symptoms in their teenage years. A survey released by the World Health Organization (WHO) in 2016 found depression to be the single most prevalent cause of illness and disability in adolescents worldwide. The World Mental Health Survey, supported by WHO, found that half of those who suffered from mental health problems—including depression—first experience symptoms at age fourteen. In high-income countries, like the United States, fewer than half of adolescents with a mental health problem receive treatment. Not surprisingly, this all too often leads to tragic outcomes.

Rates of teen suicide are rising at an alarming rate, according to an August 2017 report by the Centers for Disease Control and Prevention (CDC), with rates for girls higher than at any point in the last forty years. From 2007 to 2015, the suicide rate rose 40 percent for teenage boys and more than doubled for teenage girls. By 2011, for the first time in more than twenty years, more teenagers died from suicide than homicide; only traffic accidents led to more teen fatalities. While other causes of death are on the decline for teenagers, suicide keeps climbing. So are suicide attempts. "The deaths are but the tip of the iceberg," lamented Sally Curtain, a statistician for the CDC.

Here's what's hard to understand: All this increased anxiety seems to have little to do with real dangers in the world. The changes don't correspond with widespread famine, systemic poverty, wars, security threats, or any other such events that normally affect mental health. Rates of depression among American adolescents and young adults were much lower during the Great Depression, World War II, and the war in Vietnam—when the United States had the military draft—than they are today. Instead, the rise seems to have much more to do with the way young people experience the world.

More weight is given to tests and grades than ever before. Children today spend more hours per day in school than ever before. Outside school, they spend more time than ever being tutored, coached, ranked, and rewarded by adults. During the same half-century in which children's anxiety and depression have increased, what researchers call "free play" (and most of us call goofing around) has declined, while school- and adult-directed activities such as organized sports have risen steadily in importance. In all these instances, adults are in charge, not kids or adolescents. And this, it appears, is a recipe for unhappiness, anxiety, psychopathology—or worse.

"It's not an exaggeration to describe" younger generations "as being on the brink of the worst mental-health crisis in decades," says Jean M. Twenge, the author of more than 140 scientific papers and books on teenagers. Twenge connects the generational increases in depression to a shift from *intrinsic* to *extrinsic* goals. Intrinsic goals have to do with your own development as a person, such as becoming capable in activities of your own choosing or developing a strong sense of self. Extrinsic goals, conversely, have to do with material gains and other status measurements, like high grades and test scores, high income, and good looks. Twenge offers evidence that adolescents and young adults today are more oriented toward extrinsic goals than they were in the past. In an annual poll, college freshmen list "being well off

financially" as more important than "developing a meaningful philosophy of life." The opposite was true fifty years ago.

• • •

In pursuit of early blooming—to get the highest possible test scores
and GPAs, be admitted to the best college, and enter the right career
track—we give young adults precious little time to be kids. And the
perception that young people are "just smarter," as once declared by
Facebook founder Mark Zuckerberg (when he was twenty-two), implies they should be successful more quickly. But often they're not. For
every Zuckerberg, who made his first billion by twenty-three, or Lena
Dunham, the twenty-five-year-old creator of the HBO show *Girls*,
there are tens of thousands of twenty-somethings sitting in their parents' basements wondering why they performed poorly in school and
haven't yet made a movie, disrupted an industry, or started a fashion
line. This anxiety has paralyzed an entire generation of young people
just at the point when their lives should be dynamic.

A study by the bank UBS found that in the wake of the 2008–9
financial crisis, millennials appear more risk-averse than any generation since the Great Depression. They're making life decisions later,
delaying marriage longer, and taking much longer to settle into a career. And they are less likely than earlier generations to have three
things associated with adulthood: A spouse. A house. A child.

Yet even without these classic adult-responsibility impediments
to mobility, untethered twenty-somethings are pulling up stakes less
often than earlier generations of young adults. In 2016 only 20 percent
of adults ages twenty-five to thirty-five reported having lived at a different address one year earlier. One-year migration rates were much
higher for older generations at the same age. When members of the so-
called Silent Generation were twenty-five to thirty-five in 1963, some
26 percent reported moving within the previous year. And in 2000,
when Generation Xers were in their twenties and early thirties, 26 percent of them reported having moved in the prior year.

Today's young adults are also more likely to be at home for an extended stay compared with previous generations of young adults, according to the Pew Research Center. As of 2016, 15 percent of twenty-five-to-thirty-five-year-old adults were living in their parents' home. This represents a 50 percent increase over the share of Generation Xers who lived in their parents' home in 2000 at the same age, and nearly double the share of the Silent Generation who lived at home in 1964. Maybe the most stunning fact is that today's young adults between eighteen and thirty-four are less likely to be living independently of their families than in the depths of the Great Depression of the 1930s.

Yet our cultural obsession with early achievement creates a strong expectation that young people should be achieving more, achieving it faster, and achieving it younger. For the twenty-somethings among us, the message is clear: *Succeed right now or you never will.*

Christine Hassler's *20 Something Manifesto* is an anthology that explores the experiences of young adults, including what she calls the Expectation Hangover. "It's somewhat terrifying," said a twenty-five-year-old named Jennifer, "to think about all the things I'm supposed to be doing in order to 'get somewhere' successful: 'Follow your passions, live your dreams, take risks, network with the right people, find mentors, be financially responsible, volunteer, work, think about or go to grad school, fall in love and maintain personal well-being, mental health and nutrition.' When is there time to just be and enjoy?" A twenty-four-year-old from Virginia lamented, "There is pressure to make decisions that will form the foundation for the rest of your life in your 20s. It's almost as if having a range of limited options would be easier."

In my research for this book, I came across many twenty-somethings who expressed similar concerns. Meg, a twenty-five-year-old graduate from a good college, who lives independently and holds a promising job in a large midwestern city, spoke for many of her peers when she told me, "I feel this awful pressure, all the time, to do more than I am doing."

Some of this is not new. The United States and other affluent countries have always fetishized youth in terms of physical appearance and cultural hipness. During the 1960s cultural revolution, the hippie spokesman Jerry Rubin exhorted youth to never trust anyone over thirty. But Rubin's comment was largely a protest against the Vietnam War and the older (and presumably untrustworthy) men who were drafting teenagers into the conflict. Over the last few decades, our cultural obsession with youth has focused less on war and idealism than on external measures of success. The values have moved from exploration and self-discovery to hard, measurable achievement. Model youth are defined by their quantifiable progress toward getting perfect or near-perfect test scores and grades, entering elite universities, obtaining killer first jobs, earning lots of money, and achieving high status.

Social media platforms like Facebook, Snapchat, and especially Instagram play an outsize role in this transformation. They speak directly to the anxieties of young and old adults alike. We've long understood that movies, magazines, and television can shape self-image and enforce social ideals, but social media has now become our most toxic cultural mirror. According to an extensive survey conducted by the Royal Society for Public Health, visual platforms like Facebook, Instagram, and Snapchat allow young adults to compare themselves to one another and earn approval based on appearances. The study found Snapchat to be the social media platform most likely associated with high levels of anxiety, depression, and bullying. This ability to compare with and seek approval from others feeds into the crisis described by Twenge: Twenty-somethings are constantly comparing their extrinsic selves—their looks, wealth, status, and success—to unattainable standards of perfection.

Sadly, it's not like the older among us are faring much better.

• • •

Plenty of industries try to replace older workers with younger ones, but technology companies are particularly distrustful of long résumés. In

Silicon Valley's most successful companies, the median employee is likely to be thirty-two or younger. And these aren't a handful of unicorn startups. They are corporate—and cultural—giants like Apple, Google, Tesla, Facebook, and LinkedIn. These companies reflect a dark ethos that has been circulating around the valley for years. In 2011 billionaire venture capitalist Vinod Khosla told an audience that "people over forty-five basically die in terms of new ideas."

Journalist Noam Scheiber has channeled the ageism of Silicon Valley through the story of Dr. Seth Matarasso, a San Francisco–based plastic surgeon:

> When Matarasso first opened shop in San Francisco, he found that he was mostly helping patients in late middle age: former homecoming queens, spouses who'd been cheated on, spouses looking to cheat. Today, his practice is far larger and more lucrative than he could have ever imagined. He sees clients across a range of ages. . . . Matarasso routinely turns away tech workers in their twenties. A few months ago, a 26-year-old came in seeking hair transplants to ward off his looming baldness.

Robert Withers, a consultant who helps Silicon Valley workers over forty with their job searches, recommends that older applicants have a professional photographer take their LinkedIn photos to help disguise their age. He also advises them to spend time in a prospective employer's parking lots, cafeterias, and kitchens so they can see how people dress. This usually results in fifty-somethings trading in their suits and briefcases for hoodies and backpacks.

Laurie McCann, an attorney with the retiree lobby American Association of Retired Persons (AARP), believes that tech companies' obsession with new ideas and extreme productivity leads employers to fall back on easy assumptions about age, like "that older people can't work that fast. That they can't think on their feet in order to come up with the ideas." Further assumptions about older employees, she points out, include a belief that they're rigid in their beliefs and habits or that they're unable to get along with younger people.

Admittedly, Silicon Valley is an extreme business microcosm, but these facts speak to a much bigger problem. Getting a job today when you're middle-aged or older is harder than it should be. A 2016 AARP study found that 92 percent of adults forty-five and older think age discrimination is somewhat or very common in the workplace. Regional data on age discrimination are hard to come by, but of the 18,335 employment claims filed in 2010 with California's Department of Fair Employment and Housing, one-fifth cited age as the reason for discrimination. This puts age discrimination claims above those for racial discrimination, sexual harassment, and sexual orientation. And according to the Equal Employment Opportunity Commission, age is cited in 26 percent of total complaints in California, 22 percent in New York, 21 percent in Texas, and 37 percent in Illinois, which has the highest ratio of age-related complaints.

At first glance, older workers wouldn't seem to have it all that bad in today's economy. The unemployment rate among workers over fifty-five hovered around 4 percent in 2018, and labor force participation among older workers has been rising since the early 1990s. But the headline statistics obscure a bleaker situation: Older workers who do lose a job spend more time out of work. And when they do find another job, it tends to pay less than the one they left. A 2015 AARP study highlights the challenges of long-term unemployment still facing many older workers. Extended unemployment, coupled with age discrimination, can add to the challenges older workers face in finding a job. On average, 45 percent of job seekers fifty-five and older were long-term unemployed (out of work for twenty-seven weeks or more). And when they do find a job, it takes longer: thirty-six weeks compared with twenty-six weeks for younger workers, according to data from the Schwartz Center for Economic Policy Analysis (SCEPA), an economic think tank. Worse, older job seekers who do find work may have trouble recovering financially. Many end up accepting jobs at lower pay, with fewer hours, and with limited benefits. SCEPA data show that when older unemployed workers do find new jobs, they typically go back to work for about 75 percent of their previous salary.

One group that's hit particularly hard by this trend is women over fifty. This is surprising because many recent trends—the rise of service-sector jobs like health care and hospitality and the rising rates of women earning advanced degrees—were considered beneficial for working women. A 2015 study, though, found that the prospects for women over fifty decreased after the Great Recession. In 2007, before the downturn, less than a quarter of the unemployed women over fifty had been out of work for more than six months. By 2013, older jobless women accounted for half of all the long-term unemployed.

Add to this a recent study by the University of California at Irvine and Tulane University that found age discrimination in the hiring of older women. The researchers sent out forty thousand fake job applications that included clues to the job seekers' ages and then monitored the response rates. Measuring callback rates for various occupations, they found that workers ages forty-nine to fifty-one applying for administrative positions had a callback rate nearly 30 percent lower than younger workers. And for workers over sixty-four, the callback rate was 47 percent lower than for younger workers.

But older men are also struggling. According to Teresa Ghilarducci, a labor economist and SCEPA's director, this reality manifests itself in government numbers on job tenure. In the last five years, median job tenure for white males fifty-five and older with a high school education or less decreased to 16.7 years from 17.7 years. Conversely, job tenure for all other groups increased during the same period.

Call them the "new unemployables." A wide-reaching study by the same title found that unemployed older workers face two dilemmas. They are less likely to find new employment than unemployed younger workers and their job loss during the pre-retirement years can wreck financial security. The study concluded, "Older workers are involuntarily working part time because they cannot find full-time employment. Others are becoming discouraged and dropping out of the labor force, believing they will not find new jobs. Financial duress following job loss has resulted in devastating blows to retirement and other savings accounts. Contributing factors include limited availability of Unemployment Insurance and a lack of health care benefits especially."

The dark incongruity of this trend isn't hard to spot: Many of these people are too young to retire but too old to get rehired. It seems we now have a large class of accomplished workers who have been pushed aside. Their experience has become a liability.

For many, it adds up to a wakeful nightmare.

• • •

It was the summer of 2012. Jonah Lehrer, the wunderkind writer from the beginning of this chapter, was sitting on top of the world. His latest book, *Imagine*, was selling briskly and debuted at number one on the *New York Times* bestseller list. A staff writer at *The New Yorker*, Lehrer gave paid speeches that earned him up to $40,000 each. He was a contributor to a National Public Radio show and a television guest of Stephen Colbert. He had purchased a $2.2 million historic house in the Hollywood Hills. By thirty-one, Lehrer had earned more applause and money than most professional writers do over a lifetime. The early-blooming Rhodes scholar was sitting pretty.

Until he wasn't.

The crash of Jonah Lehrer came about because he was caught making up quotes from singer-songwriter Bob Dylan and using them in his best seller, *Imagine*. Lehrer's fabrications were caught by writer and Dylan enthusiast Michael Moynihan, who wrote:

> "It's a hard thing to describe," Bob Dylan once mused about the creative process. "It's just this sense that you got something to say."
>
> That Dylan observation can be found in the first chapter of journalist Jonah Lehrer's best-selling new book *Imagine: How Creativity Works*, an exploration of how neuroscience

explains creative genius. Lehrer has much to say on the matter, from a meditation on the inventor of the Post-It note to an investigation into the way Bob Dylan's mind works, which included the quote above.

The problem, though, is that there is no proof that Dylan ever said this.

One unattributable quote might have been sloppy but forgivable. But Moynihan documented other Dylan fabrications by Lehrer. When he tried to confront Lehrer about them, "Lehrer stonewalled, misled and eventually outright lied to me." Later Lehrer confessed to Moynihan that he just made them up, altered the wording, or patched two Dylan quotes from different times and places into one that, presto, supported Lehrer's thesis about creativity.

Months prior to his Dylan quote fakery, Lehrer had aroused suspicion of plagiarism on his Wired.com blog. Some of Lehrer's plagiarizing was of his own work, which journalists call "recycling" and which most journalistic ethicists would say is like jaywalking—more lazy than unethical. But after his Dylan fiasco, Lehrer was shown to have plagiarized the work of others, too, including *Newsweek* science writer Sharon Begley.

The reaction to Lehrer's sins was swift. *The New Yorker* and National Public Radio fired him. His publisher, Houghton Mifflin Harcourt, pulled *How We Decide* and *Imagine: How Creativity Works* from bookstore shelves. Amazon used its technical voodoo to make *Imagine* disappear from Kindles, and today Amazon sells only used hardcover and paperback copies of *How We Decide* and *Imagine* on its website.

And what of Jonah Lehrer? In 2016 he attempted a comeback with a new work, *A Book About Love*. Reaction was swift and brutal, like this review by Jennifer Senior:

> Books are still the slow food of the publishing business. Yet here is Mr. Lehrer, once again, serving us a nonfiction McMuffin. I wasn't expecting it. I was one of those weirdos

who thought Mr. Lehrer would make a respectable comeback. He's bright. He's a decent stylist. He languished in the public stockade for weeks for his sins. Why wouldn't he try something personal, something soulful, something new? No clue. But he didn't. His book is insolently unoriginal.

How did Jonah Lehrer, early bloomer and wunderkind, fall so fast and so far? The best explanation comes from literary agent Scott Mendel: "You know, I do think in some level this is the predictable outcome of expecting a young journalist to be the next Oliver Sacks." Sacks spent decades as a practicing neurologist and psychologist before turning his hand to write bestselling books and articles for *The New Yorker*, Mendel says. But Lehrer benefited too quickly from a system that likes its stars young.

There's no joy in cataloging Lehrer's missteps. I don't believe he's a bad person who tried to dupe agents, publishers, editors, and the public. I see him as a victim of today's social pressures and expectations, a canary in the coal mine of our wunderkind obsession. Most of all, though, I see him as an embodiment of a line from novelist Walker Percy's *The Second Coming*: "You can get all As and still flunk life."

. . .

In the Introduction, I defined a late bloomer as a person who fulfills their potential later than expected; often their talents aren't even visible to others initially. The key word here is *expected*. And second, they fulfill their potential while marching to their own drummer. They don't grit their teeth to try to meet the expectations of their parents or society. A late bloomer can be the apparently listless teenager like record-setting astronaut Scott Kelly, who could not pay attention in high school to save his or her life, but later finds motivation in a book, a subject, or a person. A parent might jump back into the workforce after a decade of child-rearing, feeling ten years behind but being ten years wiser. Or a retiree might find a deeper meaning in life by finally pursuing a childhood dream or mentoring others. Late blooming can happen at any age, and it can happen more than once in a person's lifetime.

Think of it like a ski race on a slalom course. The skiers go one at a time, but based on how fast each one goes through the first, second, or third gate, you can tell where she or he is relative to the competition. You can tell if a skier is behind or ahead of the expected time. When you expand the concept of late blooming to all ages, there are slalom gates that society has set up—people are expected to hit certain marks at certain times. Some people get through the gates faster than others: In grade school, junior high, and high school they get perfect grades, they ace the SATs, and then they get into an elite college and get the right job. Those people hit the slalom gates early, beat the clock, and take a spot on the podium.

Life is not an Olympic slalom event, but if you're not one of those elite racers, if you fall behind at some of the slalom gates of life, it is difficult to catch up. This is an enormous problem in society today because it affects so many of us.

Truth is, many factors can slow our blooming early in life, including delayed physical or neurological development, early childhood trauma, nonstandard learning styles, socioeconomic status, geographical restrictions, illness, addiction, career turbulence—even plain bad luck. Many of us, growing up, are unable to reach our full potential at school—and therefore fall short of our university and professional potential—because we're fed negative messages about our learning abilities. We're told, "You just don't have a mind for science," or, "You'll never be a good writer."

Then as we age, marriage, pregnancy, child care, and other family obligations with competing urgencies limit our opportunities and affect our career trajectory. Other obstacles to blooming include accidents and illnesses, depression and addiction. These all-too-common setbacks delay a real blooming of our talents and purpose, leaving us to face a culturally induced sense of marginalization.

Many people, like me, recognize themselves as late bloomers.

Others may feel a vague sense that their careers haven't quite clicked yet. All of us know someone, care about someone, or love someone who seems stuck in life. The critical thing to remember is—we cannot give up on ourselves, or on others, even (and especially) if society has made it harder to catch up.

As society celebrates the early bloomers, countless examples of late bloomers can be found in virtually every field. International star Andrea Bocelli began singing opera at thirty-four; James Murphy, founder of LCD Soundsystem, released his first album at thirty-five, ancient in the world of electronic dance music; Lucinda Williams broke through at forty-five with *Car Wheels on a Gravel Road*, her fifth stab at recording success; and Susan Boyle, the surprise star of *Britain's Got Talent*, was discovered at forty-eight. Martha Stewart was thirty-five when she started her catering business in a friend's basement, and forty-two when her first book of recipes was published. Even a field as avant-garde as fashion has its surprising late bloomer stories: Rick Owens broke out at age thirty-nine, Vera Wang at forty-one, and Vivienne Westwood at forty-two. Acclaimed artist Marina Abramovic didn't find her way in the art world until her thirties, achieved national recognition at fifty-four with her performance piece "Seven Easy Pieces," and became famous at fifty-nine with a Museum of Modern Art retrospective titled *The Artist Is Present*.

The list of late-blooming writers is as diverse as it is illustrious. Chuck Palahniuk published his first novel, *Fight Club*, at thirty-four; David Sedaris, the humorist, published his first collection of essays at thirty-eight; Toni Morrison published her first novel, *The Bluest Eye*, at thirty-nine and won the Pulitzer Prize for *Beloved* at fifty-six; Janet Evanovich launched her bestselling Stephanie Plum series of crime novels at forty-four; and Frank McCourt published his Pulitzer Prize–winning memoir, *Angela's Ashes*, at sixty-three.

In business, Tom Siebel founded his first successful tech company, Siebel Systems, at forty-one, and his second, C3, at fifty-seven; Dave Duffield launched tech firm PeopleSoft at sixty-six. Gary Burrell, after decades of working for engineering firms like Allied Signal, cofounded Garmin, the GPS device maker, at fifty-two. John Torode started an airplane company, Vashon Aircraft, at seventy. Billionaire Dietrich Mateschitz, who spent ten years in college and worked as a ski instructor, founded energy drink maker Redbull at forty. And let's not forget the greatest innovator of recent times: Steve Jobs. While not technically a late bloomer, his unparalleled second act, in which he launched the iPod, iTunes, iPhone, and iPad at Apple, came after he was forty-five.

Can you imagine getting your big break in Hollywood at fifty-two? That's what happened to Morgan Freeman. After years of toiling in community theater and small stage productions, he broke through in *Driving Miss Daisy*, with eighty-one-year-old Jessica Tandy—who, by the way, received her first Academy Award nomination for the film. Famous movie villain Alan Rickman owned a graphic design studio for years before he got his first taste of fame at forty-two for his role as Hans Gruber in *Die Hard*. Jon Hamm, after being dropped by an agent and working in the art department of a soft-core pornography company, secured his breakthrough role on *Mad Men* at thirty-six; Bryan Cranston, who bounced around during a hardscrabble childhood, gained recognition on the TV show *Malcolm in the Middle* at forty-four; Jane Lynch broke through at forty-five in Judd Apatow's *The 40-Year-Old Virgin*; and Margo Martindale, after decades of work in community theater, made her breakthrough appearance on TV at sixty in the FX show *Justified*.

These are just some of the famous late bloomers. There are millions of others who aren't famous but are highly accomplished and personally fulfilled. They just don't get publicized.

Creativity is not the sole province of the young. Some of us simply need more time, experience, and experimentation to develop a path and realize our talents. Life is often defined by snags and setbacks, by detours and disappointments. Purpose and wisdom, strengths of the late bloomer, come from a portfolio of these experiences, making late bloomers more reflective, more considerate, and more patient. Late bloomers often have a higher level of empathy. They are usually better at regulating their emotions. They have higher levels of emotional intelligence, and they have better coping skills (as I'll explore in greater detail in Chapters 3 and 4). Not surprisingly, handling adversity and setbacks is something late bloomers do better than early achievers. As Stanford's Carol Dweck notes in *Mindset*, early bloomers are at risk for developing a fixed mindset about how they achieved their early success. Puffed up with overconfidence, they stop learning and growing. Tennis early bloomer John McEnroe, for example, became more and more enraged as later-blooming tennis pros surpassed him on the courts.

• • •

We are in danger of losing a valuable narrative about our lives: that we are capable of blooming at any age and in any stage of our lives. Late bloomers are disappearing from the stories we tell about ourselves, as we become trapped by our cultural worship of the precociously talented, the youthfully ambitious, and the extraordinarily smart—the wunderkinds. This new ideal has become so pervasive, I would argue, that it has chipped away at our feelings of worth and security. For some, it may have narrowed, or even eliminated, traditional pathways to success. It's robbed too many of us of a sense of control over our lives and our destinies.

Our mad drive for early achievement—and the taint of failure that colors those of us who do not attain it—has squandered our national talent and stunted our creativity. A healthy society needs all its people to realize they can bloom and rebloom, grow and succeed, throughout their lives.

This should be obvious. But we've made it terribly hard. Why is that?

. . . .

CHAPTER 2

The Cruel Fallacy of Human Measurement

For a lowbrow comedy starring second-rate actors, *Revenge of the Nerds* was a surprise hit that created a cultural moment. Set at fictional Adams College, it pitted some computer science majors against the campus jock fraternity, Alpha Beta. Who wins? The nerds, of course.

When the movie came out in 1984, the nerds in the real world were starting to win, too—bigtime. In 1975 a precocious Bill Gates dropped out of Harvard after his junior year. Gates had scored 800 on his math SAT and was bored by the pace of Harvard's academics. He left Harvard and, along with his Seattle suburban friend Paul Allen, started Microsoft (called Micro-Soft then). In 1986 Microsoft sold stock to the public, and by 1998 it was the highest-valued company in the world. Until 2017, Bill Gates was the world's richest man.

During the early 1990s, I interviewed Gates several times and once spent five days traveling with him. He still displayed his odd habit of rocking back and forth in his chair while he talked, which some have speculated is evidence of borderline Asperger's Syndrome. Back then Gates was far brasher and more outspoken than the circumspect global philanthropist he's since become.

In the 1990s Gates fancied Microsoft as an IQ factory. "We beat everybody in IQ," he told me. "We beat Oracle, we beat Sun. We compete with Goldman Sachs." The value of having world-class IQ throughout a software company, he said, is that "one really great programmer is worth a thousand average ones." The really great programmers had the highest IQs, he said. His logic: High IQ in a software programmer was like a fast forty-yard-dash time in a pro football player. Nobody who is physically slow will ever play in the National Football League. And nobody who is mentally slow will ever work for Microsoft.

This was an American cultural moment: The world's richest man was a wunderkind, a member of the cognitive elite, with a perfect SAT math score to prove it. He had built the world's most valuable company with an army of software programmers specifically selected for high IQ.

What do you suppose this did for the image of the SAT as the gateway not only to Harvard, Stanford, MIT, and Caltech but also to the Forbes 400 list of richest people? Did IQ and SAT scores become less or more important in our culture?

Okay, that was a softball.

We now live in a world where the highest-IQ people earn the greatest financial rewards. And they earn them blindingly fast—not over a lifetime but in a decade or less. I've met many high-wattage early achievers, and I have great admiration for their talents, work ethic, and vision. But their preeminence should raise a number of concerns. A rapidly growing percentage of society's riches now go to those who've demonstrated ninety-ninth percentile IQ on a standardized test—a test, may I remind you, that's taken over a few hours at age sixteen or seventeen.

How did this happen?

• • •

In 1905 a German-born Swiss patent application examiner—a late bloomer who didn't speak until age six and now at twenty-five was so easily distracted at work that he was repeatedly rejected for promotion at the patent office—wrote, during his nonwork hours, a series of papers that would profoundly change the world. They included a Ph.D. thesis and four additional papers on the photoelectric effect, Brownian motion, special relativity, and the relationship between mass and energy. The author summarized the last paper with the famous equation

$E = mc^2$. And with them, Albert Einstein altered the foundations of the world as we know it.

But 1905 was also notable for another series of papers that continue to define our world today. The author, like Einstein, was a self-taught outsider. Born in Nice in 1857, Alfred Binet was educated as a law-yer, but his interests were varied and quirky. He became a researcher in a neurological clinic and developed a lifelong interest in how the brain worked. Binet pursued his brain work with creative whimsy. He once devised a memory test to see how chess players performed when blindfolded. He dabbled in hypnotism, which threatened his scholarly reputation. He taught himself psychology, an emerging academic dis-cipline, by reading papers at the National Library in Paris.

In 1899 France passed a law that made school mandatory for chil-dren six to fourteen. The eclectically educated Binet was asked to join a commission called the Free Society for the Psychological Study of the Child to assess children's capabilities and learning modalities. He soon discovered that some children, sadly, could not keep up with any of the curricula being assessed. What to do about these slower chil-dren? Well, first you needed some facts about their capabilities—how impaired were they? So in 1905 Binet and a young medical student, Theodore Simon, devised a test to measure the mental capabilities of children ages three to thirteen. They studied a sample of fifty chil-dren to determine the median scores and the extreme ends of bright to slow. It was called the Binet-Simon Scale, and we know it today as the world's first intelligence test.

Here is the really important thing to remember about Binet and his 1905 test: He saw it as a snapshot in time. The test would reveal where a child stood on the scale of mental capability relative to that child's peers—*at a moment in time*. Nowhere did Binet write or imply that his IQ test, given once to a child between three and thirteen, would project that child's intelligence over his or her entire lifetime. It was an American who made that unfortunate leap.

• • •

In 1999 journalist Nicholas Lemann (now a dean emeritus at Columbia University's school of journalism) wrote *The Big Test: The Secret History of the American Meritocracy*, which looks at the origins of the SAT and its direct roots in IQ testing. As Lemann tells it, it was the American psychologist Lewis Terman, based at Stanford, who saw testing as a tool of vital national importance in the dawning twentieth century. Writes Lemann:

> Lewis Terman thought of the IQ test as a much more significant and widely applicable scientific breakthrough. He believed it could quickly, almost miraculously, measure the innate capacity of the brain, a quasi-biological quality that he considered the essential human attribute of the modern age. Terman was a tireless advocate of the widest possible use of IQ testing, so that students could be assessed, sorted and taught in accordance with their capabilities.

Terman believed that the IQ test, which he revised into the Stanford-Binet test, would improve the human condition—and humans themselves—over generations. But his belief was rooted in a bad seed, one shared by many early twentieth-century leading academics. The bad seed was eugenics, the idea that humans with good qualities (like high intelligence) should be allowed to breed and pass on those qualities. Humans with bad qualities (which in early twentieth-century America meant anyone who was not a northern European) should be discouraged from having children. People with "defective" qualities, such as those with mental disabilities, should be sterilized. Twenty years after Terman revised Binet's intelligence test into the Stanford-Binet IQ test, Terman cofounded the Human Betterment Foundation—which advocated the sterilization of "inferior" races.

Sadly, those kinds of beliefs went unchallenged back then. But they do not negate Terman's positive contributions to psychology. When the United States entered World War I in 1917, the Stanford-Binet test was given to 1.7 million soldiers. The idea was to quickly identify the mental abilities of soldiers, to better determine where they might best fit in the war machine. The high scorers were funneled into army intelligence and officer training. The low scorers went to the trenches. A starkly different sorting mechanism was used in England, where the wellborn went into intelligence and officer training, while the poor and working classes went to the trenches. Terman's test for American soldiers was not only more effective, it also seemed fairer, less rooted in the happenstance of birth.

Terman's IQ test was a raging success. The U.S. Army got what it wanted, and now it wanted more. But Terman's embrace of eugenics eventually proved toxic, even by early twentieth-century standards. In 1916 he wrote in *The Measurement of Intelligence*: "Border-line deficiency . . . is very, very common among Spanish-Indian and Mexican families of the Southwest and also among negroes. Their dullness seems to be racial, or at least inherent in the family stocks from which they come. . . . Children of this group should be segregated into separate classes. . . . They cannot master abstractions but they can often be made into efficient workers. . . . From a eugenic point of view they constitute a grave problem because of their unusually prolific breeding." It is painful to read.

Unfortunately, almost all the top researchers in IQ testing in the 1920s were attached to the eugenics movement. Carl Brigham, a psychology professor, carried Terman's torch and developed the SAT out of Princeton University in 1926 for the U.S. Army; he was a eugenics enthusiast, if not a zealot like Terman. Years later he would change his mind about testing. In fact, he would come to hate the very thing he created, that continues to drive our obsession almost one hundred years later: the SAT.

• • •

Brigham's 1922 book, *A Study of American Intelligence,* quickly became a sensation in academic circles. Like Lewis Terman and the other noted American IQ researchers, Brigham embraced the idea that some races were superior to others. He wrote such cringeworthy lines as "Our figures, then, would tend to disprove the popular belief that the Jew is highly intelligent." He sourly lamented the high immigration numbers of the time, particularly dark and swarthy immigrants from "Mediterranean" countries. "American intelligence is declining," he wrote, "and will proceed with an accelerating rate as the racial admixture becomes more and more extensive. These are the plain, if somewhat ugly facts that our study shows."

Sadly, it was a typical sentiment of the day. Nor did Brigham's claims hurt his career. (What did hurt his career was taking the opposite view, as I shall get to in a bit.) On the contrary, he was propelled to the forefront of IQ researchers. And when the U.S. Army came looking for improvements to its First World War intelligence test, it included Brigham in the list of potential contributors, along with Stanford-Binet creator Lewis Terman and psychologist Edward Lee Thorndike of Columbia University. The army liked Brigham's adaptation of and refinements to the original army intelligence test. Brigham called it the Scholastic Aptitude Test, or SAT. In 1926 he made no effort to hide the fact that the SAT was a longer and more practical version of an IQ test.

With the army's embrace of the SAT, and Brigham's impressive academic credentials as a Princeton psychologist, universities soon embraced it as well. First to adopt it were the military academies of West Point (army) and Annapolis (navy) in 1930. Then Yale jumped in. Soon most universities in the U.S. Northeast followed suit.

The SAT became a huge hit. But only two years after designing the test, Brigham developed grave doubts about it. He was less convinced that the SAT measured raw intelligence and more certain that it measured what a child or young adult had been exposed to. In 1928 he was invited to speak to a group of eugenicists, to whom he expressed his doubts. In 1929 he wrote, "The more I work in this field, the more I am convinced that psychologists have sinned greatly. I feel we should all stop naming tests and saying what they measure . . . if we are to proceed beyond the stage of psychophrenology." In 1934, shortly before his death, he called his test a "glorious fallacy":

The test movement came to this country some twenty-five or thirty years ago accompanied by one of the most glorious fallacies in the history of science, namely that tests measure native intelligence purely and simply without regard to training or schooling. I hope nobody believes that now. The test scores are very definitely a composite including schooling, family background, familiarity with English, and everything else, relevant and irrelevant. The "native intelligence" hypothesis is dead.

But the "native intelligence" thesis wasn't dead at all. In fact, it was just getting under way. Two Harvard University revolutionaries would rescue the SAT's reputation and kick it into high gear.

Revolution was in the air in the 1930s. Stocks fell 86 percent from October 1929 to July 1932. Unemployment hit 25 percent, and soup lines of hollow-cheeked citizens became a much-photographed symbol of hard times. Capitalism appeared to have failed. But America's old-money rich (as opposed to 1920s go-go stock and bond millionaires) were relatively untouched by the Great Depression. Many still had their mansions and servants, private clubs and luxurious yachts.

The incoming president of Harvard University, James Bryant Conant, was angry about the gross inequality. His family was not from East Coast old money. His father was a merchant who owned a photoengraving shop. Conant, despite his good grades, felt like a second-class citizen amid Harvard's wealthy set. The chip never fell off his shoulder, even when he became Harvard's president in 1933. The rich boys there lived different lives, and it infuriated him. As Lemann observes, "Rich young men at Harvard conducted a life barely recognizable today as college students. At a time when a quarter of the American workforce was unemployed and desperate, they lived in private apartments, attended by butlers and maids, in a [Boston] district called The Gold Coast, went to debutante balls in Boston, did not customarily attend classes, and enrolled briefly in special tutoring schools at the end of each semester so they would be able to pass their exams."

Conant was determined to shake Harvard's class system to its roots. What would replace wealth and aristocracy as the natural pecking order? Conant believed in a different aristocracy: an aristocracy of the intellect. It was not a new idea; he borrowed it from Plato's *Republic*. It was an idea that had been tried, to great success, in China. In the sixth century, high-ranking Chinese government officials, called mandarins, were chosen by examination. And the idea had American roots as well. Thomas Jefferson had argued for an aristocracy not of inherited privilege but of "merit." Ever an inventor as well as a thinker, Jefferson proposed a device called an "anthropometer" that would measure human merit. "I should like to see that appraisal applied to every man, that he be placed where he belongs," he wrote.

Class resentment might have driven Harvard's president, but a sense of moral righteousness pulled at him. Conant found an ally in assistant dean Henry Chauncey, whose grandfather had been a New York aristocrat, but whose family money had been lost in a swindle. By the time Henry was born, the family was living in genteel poverty on a minister's salary. Chauncey couldn't afford Harvard and so attended Ohio State University, then a hotbed of psychology. Chauncey loved the field, and when he transferred to Harvard, thanks to a benefactor's scholarship, he pursued psychology and its new branch, intelligence measurement.

These two Harvard revolutionaries, James Conant and Henry Chauncey, promoted the SAT as a weapon against the lazy aristocracy. Their efforts were what established the SAT as a permanent fixture in American life. Conant and Chauncey were untainted by the eugenics movement; their politics, unlike the eugenicists', were not based on social Darwinism and racism. Conant and Chauncey were FDR-era left-wing reformers.

Conant, in particular, became convinced that IQ testing was crucial for America's national defense. In 1940 he was appointed to the National Defense Research Committee. He became the NDRC's chairman in 1941 and presided over the Manhattan Project, which developed the atomic bomb in 1945. Conant even attended the Trinity test in Alamogordo, New Mexico, on July 16, 1945, where he witnessed the atomic bomb's first detonation.

Unlike Carl Brigham, the SAT's anti-Semitic inventor, Conant saw that Jewish refugees from Nazism had been indispensable contributors to the Manhattan Project's success. Hitler's virulent anti-Semitism and Nazi policies had driven some of Germany's top physicists out of the country and into the hands of the Americans. The Americans were lucky beneficiaries of Hitler's racism.

But next time, Conant knew, America might not be so lucky. Thus he became an even more fervent believer in the idea of giving IQ tests to every American child, to ensure that gifted mathematicians, physicists, and engineers from minority groups, poor families, and rural areas could be identified and supported. America's national defense and survival, he believed, depended on the use of an IQ test.

At this point, there was no stopping the SAT's widespread use. Its effects on American culture were rapid. At the beginning of the 1950s, Harvard and the other Ivy League schools still favored legacy kids from elite northeastern families and prep schools. But in the 1960s, Jews and small-town kids who had tested well began pouring into the Ivies. African Americans, Asian Americans, and members of other ethnic minorities would soon follow.

Between the 1950s and 1990s, the SAT replaced membership in old-money aristocracy as America's official gatekeeper of elite university admissions. SAT prep courses naturally followed, as the test grew in importance. Amazingly, by the 1990s, the *Washington Post* newspaper company derived most of its market value not from the newspaper but from its ownership of an SAT prep course vendor, Kaplan Testing Services. Along the way, the SAT weathered some notable controversies, including whether a high test score should earn draft deferment in the Korean War and, reprising Carl Brigham's concern, whether the SAT discriminated against poorer ethnic minorities. In the end, however, the most withering indictment of this measuring and testing craze came from one of its earliest proponents, Lewis Terman himself.

. . .

Today, when testing of intelligence or aptitude or personality type penetrates almost every corner of American life, it's difficult to imagine that such measurements once didn't exist here. People might be known as brilliant or dull, clever or slow, talented or plodding, but there was no empirical yardstick by which to compare and rank them against one another. Lewis Terman's Stanford-Binet test did just that—and was the precursor of scores of such tests for both native aptitude and acquired knowledge. Few people living in the United States today have not experienced at least one IQ test, or a personality test, or an educational test such as the SAT or ACT in high school or the GRE, MCAT, or LSAT in college.

All these tests are descendants not only of Lewis Terman's pioneering work but also of his zealous efforts to standardize testing across the population and drive its adoption by key national institutions, including the civil service. Terman wasn't just an IQ advocate, however, he was also a key researcher.

In 1921 he embarked on the Terman Study of the Gifted, the first and now longest-running longitudinal study of high-IQ individuals in psychology. With a team of assistants, he combed California's public schools with the goal of finding one thousand gifted children to study. In the end, they found more than fifteen hundred, all born between 1900 and 1925, slightly more males than females, most of them white, and nearly all from middle-to-upper-class families.

As the decades passed, however, and the gifted test subjects passed through their prime productive years, it became increasingly apparent that these individuals weren't really special after all—they just had higher IQs. Sure there were a few success stories among them, including a number of college professors, but overall they were almost indistinguishable from their less gifted counterparts—a result that is unlikely to change as the last of the subjects pass from the scene. Most proved to be housewives or had professions "as humble as those of policeman, seaman, typist and filing clerk."

Though Terman was still convinced of the heritability of intelligence, it was a chastened man who later wrote: "At any rate, we have seen that intellect and achievement are far from perfectly correlated."

Neither the stench of eugenics nor the failure of the Stanford-Binet IQ test as a predictive instrument, however, dampened America's zeal for intelligence testing. Just 80,000 students took the SAT in 1951; that number jumped to 1.7 million in 2015. And in the twenty-first century, the SAT is being administered and used by universities around the world.

This explosion in usage has had a secondary effect. The logistical challenge of processing so many examinations in a timely way all but guaranteed that subjective grading by hired readers would give way to the machine grading of multiple-choice answers. The essay section managed to survive, but the rest of the SAT lost all nuance and became a strictly empirical process.

Because the theory behind IQ tests and other "talent" metrics like the SAT and ACT is faulty, their results are generally at odds with expectations. In 1975 two scientists working separately, on different continents, articulated the clear dysfunction of this type of human measurement. The American social psychologist Donald T. Campbell formulated what's come to be called Campbell's Law, which asserts that "the more any quantitative social indicator is used for social decision-making, the more subject it will be to corruption pressures and the more apt it will be to distort and corrupt the social process it is intended to monitor." In other words, the more important we make the SAT and its ilk, the more corrupt and distorted the results become. And the British economist Charles Goodhart formulated Goodhart's Law, which states, "Any measure used for control is unreliable." Put another way: Once attaining a high score becomes the goal of a measurement, the measurement is no longer valid. Put even more simply, and crassly: Anything that is measured and rewarded will be gamed.

These two statistical realities create a perverse outcome. As both laws predict, our obsession with testing—and especially with attaining high scores—destroys any possible predictive validity for the tests.

A test of long-term performance like the SAT is designed to evaluate the knowledge and ability that students have acquired over years of learning and development. When the focus becomes taking the test— rather than the years of learning and development—the test no longer measures what it was created to quantify. Instead, it becomes a competition against a clock, a test of one's ability to answer multiple-choice questions in a specific amount of time.

As Goodhart's Law makes clear, the more we incentivize test results, the more people will beg, borrow, and steal to game the tests. So people with the economic resources for private tutoring and extensive test preparation will attain significantly higher scores—without having actually learned much more about the subjects being tested. This seems like a lousy, and unfair, method for determining the future of a sixteen- or seventeen-year-old.

• • •

Yet another test of human traits that originated in the same era is the now-popular business personality test known as the Myers-Briggs Type Indicator. Its grid of sensation, intuition, feeling, and thinking is believed to define how individuals perceive the world, then make decisions based on those perceptions.

In 1917 Katharine Cook Briggs noticed distinct differences between the personality of her daughter's beau and those of his family members. Largely self-taught, Briggs pursued her inquiry by reading biographies of famous figures and slowly constructed a theory of four temperaments. In 1923 she had an epiphany: Reading the recent English translation of *Psychological Types* by the legendary Swiss psychologist Carl Jung, she learned about Jung's model for human personality types and realized that it seemed to mirror her own. She was soon publishing articles on the rudiments of her theory.

By the end of the 1920s, Briggs's daughter, Isabel Briggs Myers, joined her in her work. A writer, Myers not only helped her mother with her work in "typology" but helped promote the theory in a 1929 award-winning mystery novel. Once a top student at Swarthmore, Myers now apprenticed herself to a noted management consultant, Edward Hay, and learned the arts of testing, statistical analysis, and data validation—all skills she rightly assumed would assist her in developing her mother's test.

Mother and daughter introduced the Myers-Briggs Type Indicator in 1944. They hoped it would help the army of women who were entering the workforce to replace their husbands while they were off at war. The business roots of the Indicator touched a chord in the corporate world—and within a decade Myers-Briggs was a standard tool of the HR/personnel/recruiting professions. Appropriately enough, in 1962, the manual written by Myers was acquired by the Educational Testing Service, the people who administered the SAT.

Myers-Briggs has never been adopted by the psychology profession— critics note its subjectivity, its user bias, and its lack of falsifiability. The researcher Annie Murphy Paul called it an "act of irresponsible armchair philosophy" and Adam Grant, the bestselling social science writer, claimed, "When it comes to accuracy, if you put a horoscope on one end and a heart monitor on the other, the MBTI falls about halfway in between." But with its ninety-three questions and its four-square grid, it remains the world's most popular personality test and is still administered thousands of times every day around the globe.

By the 1950s and 1960s, the use of these archetypical instruments (not to mention scores of others) made American life seemingly test-crazy. IQ tests were administered to children even before they entered school, and the results were used to place them in tracked classes according to their perceived aptitudes. Their SAT or ACT results increasingly determined, even over grade-point average, where they would be accepted to college. And over the course of their adult careers, they faced batteries of personality and aptitude tests for every job to which they applied.

Ranking individuals on a handful of metrics—or even a single metric—is common practice when categorizing not only students but employees. In the early 1990s, General Electric, Microsoft, and others popularized the ranking of all employees on a bell curve. GE's CEO and chairman, Jack Welch, even talked openly about firing the bottom 10 percent every year. Understandably, many businesses subsequently adopted ranking since GE and Microsoft were among the five most valuable companies in the world. They must know what they're doing! Testing and ranking offer the illusion of objectivity and mathematical certitude. In a litigious workplace, they can make a denial of a promotion or pay raise look objectively based and therefore defensible. They seemed to make perfect sense.

Some companies, including Google, have formally moved away from rank-based hiring and promotion systems. Logic-based puzzles and mathematical word problems—designed, in essence, to measure the same capabilities as standardized tests—have replaced GPAs and SAT scores. Thus many applicants and critics claim the change is merely cosmetic. Even in trying to do the right thing, it seems, many companies have failed to wean themselves from the comfort of crude metrics.

Even though the IQ test, the SAT, the ACT, and personality tests like the Myers-Briggs have faced criticism or been proven inaccurate, they've continued to survive—and even flourish. In the twenty-first century, the SAT and ACT standardized college tests loom larger than ever in the lives of American high school students and parents. And the success of Myers-Briggs has spawned a spate of other personality tests, such as the Big Five Personality Test, the Enneagram Type Indicator, and DISC (Dominance, Influence, Steadiness, Conscientiousness). Maybe this resilience shouldn't be surprising. Just as Lewis Terman, Carl Brigham, and Edward Lee Thorndike were working to quantify the potential of each individual, another powerful trend was taking shape in the United States.

• • •

Does this sound familiar? A new technology is created and connects the world. It creates enormous first-generation wealth for its visionary leaders but crushes the working poor in locations far from the technology grid. The gap between rich and poor grows to record proportions. The dispossessed rural poor crowd into cities, which creates epidemics of disease and crime. Angry populism, on both left and right, catches fire. Growing numbers of people suspect the American dream is a myth.

The technology I'm referring to is the late nineteenth-century technology of railroads. The 1890s are often called the Gilded Age for the spectacular wealth and mansions and yachts the railroads produced. But the 1890s also gave us the 1894–97 depression, the worst financial calamity the American economy had suffered to date. (It would be eclipsed in sheer misery by the Great Depression in the 1930s.)

During and after the brutal 1894–97 depression, a growing number of educators and social scientists searched for better ways to rein in corporate greed, the boom-bust economy, and the social ills it produced. Popular feeling gave rise to what historians call the Progressive movement. (The word *progressive* today stands for liberal-left ideas popularized by Democratic senators Cory Booker and Elizabeth Warren, but in the 1890s it stood for applying science-based management to everything from the economy to corporate behavior, education, public health, sociology, and psychology.) Politically, Progressivism rejected both social Darwinism and the collectivist and anarchist schemes arising in Europe. In fact, it was politically bipartisan and was supported by Republican president Theodore Roosevelt and Democratic president Woodrow Wilson.

Progressivism was well-intended and produced many needed reforms, notably in public health, worker safety, antitrust regulation, and the right of women to vote. Its effects in education and business management were also profound but more mixed. In business, Progressivism imposed a rigid conformity that reduced human beings to moving parts. To see how, let's look at the work of Frederick Winslow Taylor, the era's most influential business thinker.

"In the past, man was first; in the future, the system must be first," Taylor wrote in *The Principles of Scientific Management*, published in

1911. His simple and appealing idea was that managers could boost labor productivity on the factory floor if they could identify, then remove, the irrational time wasters. So managers took to watching, recording, measuring, and analyzing the actions of their workers. No more employee freelancing on the factory floor. No more dawdling between tasks. No more artisanal craftsmanship and make-it-up-as-you-go. Taylor wanted to reduce complex manufacturing processes to the smallest repetitive steps that any worker could do quickly.

Taylorism, predictably, required an authoritarian level of control over workers and work practices. But Taylor felt his ideas would be the savior of workers, since more productive workers could earn more money. His influence peaked in the first decades of the twentieth century, as his theories found their greatest realization in the auto assembly plants of Henry Ford. Just as Taylor had predicted, Ford paid his most productive workers twice the going rate for factory work. He said he wanted his employees to be able to afford a Ford.

Taylor had let the scientific management genie out of the bottle. Taylorism spawned many new timing, bookkeeping, and accounting methods, as well as workflow charts, machine-speed slide calculators, motion studies, and assembly pacing metrics. He gave managers permission to observe, measure, analyze, and control every minute of a worker's time on the clock. That was the core of Taylor's scientific management, and it was hard to argue against its value. Today's technology—including cloud computation, the Internet of Things, big data analytics, artificial intelligence, workflow apps, and robots—may seem centuries removed from Taylor and his stopwatch, but many of his ideas still dominate the business world.

Oddly enough, Taylor's system of scientific management has also become firmly entrenched in education. A century ago American educators adopted it as the best way to deal with the large influx of immigrant children. In 1912 the publication of *The Elimination of Waste in Education*, by John Franklin Bobbitt, set the stage for the adoption and implementation of scientific management in schools. Bobbitt argued that schools, like businesses, should be efficient, eliminate waste, and focus on outcomes. Curricula should mold students into effective workers.

Like Taylor, Bobbitt believed that efficient outcomes depended on centralized authority and precise, top-down instruction. Other educational leaders, such as Columbia University's Edward Lee Thorndike, openly advocated the conveyor-belt-like structures. Thorndike, especially, shaped society's views on curriculum, pedagogy, and organizational structure to fit the principles of scientific management. Very quickly this became the dominant model for education.

As Harvard's Todd Rose writes in his brilliant book on differing human talents, *The End of Average*, the rigid pathways of today's educational system stem from ideas about factory management:

> Our schools still follow the same [Tayloristic] rigid march through time as they did a century ago, with fixed class durations, and fixed semesters, proceeding through the same unyielding sequence of "core" courses, all of which ensure that every (normal) student graduates from high school at the same age with, presumably, the same set of knowledge.

In 1962 the historian Raymond Callahan discussed how scientific management had affected American schools. His *Education and the Cult of Efficiency* recounts the influence of Taylor's ideas on educational administration—everything from making better use of buildings and classroom space to standardizing the work of janitors. Another line of reforms required teachers to document their teaching activities in order to minimize "waste."

Lest we think we've become more enlightened since the days of Taylor, recent educational reform initiatives like No Child Left Behind, Common Core, and Race to the Top have all increased the role of standardized testing in public education. High-stakes standardized tests, however, are just the most visible example of Frederick Taylor's ideas at work in education. In reality, our educational system operates largely according to the dictates of an industrial system: a consistent drive toward greater standardization and measurement, an overt promotion of a utilitarian STEM-focused curriculum, and even a physical synchronization through the use of bells to signal changes and breaks—all as if kids are little Ford Model T's rolling off a Frederick Taylor–designed assembly line.

To most people, this sounds ridiculous. It's common knowledge that we all learn in different ways. Learning is a cumulative process that involves neurological, physiological, and emotional development. This means we all absorb, incorporate, and apply knowledge at different paces. Some people start applying knowledge as soon as they're exposed to the foundations. Others, late bloomers in particular (myself included), apply that knowledge only after the final piece clicks into place. This moment when something complex suddenly makes sense often feels like an awakening. But this pattern can skew the process of tracking, ranking, and categorizing students along the way. Though some kids have profiles that fit neatly into the learning templates, many others possess profiles that are not well matched to expectations.

Standardized tests simply can't measure students' critical thinking skills or true engagement with a topic. And forcing teachers to address only content that can be measured in standardized tests, while avoiding more analytical material, hinders learning. It also devalues the profession of teaching, the way that Taylor's theories devalued the role of skilled craftspeople in factories. Reducing education to test preparation jeopardizes the quality of curricula and the craft of teaching. It drains education of humanity.

• • •

The outcome of our obsession with measurement?

Success today is represented by the high-IQ, high-SAT wunderkind test takers beloved of Bill Gates and other IQ farms like Goldman Sachs, Google, and Amazon. The most successfully measured among us make the most money, and they make it the fastest. Today IQ and data dominate academic sorting, which has put unprecedented pressure on kids to be early bloomers. And thanks to our pressure-cooker education system that picks "winners"—that is, students with high GPAs and SAT scores—generations of young women and men find themselves left behind before they even reach adulthood. Young adults, men especially, look at the adult world, reject it, and live in their parents' house playing computer games for hours every day. We see it in binge drinking and opioid addiction—all manner of ways in which people seek relief from their confusing, stressful, and unsatisfied lives. We see it in surveys that indicate a majority of employees feel underappreciated and disengaged. We see it in the stigmatizing of diverse skills, atypical development, and late blooming.

The continued use of intelligence-based tests by many schools and businesses speaks more to our need to have a seemingly objective and defensible system of defining people than to any provable efficacy. If there's one key takeaway here, it's that no one has yet been able to devise a test that can accurately measure the potential or talent of an individual. The simple fact is, it's impossible to apply a single metric or one-dimensional scale to something as intricate and multifaceted as human development.

And yet we as a society measure, rank, and sort ourselves more than ever before. Why?

• • •

Earlier in this chapter, I mentioned that the world's second-richest man, Bill Gates, scored 800—a perfect score—on his math SAT. I explained how his belief in the moneymaking magic of high IQs drove Microsoft's early hiring and staffing decisions, and that Microsoft's reliance on IQ as a predictor of code-writing talent and business acumen was followed by many other companies.

Larry Page and Sergey Brin, who founded Google, also scored at or near 800 on their math SATs. They started Google as Stanford graduate students in 1998, and until 2014, both were known to ask Google job applicants for their SAT scores. (Alphabet, Google's parent company, now goes to great lengths to say it no longer does this. But the reality is that Google still uses various puzzles, riddles, and other means to evaluate a job applicant's fast-twitch cognitive giftedness.)

Amazon's founder and CEO, and the world's richest man, Jeff Bezos, also scored 800 on his math SAT. According to reporter Brad Stone, Bezos "felt that hiring only the best and brightest was key to Amazon's success. Early on, he conducted job interviews himself; and he too asked candidates for their SAT scores. Bezos said: 'Every time we hire someone, he or she should raise the bar for the next hire, so that the overall talent pool is always improving.'" Bezos jokingly told a reporter that his wife's high SAT scores made the pair compatible.

Facebook founder Mark Zuckerberg scored a perfect 1600 on the math and English parts of his SAT. And Apple cofounder Steve Wozniak? He, too, scored an 800 on his math SAT.

Two more eye-opening numbers: The combined personal wealth of our six wunderkinds math SAT test takers is more than $300 billion. And the companies they created are worth $3.6 trillion, more than the GDP of all but nine countries.

Surely this is worthy of applause. But let's stop and consider the price. One well-known contrarian thinker argues that today's obsession with SAT scores and the wealth-generating mojo of algorithmic genius has left the U.S. economy in a decades-long state of underperformance and a society desperate for answers. Lest you think this contrarian thinker is hostile to Silicon Valley and its wunderkinds getting obscenely rich, he's actually one of them.

Peter Thiel, a cofounder of PayPal and board member of Facebook (and himself a high school chess prodigy, Stanford law school graduate, and 800 math SAT scorer), claims there is a mismatch between what is good for overall economic prosperity and what gets easily funded by investors. In Thiel's mind, the U.S. economy has too much investment capital flowing into "bits" companies. Using terminology coined by MIT's Nicholas Negroponte in the 1990s, "bits" companies are those that earn their profits by writing algorithms to provide a service (think Google, Facebook, and Amazon) or that use them to outsmart financial markets (think Morgan Stanley, Goldman Sachs, and countless hedge funds). What "bits" companies mostly don't do is make physical products. They use their clever algorithms to create markets, not products.

An "atoms" company, in Negroponte's and Thiel's vernacular, is the older kind of company that manipulates physical objects—harvests crops, extracts fuels, forges steel, manufactures cars, binds books, assembles TVs, and transports goods over land, sea, or air. General Motors is a quintessential "atoms" company. It operates dozens of factories in seventeen countries, employs over 200,000 people, and produces ten million cars and trucks per year.

But because atoms companies use physical resources, require factories and stores, generate waste, and occasionally result in job-related injuries, they are heavily regulated and taxed. By contrast bits companies, whose employees write algorithms while seated at computers, use minimal resources (with the exception of electricity, whose regulatory burdens are assumed by fuel companies and utilities), generate little pollution, and rarely have accidents on the job. So they are barely regulated at all. Bits companies that challenge older atoms companies, such as Uber and Airbnb, are so new and disruptive that the old regulatory structures haven't caught up. Another advantage enjoyed by bits companies is favorable tax consequences. Their founders and investors are taxed at the lower capital gains rates as opposed to higher personal income tax rates. Corporate profits of bits companies typically are kept offshore. Facebook and Google pay effective corporate income taxes of 15 percent, versus the Standard & Poor's 500 company average of 21 percent.

Thiel's view of the present-day economy, with skewed rewards going to bits companies, is not partisan. (He is a noted libertarian/conservative.) Democratic pollster Mark Penn agrees with him: "The old brick-and-mortar economy is being regulated to death. The new tech-driven economy has been given a pass to flout regulation and build vast value."

It's no surprise, therefore, that investment capital pours into the bits economy and prefers to avoid the atoms economy. Uber, the on-line car-sharing service, had, in 2018, a shareholder value of $72 bil-lion, even though it was only nine years old and retained around ten thousand full-time employees. General Motors, a 110-year-old com-pany, has a current market cap—or valuation—of $52 billion. Stop and think about this. Uber is worth $20 billion more than GM. The enormous market cap advantage held by bits companies becomes self-perpetuating. As richly funded bits companies look to the future, they can invest more, acquire more, and pay more for talent than atoms companies can. The lopsided advantages in market value held by bits companies has been gaining momentum for the last thirty years.

What does this mean for early achievers and late bloomers? When you see these types of discrepancies in rate of return, if you're an am-bitious teenager—or a parent—a natural question is: *What will it take to get a job at a bits company?* That's easy. As we've seen, bits compa-nies want the cognitive elite. They want the measurably smartest and quickest, the very best of the best. And no single test or evaluation, in their minds, gives a snapshot of supercharged algorithmic skill as well as the math portion of the SAT. Young adults, parents, teachers, and employers—no one can escape the fact that the world's most valuable companies in the twenty-first century were started by people who were SAT math whizzes. Few articulate this, but we all know it's true. In a highly uncertain economy, society has put tremendous pressure on children to achieve the test scores that make them hirable by the most profitable companies in the most lucrative industries.

But this pressure for high test scores and early achievement has created its own perversities.

• • •

In 2014 *Forbes* magazine named a thirty-year-old Stanford dropout as the richest self-made woman in the world. Elizabeth Holmes and her company, Theranos, had developed a "technology that could take a pinprick's worth of blood, extracted nearly painlessly from the tip of a finger, instead of intravenously, and test for hundreds of diseases." Holmes speculated that her company could save millions of lives.

Investors speculated, too, believing that Theranos could make them billions of dollars. They poured in rounds and rounds of private capital investment and bid the company's value to $10 billion. Holmes was in the catbird seat. She used her leverage to maintain half the Theranos shares, thus accounting for her $5 billion net worth, which propelled her to the top of the *Forbes* list.

But in 2016 it all came crashing down. As *Wall Street Journal* reporter John Carreyrou revealed in more than two dozen articles, the Theranos technology did not work. Those tiny pinpricks of blood were often contaminated by broken skin from the fingertip. Worse, even clean pinprick test results failed to match up with the older, time-proven method of drawing vials of blood intravenously. In other words, the pinprick samples were useless and possibly dangerous if they missed a fatal symptom or led to a wrong treatment. The first to notice the problem was Theranos's chief scientist Ian Gibbons. The Theranos chief operating officer, who reported to Holmes, told Gibbons to button his lips. But word of Theranos's secret deception got out, and soon the FBI was investigating. On the eve of being summoned to Holmes's office presumably for his firing, Gibbons took his own life. If his widow, Rochelle, was expecting condolences from Holmes and Theranos, she was in for a shock. Theranos lawyers quickly sent Rochelle Gibbons a letter threatening legal action if she talked to a reporter.

Holmes, obsessed with achieving early success, at first seemed destined for it. When she was nine years old, she wrote a letter to her father: "What I really want out of life is to discover something new that mankind didn't know was possible to do." She studied Mandarin as a child, and in high school in Houston, she started her first business, selling a computer coding language to Chinese universities. Her acceptance into prestigious Stanford University was accompanied by a President's Scholar award and a stipend for a research project of her choosing. Her summer job upon completing her freshman year at Stanford was at the Singapore Genome Institute. At eighteen, she applied for her first patent, a wearable drug-delivery patch.

Exceptionally gifted, Holmes was also exceptionally driven. Her business hero was Steve Jobs, the prodigy who cofounded Apple and later led it to glory. She quickly adopted Jobs's tropes and mannerisms. She wore black turtlenecks. She steepled her hands. Her slow-blinking stare, it was said, could bore holes through your eye sockets. She also took on Jobs's less admirable traits. She ran Theranos like a police state, obsessed with preventing employees from talking about their work with each other. She became a master at employing Jobs's "reality distortion field"—a fictional narrative about her own genius and wondrous Theranos products that were unyielding to the facts.

Jobs was only twenty-one when he cofounded Apple, and twenty-five when Apple first sold its stock to the public, making Jobs a young celebrity and centi-millionaire. Holmes felt increasingly pressured in a race to glory and early wealth against her old idol. As the Theranos pinprick blood tests proved worthless, she pushed ahead instead of getting the technology right. She traveled the world in a leased Gulfstream 150, often alone, to make speeches. She threatened critics with lawsuits; she visited *Wall Street Journal* chairman Rupert Murdoch to try to stop Carreyrou's reporting; and she directed Theranos to secretly test its blood samples with old technology to keep customers like Walgreens happy.

But those investigative articles by the *Wall Street Journal* and later by *Forbes* and *Vanity Fair* would not wait. By 2016 the word was out. Theranos had failed to do what it purported to do, it lied about it, and it threatened anyone who reported the truth. Two years after declaring Elizabeth Holmes the richest self-made woman in the world, *Forbes* calculated that her stock in Theranos was worthless.

What can we say about Elizabeth Holmes? She was tremendously gifted. Her one-in-a-million algorithmic skills made her fluent in Mandarin and an expert computer programmer in high school. She was a President's Scholar at Stanford, a patent applicant at eighteen, and as an entrepreneur was so smart and charismatic that at nineteen she was able to talk her Stanford adviser into joining her company. But is she actually a born liar and a con artist, a Bernie Madoff wannabe? Here I speculate, but I don't think so—or at least she didn't start out that way. I think her fatal flaw was an obsession with early success and the impatience that goes with it. When Theranos didn't succeed on her magical schedule, she didn't stop to fix the technology but rather doubled down on her young genius narrative, her TED talks, her private jet trips, and her legal threats to doubters.

Is Elizabeth Holmes a bad person? Millions think so. I'm guessing her actions are more complicated, not so black-and-white. More likely she got trapped by her own story of early achievement—a story that was cheered in a society that promotes a narrow view of success.

• • •

In countless ways, America and rich countries around the world celebrate a diversity of ethnicities and lifestyles that were not accepted a generation or two ago. For many people who have historically been marginalized, this progress has been significant. University graduation rates for African Americans have doubled in the last three decades. Prominent African Americans like Michael Jordan and Magic Johnson aren't just former athletes, they're now team owners. The most recent *Forbes* list of "America's Richest Self-Made Women" includes seventeen billionaires, with businesses ranging from roofing to trucking to retail. Same-sex marriage is now a federally mandated constitutional right in all fifty states, and high-profile business leaders like Apple CEO Tim Cook openly identify as gay.

And even though we've lately taken a step back as a society in terms of public and political tolerance, polls confirm that over recent decades, attitudes toward diversity in education and the workplace, gender equality, and same-sex marriage have shifted steadily. This growing sense of social acceptance has stretched to include personal style, unusual interests, and radical identity politics. We now can have tattoos and multiple piercings and still hold good jobs. We can bend genders and be sexually fluid, we can wear flip-flops and hoodies to work, we can collect comic books and play video games as adults—and it's all much more culturally accepted than it was before.

And yet when it comes to early achievement and cognitive diversity, we've done the exact opposite. We've become less tolerant of those with different cognitive profiles—of those with slower rates of development or skills not recognized by the job market.

Society flatters itself with the idea that we've become wonderfully independent and more diverse thinkers. We assume that because we celebrate different identities and lifestyles, we also celebrate different learning profiles and cognitive development schedules: We assume that there's more opportunity for more of us now than ever before. But this assumption is deeply flawed, a misconception that blinds us to the rigid conformity that vastly overvalues the rapid algorithmic skills coveted by Web companies and financial firms. Maybe more damaging, this conformity is often built on a single metric or a vague percentile, hardly the type of data needed to map something as complex as human potential.

Look at how all-determining the IQ test and the SAT have become. They were never meant to be the final arbiters of success in life. Just a few decades ago, possessing decent grades and middling test scores wasn't likely to limit your life's trajectory. Your SAT scores weren't a big driver in how much money you made, whom you married, or what others thought of you. The qualifications for a good job, whether on a factory floor or behind a desk, mostly involved integrity, eagerness, experience, work ethic, reliability, teamwork, and stick-to-it-iveness. It was about emotional intelligence, not just IQ. Compare that with the present moment. Today the bottom 75 percent in standardized test results—three-quarters of all test takers—have a rough time. It's hard to have a nonstandard learning style if your parents can't afford to send you to an alternative school or hire a battery of tutors, or haven't the time to homeschool you.

And whether we recognize it or not—whether we want to admit it or not— this constitutes a significant cultural regression.

Today you can do all the right things—study hard, take the SAT, go to a local or state university—and still be left behind. You can follow the path that for generations was the "escalator to success," yet still be pushed to the margins or be economically excluded. And why? Well, you didn't do it brilliantly enough or fast enough; your standardized-test-taking skills were not stellar at seventeen. Ergo, you are probably one of life's unfortunate also-rans.

In the past, if you hit a snag in high school or college, you had more ways to catch up. For example, the U.S. military was once a readily available route to reinvention. The military used to be a place where people, men mostly, particularly from the working class, could gain discipline and maturity, discover role models, and raise their sights. But you rarely hear such stories anymore—they've faded from the American conversation. Consider J. D. Vance, the author of the surprise 2016 best seller *Hillbilly Elegy: A Memoir of a Family and Culture in Crisis*. After a troubled childhood and adolescence, he joined the Marine Corps. Once his military stint was up, he enrolled at Ohio State, moved on to Yale Law School, then became a principal at a leading Silicon Valley investment firm. It's an extraordinary story of exploration, growth, and self-development. But what's most extraordinary about Vance's story is the very fact *that it is extraordinary*. It used to be commonplace. Today a rigid conformity underlies our surface tolerance, a tacit cognitive tyranny that excludes many alternate pathways to success and fulfillment.

Worse, this conformity has blinded us to a universal, profound truth that hides in plain sight—that human potential is wonderfully wide-ranging. Some people are lucky that their skills are noticed early in their school years, that their best talents get discovered through one-dimensional, standardized tests. They are the fortunate ones. For the unfortunate majority, however, our latent skills are neither discovered nor recognized nor encouraged until much later, if ever. As a result, most of us are falsely labeled as having less talent or ambition; we're written off as lazy or apathetic. But in reality, the light simply isn't shining on our true abilities, on the things we can do uniquely well. The toxic combination of early pressure and conformity is turning us into machines.

And this sets up a competition we're guaranteed to lose.

• • •

Our dilemma is scary: Machines are inexorably getting smarter, year after year. In the last century, when modern automation first appeared, it didn't seem like much of a threat to the knowledge-based economy because the gains it offered were mostly at the expense of raw manual labor. Automobile assembly-line workers worried when robots began welding and assembling more and more car parts, but when robots and AI began to invade the professional workplace, people in universities and the media took notice. Only now is the magnitude of the crisis becoming clear.

In the fall of 2016, former treasury secretary and chief economist of the World Bank Lawrence Summers wrote: "I expect that more than *one-third* of all men between 25 and 54 will be out [of] work at midcentury. Very likely more than half of men will experience a year of non-work at least one year out of every five." His assessment is based on work by Nicholas Eberstadt, one of America's leading demographers, who calls this coming displacement "America's invisible crisis."

Just before Christmas 2016, the White House released a fifty-page report titled *Artificial Intelligence, Automation, and the Economy* that suggests that "the U.S. should invest in and develop AI, because it has 'many benefits,' including educating and training Americans for the jobs of the future, and aid workers and empower them to share in future growth." That doesn't sound so bad, right? But read on: "But the authors of the report acknowledge that there are countless unknowns, from what the effects could be, to how quickly they'll arrive. Researchers' estimates on the scale of threatened jobs over the next decade or two range from 9 percent to 47 percent." In reporting the story, the website MarketWatch headlined tongue-in-cheek: "White House: Robots May Take Half of Our Jobs, and We Should Embrace It."

In the years ahead, millions of white-collar workers who thought their careers were immune to automation will learn that their highly respected jobs can be performed by a cheap software program. Indeed, it's hard to identify a career that isn't at risk of being supplanted by AI and computer automation. Medicine, radiology, oncology, and even some kinds of surgery are all vulnerable to automation. That means saying goodbye to six-figure careers in some of the most distinguished professions. Tenured college professor? Digitized lectures are already being offered via online learning. Lawyer? The website LegalZoom can help consumers write a will, create an LLC, file for divorce, or register a trademark. How about architect or engineer? BIM (building information modeling) and VDC (virtual design and construction) programs like Autodesk and Revit are already designing structures and creating blueprints.

In speculating about which jobs are at risk, MIT economist Frank Levy pinpoints white-collar jobs that are "rules-based." They require following complex directions or rules, such as filing legal briefs, reading schematics, or creating structural designs. Up until now, someone could make a good living doing such jobs, but now they are under attack—and probably doomed.

Now, I'm optimistic that most people will successfully adapt in time. Still, one can see the trap. Society's currently favored STEM track (science, technology, engineering, and math) encourages young people to go into jobs that AI, ironically, may soon destroy. Many rules-based jobs, from engineering to banking, from lab work to computer coding, once seemed future-proof or disruption-resistant. But in fact they are a trap. And the coming dislocations will be profound.

• • •

Society is in a crisis. Our obsession with test scores, perfect grades, and measurable early achievement developed from a good idea that has been way overshot. Instead of a meritocracy that rewards a variety of human talents, we have created a narrowing IQ/SAT oligarchy. A cohort of early bloomers win big in this new order, but most young men and women find themselves left behind before they even reach adulthood, their natural abilities lying fallow and undiscovered by the algorithm-biased conveyor belt of success. Such outsize emphasis on early achievement is misplaced. Human life spans are lengthening. Most people recently born will live into the twenty-second century. The vast majority of us will be better served not by high SAT scores or STEM degrees but by discovering and embracing our true talents, so we may bloom at any stage of our lives.

Expensive four-year universities and soaring college debt are just one symptom of our current dilemma. There is $1.3 trillion in college debt in the United States today (see the Introduction), with an 11.5 percent default rate. That's greater than the 2008 housing bubble. Fear that our children will miss the first and only on ramp to adult success is driving this fiscal insanity. And in the absence of a system of hereditary titles, with no officially mandated status ladder in place, we've created a new system of snobbery based on IQ scores and elite university degrees.

To mitigate this crisis, we must stop excessively glorifying precocious achievement and seeing human development as a "fast track" on ramp for early success. Not only is it unjust to the majority of us, it's profoundly inhumane. It ignores the natural-born gifts that we all possess. It cuts off paths of discovery for our more latent or later-blooming gifts and passions. It trivializes the value of character, experience, empathy, wisdom, reliability, tenacity, and a host of other admirable qualities that make us successful and fulfilled. And it undercuts the majority of us who are potential late bloomers.

Instead, we should celebrate the full range of human ability and diverse timetables for individual success and achievement. Instead of arbitrarily cutting off paths of discovery at early ages, we should be opening paths up. This is essential if we're to thrive in a future defined by intelligent machines and ubiquitous automation. And it better corresponds with the fact that each of us develops on an individual timetable, in distinctive ways.

But rather than celebrate the fact that we're all different, our society overwhelmingly favors people who prove to be algorithmically exceptional or precociously focused—people with early-manifesting gifts for taking tests who have the resources to go to the right schools, take the right classes, and find the right coaches.

In the past, success was not about becoming rich or famous, or about achieving as much as possible as early as possible. Rather, it was about having the opportunity to live to our fullest potential. It was about being appreciated for who we are as individuals. But that's been corrupted by the Wunderkind Ideal and our obsession with testing, ranking, and sorting young adults; by our cultural fascination with youth, particularly youthful *über*-achievement; and by an increasingly algorithmic economy that rewards raw synaptic speed instead of experience and wisdom.

Unfortunately, most of us didn't score outrageously high on the SAT, or have the insider's advantage to attend a $40,000-per-year preschool. Most of us don't fit the latest learning template or develop according to principles of scientific management. Most of us are not athletic phenoms or extreme extroverts, ruthlessly ambitious climbers or cognitive standouts.

Where does that leave us, the unconnected, the high or middling scorers who didn't get 800 on our math SAT, the slower and more typical learners—the late bloomers?

That's the focus of the rest of the book. And the good news is, our situation is wonderfully more encouraging than today's wunderkind culture would suggest.

• •

CHAPTER 3

A Kinder Clock for Human Development

At fifteen, Ashley cut her wrists, ran away, and engaged in dangerous trysts with older men. She was trapped in a cycle of depression, self-abuse, and paralysis. Today she's a professional counselor and public speaker.

Now thirty-two, Ashley shares her story from a ballroom stage at a resort hotel. It's a Saturday evening in January, and the roughly six hundred attendees have just finished their chicken dinner and dessert. They've turned their chairs to watch Ashley. She projects health and confidence. She seems the opposite of a person who once, as she put it, "habitually bailed on responsibilities and cut and run."

To be clear, Ashley is not using "cut and run" as a metaphor. She tells the audience that she began cutting her wrists with razor blades in junior high school. Her alarmed parents tried to stop the cutting and whatever compulsions propelled it. They tried discipline, rewards, and counselors. Nothing worked. So they plucked Ashley out of tenth grade and enrolled her in an experimental girls' boarding school, an hour north of Phoenix, Spring Ridge Academy.

At Spring Ridge, Ashley liked to run away and hitchhike. Her longest disappearance was an almost-twenty-hour overnighter in Phoenix. Her compulsive streak reached the point where it was placing her in real danger. After being intercepted by a Spring Ridge counselor who was genuinely willing to listen, Ashley began her journey back to health and functionality. She got her high school diploma, then went to college and earned a master's in clinical psychology. Nearly two decades have passed since Ashley ran away to Phoenix; she is now a counselor to troubled teenage girls. "I always wanted to be fearless," she says. "But that desire once took unhealthy paths. Now I've learned I can be fearless in a much healthier way. And I can be a leader, helping others."

As Ashley's story suggests, our present-day mania for early blooming is on a collision course with real life—and with three major trends. First, an expanding body of evidence suggests that adolescents generally are maturing into cognitive and emotional adulthood later today than in previous generations. Second, technology's relentless march demands ongoing personal and career reinvention. The truth is inescapable; the skills young people demonstrate in college or on the SAT are more perishable in an age of faster change. And third, recent research suggests that the cognitive abilities we lose as we age are offset by abilities we acquire up until the end of our lives. Nearly all reasonably healthy people are capable of blooming in different ways at different ages. To create a prosperous society of fulfilled individuals, it makes sense, therefore, to have a kinder clock of human development. Every person needs to have the chance—multiple chances, really—to follow their unique timeline of evolving brains, talents, and passions.

• • •

Teenagers and young adults mature at different rates. Every parent knows this, and a growing number of neuroscientists and psychologists now confirm it. Many psychologists believe that ages eighteen to twenty-five form a distinct period that is neither truly adolescent nor truly adult. By law, we label eighteen-to-twenty-five-year-olds as adults, but in reality many of us, late bloomers especially, lack important elements of functional adulthood.

My own rather embarrassing story reflects this fact.

I loved being a kid. I excelled in grade school, had fun playing all sports, and recall with affection my parents, siblings, and friends. Then adolescence arrived and upended my little world. Junior high school felt like a prison. The other boys began to mature physically while I seemed stuck in a snowbank. They got interested in girls, and girls in them. Many boys and girls in my class suddenly understood algebra and geometry in ways I couldn't begin to comprehend, leaving me behind. I could not bring myself to read serious books like *To Kill a Mockingbird*. I got by in school but no longer excelled, falling from straight A's in the fifth grade to mostly B's in junior high. In sports I was a benchwarmer. In social life I was picked on, pushed around, yanked up by the underwear, and flushed. One afternoon a ninth grader took a swing at me and broke my glasses. I did nothing to retaliate and became a loser in the eyes of those who stood by.

In high school I won back some shred of dignity by trying out for the track and cross-country teams. Distance running favors skinny kids who can channel their anger into pain tolerance. I ran the mile in 4:36, not a bad time, but we were a state championship team, and my time was only fourth best on the team. The coaches seemed to hardly notice. Academically, I finished something like ninety-fourth out of 521 in my senior class, with a 3.2 grade point average. I was the worst student in my advanced math class.

High mediocrity and alienation seemed my fate. At the local junior college, three blocks from my house, I struggled with economics, calculus, and chemistry. I ran track and cross-country and even won a race, but our small team competed at the very lowest of the varsity collegiate levels—junior college in the sparsely populated states of the Upper Midwest.

Then I transferred to a four-year college, the lucky beneficiary of a cosmic mistake. My junior college track time in the obscure thousand-yard indoor run was 2:21, an average high school effort. But it qualified me for the junior college national indoor meet, which caught the eye of Stanford's distance coach, who—because I had run in the nationals— misread it as a thousand-*meter* time, portending my promising future as an NCAA runner. The coach thought I was 10 percent faster than I really was. While 10 percent faster wasn't good enough to win me a track scholarship, the mistaken Stanford coach did me a favor of another sort. He called the admissions department and asked them to overlook my B grades in junior college and my less-than-stellar SAT scores in lieu of my promising potential as an NCAA-level middle distance runner. (I later learned of the coach's mistake while chatting with him at the university's intramural track meet.)

At this point, I'd love to say that I took advantage of my outrageously lucky break and blossomed into a varsity track athlete and Rhodes scholar candidate. But no, I squandered the golden opportunity. My academic lethargy continued. I learned to follow football players around on class signup days, figuring (correctly) that some took the easiest classes, nicknamed the Mickey Mouse curriculum. Yet I still managed no better than B's pursuing the Mouse major—though I got an A minus, once, in film aesthetics. After graduation my roommates went off to grad school with grand plans—law, chemical engineering, divinity. I went off to become a security guard, dishwasher, and temporary typist. For seven months, I was an editorial assistant at *Runner's World* magazine, which gave me a potential footing on a real career. But I quit ahead of a firing for being a stoner and a slacker, picking fights with colleagues, and misspelling names on race results. I lived hand to mouth. Months after leaving *Runner's World*, I would steal wine bottles at my night watchman's job at a winery and get drunk on the job. On the way home to my shabby apartment in my old Ford Falcon, I would stop by a convenience store for a junk food breakfast.

One cold night my failure to bloom led to a humiliating insight.

Dark had settled in as I walked out of the guard shack to start my hourly patrol. I wore the uniform of American Patrol Services, black slacks and a gray short-sleeved collared shirt with a shiny badge over the breast pocket. I looked like a mall cop, except my security guard "post" that night was a rent-a-truck yard in north San Jose, California. I carried no weapons, but rather a Detex clock shaped like a large hockey puck. My job was to walk the perimeter of the fenced yard and insert the Detex's key into a dozen or so boxes bolted to the fence, thus proving I had made my appointed patrol rounds each hour.

Somewhere in the night a dog began to bark. It was a large dog's bark, meant to frighten, and it would not stop. I swung my flashlight around for the source and soon found it—a Rottweiler in the lumberyard next door.

Then it hit me. The security guard in the lumberyard next door was not another person, but a dog. The implication was sobering. I was twenty-five years old, a Stanford graduate. In a few months, Steve Jobs, also twenty-five, would take Apple public, change the computer industry, and become fabulously rich. I, on the other hand, was poor and stuck, and my professional colleague was a dog.

That was me at twenty-five.

Then everything changed for me. At twenty-six, my brain woke up—yes, it felt like that—and I managed to win a job as a technical writer at a research institute. At twenty-nine I got married. I started, with a friend, what would become the top public affairs organization in Silicon Valley. At thirty-four I cofounded Silicon Valley's first business magazine. At thirty-eight *Forbes* hired me to launch a technology magazine. At forty-four I became the publisher of *Forbes* and began a speaking career that would take me around the world. At forty-six I learned to fly an airplane, and at forty-nine I wrote a bestselling book about my flying adventures. My fifth-grade dreams that I might amount to something were coming true.

Looking back, the hinge point in my career was my late twenties. Somehow, during those years, I awoke from a long slumber that had begun in junior high school. And by twenty-nine, I began to feel like I had a fully functioning brain at last. I read the *Wall Street Journal* and the *New York Times* instead of watching TV news. I read political journals across the ideological spectrum. I could think both intuitively and logically and see the difference. I could write sentences, paragraphs, and whole papers. I learned to plan and run my own business. I could foresee entrepreneurial opportunities and write proposals. I could conduct myself professionally with people older and more accomplished than I was.

A whole new world opened up.

What caused me to awaken in my late twenties? What shook me

out of a dopey postadolescence and propelled me toward an adult's sense of possibility and responsibility?

. . .

Emerging research suggests that the accepted human maturation sequence, from adolescence to adulthood, misses a step. Between the ages of eighteen and twenty-five, most people are not yet fully adult but rather are living in a volatile postadolescence, a few cognitive processes short of a fully functioning adult brain. In adolescent and young adult brains, the prefrontal cortex—the processing center of our frontal lobe—is the last part to fully develop, often in our mid-twenties or later. Located just behind the forehead, the prefrontal cortex is responsible for complex processes like planning and organizing, problem solving, memory recall, response inhibition, and attention allocation.

Cognitive researchers have used neuroimaging studies to determine two important characteristics of the prefrontal cortex: It's late in developing, and it's large. In essence, cognitive development in our frontal lobe, home to the prefrontal cortex, progresses in a back-to-front direction. It begins in the primary motor cortex, spreads to the parietal and temporal cortex, and finishes with the prefrontal cortex.

Maybe this shouldn't surprise us. Our prefrontal cortex is massive compared to that of other species. In the human adult, the prefrontal cortex constitutes nearly one-third of the neocortex, which is the entire part of the brain involved in higher-order brain functions. By comparison, the prefrontal cortex makes up just 17 percent of the neocortex in a chimpanzee, 13 percent in a dog, and 4 percent in a cat.

What's important to know is that many critical prefrontal cortex changes occur during our late teens and early twenties. Myelination, for one, is a process in which nerve fibers are more extensively covered with myelin, a substance that insulates the fibers so that nerve signals can be more efficiently transmitted. Extensive synaptic pruning also occurs during this period. This may sound like a bad thing, but it's not. Through synaptic pruning, the tangled web of possible connections resulting from explosive nerve growth is pruned back, allowing the remaining ones to more effectively transmit signals. At the same time, the prefrontal cortex develops the ability to better communicate with other parts of the brain—especially those associated with emotions and impulses—so that all areas of the brain can be included in complex processes such as planning and problem solving.

These are the defining abilities that make us adults: controlling for emotions and impulses, planning complex processes, and anticipating problems. But they are ill-formed in most eighteen-to-twenty-five-year-olds. Psychologists use another term for neurological maturity: executive function. The lack of executive function is what led to Ashley's compulsive cutting and running streak and my own raging immaturity. Executive function has nothing to do with IQ, potential, or talent. It is simply the ability to see ahead and plan effectively, to connect actions to possible consequences, to see the probabilities of risk and reward. It includes developing a sense of self (self-identity, individual beliefs, and personal values), regulating emotions, and setting goals. Most of these executive function skills are coordinated and controlled through our prefrontal cortex—precisely the slowest, largest, and last region of the brain to develop.

A longitudinal study of brain development sponsored by the National Institute of Mental Health (NIMH) followed nearly five thousand children at ages three to sixteen (the average age at enrollment was about ten). The scientists found that the children's brains were not fully mature until twenty-five or later. They also found a time lag between the growth of the limbic system, where emotions originate, and the growth of the prefrontal cortex, which manages those emotions. The limbic system explodes with activity during puberty, but the prefrontal cortex continues to mature for another ten years. When the limbic system is fully active but the cortex is still maturing, emotions may well far outweigh rationality, strategic thinking, and the consideration of consequences.

Think about it this way: Most eighteen-to-twenty-five-year-olds are literally incapable of making responsible judgments, paying sufficient attention, or managing their emotions. Yet at this age they're being measured and fitted (via tests, grades, and job interviews) for the trajectory of the rest of their lives. This makes no sense.

And remember, twenty-five is the median age when full executive functioning takes root. In some people, it is fully developed at twenty-one. In others, it occurs well past twenty-five and into the thirties. I was in my late twenties when I finally gave up the ghost of postadolescence. If you, like me, were an immature teenager and a minimally responsible young adult, it likely happened later for you, too. As a parent, do you worry that your own teenagers lack focus and discipline, or that your adult children haven't yet launched into productive and responsible lives? Welcome to the twenty-first-century human race.

Psychologists now debate whether young people are fully adult without the onset of executive function. Yes, we see eighteen-year-old math prodigies and chess masters. We can witness an array of great athletes, brave soldiers, actors, singers, and entrepreneurs in the eighteen-to-twenty-five-year-old age range. But their successes do not typically depend on their executive function decision-making. Car rental companies know this; they charge a stiff premium to rent a car to people under twenty-five. For most of us, well-developed executive function skills don't arrive until our mid-to-late twenties—consistent with the maturation age of the brain's prefrontal cortex. For a sizable group, that does not occur until even later, our late twenties and early thirties.

The slow development of the prefrontal cortex is in stark contrast to societal efforts to test children at younger ages, and more rigorously than ever, in an attempt to discover their abilities. No youngster who is serious about participating in high school sports would dare wait until high school to attempt the sport. If you want to play a team sport like football, basketball, soccer, or baseball, you need to start in an organized program much earlier. And if you compete in an individual sport like tennis, swimming, or gymnastics, you'll need to invest in expensive personal coaching, workouts, summer camps, and meets or tournaments.

The same is true for academics. If you hope to send your child to a top-notch university, you don't wait until high school to plan for it. Admissions to top universities require top grades, near-perfect SAT scores, and a record of leadership, community involvement, and accomplishment. Seventh or eighth grade is not too early to begin planning. Millions of parents collectively spend nearly a billion dollars a year on tutors and SAT prep courses.

These two trends—the later onset of adult maturity, and the earlier testing of children's abilities—are in clear opposition. Only a small percentage of those under twenty-five thrive in this race for early blooming. Most don't and are at risk of being scarred by what they correctly intuit as a high-stakes pressure-filled race, with rules set by educators and anxious parents. When we fail in a race in which our parents and other adults place so much value, some of us risk dropping out altogether. Yet our society persists in testing, tracking, and ranking teenagers and young adults about their future potential even as they're only just starting a cognitive maturation process that won't end until their mid-twenties or later.

• • •

It takes longer for each successive generation to finish school, become financially independent, get married, and have children. A large-scale national study conducted since the late 1970s found that today's twenty-five-year-olds, compared with their parents' generation at the same age, are twice as likely to still be in school, 50 percent more likely to be taking money from their parents, and only half as likely to have a spouse.

Why are so many people in their twenties taking so long to grow up? This question pops up everywhere, underlying familiar parental concerns about their children's "failure to launch" and the increase in "boomerang kids"—kids who return home.

The traditional cycle seems to have gone off course. As more young people remain untethered to romantic partners or to permanent homes, they go back to school for lack of better options. Others travel, avoid commitments, compete ferociously for unpaid internships or temporary (and often grueling) gigs, and otherwise forestall the beginning of adult life. The median age for a first marriage in the early 1970s, when the baby boomers were coming of age, was twenty-one for women and twenty-three for men. By 2009, it had risen to twenty-six for women and twenty-eight for men. Because the brain continues developing well into our twenties—or even early thirties—it appears that what we would generally call adulthood is happening later than ever.

What does this mean? It suggests that our twenties are a time of discovery, when many different outcomes are possible. It's a time when people acquire almost all their formal education; when they meet their future spouses and the friends they'll keep in adulthood; and when they start on their careers. They also embark on adventures, travels, and relationships with a sense of freedom that they'll likely never feel again.

Jeffrey Arnett, a psychology professor at Clark University, is urging society to recognize what he calls "emerging adulthood" as a distinct life stage. Arnett believes that social and economic changes have caused the need for a new, distinct stage between the ages of eighteen and thirty. Among the cultural changes that have led to Arnett's concept of emerging adulthood are the need for more education, the availability of fewer entry-level jobs, and less of a cultural rush to marry while young.

Arnett, who describes himself as a late bloomer, says that emerging adulthood is an important period for self-discovery. Emerging adults often explore identity, experience instability, and focus on themselves during this time. Exploration is part of adolescence too, but in the twenties it takes on new importance. The stakes are higher as people approach the age when their possibilities narrow and they need to make long-term commitments.

Arnett proposes, controversially, that prolonging adolescence actually has an advantage. If this sounds like coddling, rest assured; that's not what he means. Rather, he argues for a super-adolescent period involving continued stimulation and increasing challenges. Maintaining brain plasticity by staying engaged in new, cognitively stimulating, and, yes, highly demanding activities can actually be a boon, as opposed to falling into repetitive and more predictable jobs and internships that close the window of plasticity. In other words, delaying adulthood may actually be desirable. It can foster independent thinking and the acquisition of new skills. More than that, it can boost motivation and drive.

There is a compelling neurological rationale for taking a year or two off before, during, or after college. People who prolong adolescent brain plasticity for even a short time enjoy intellectual advantages over their more fixed counterparts in the work world. Studies have found that highly accomplished people enjoy a longer period during which new synapses continue to proliferate. The evidence is clear: Exposure to novelty and challenge while the brain's frontal cortex is still plastic leads to greater long-term career success.

Some organizations and institutions inherently understand this. The Mormon religion encourages young men and women to take a break from college and go on two-year missions. As a result, young adults graduate from college at twenty-four instead of twenty-two. In a neurological sense, they are that much closer to full adult capability before they search for a job or get married or decide to go to graduate school.

Aubrey Dustin, a Mormon, did his two-year mission in Japan. He had struggled with his K–12 education; he was a poor reader, writer, and speller. But in Japan, away from his doubting teachers and peers, he bloomed. He became a determined student. He memorized two hundred Mormon verses of scripture in Japanese, then learned Portuguese so he could teach the Japanese language to immigrants from Brazil. This same teenager, two years before, had struggled with his own language. Returning from his mission, Dustin was accepted into the U.S. Army's Defense Language Institute. He's now an army officer

and a graduate student in engineering. Dustin explains his late blooming this way: "The skills I developed working with people on my mission have played a part in everything I've done since."

Nike founder Phil Knight, in his brilliant (and wonderfully con-
fessional) autobiography, *Shoe Dog*, describes how taking a break between college and career gave him the idea to start a shoe company.
Knight was a varsity track runner at the University of Oregon. He
served two years in the army, then went to Stanford Business School,
where he wrote a master's thesis on why he thought 1960s Japan—less
than twenty years after the destruction of World War II—could be
a big force in the growing sporting goods market around the world.
Knight talked his father into bankrolling him for a trip around the
world after he got his Stanford MBA. Afterward, Knight promised, he
would settle down and find a career in accounting. But while he was in
Japan, he tested his MBA thesis, visiting athletic shoe factories. And so
he ended up starting his business, originally as a U.S. importer of Japanese running shoes called Onitsuka Tigers (today known as Asics).

Knight would not make his own branded shoes—Nike—until ten
years later. For him, business was a path of discovery. Had he gone
straight from graduate school into business, he muses, he might have
become an accountant working for an existing company, just as frustrated and unfulfilled as his father.

Knight actually took two gap breaks. He did a two-year stint in
the army after completing his undergrad degree. As a result, he was
twenty-four, rather than twenty-two, when he entered Stanford Business School. His second gap break, at twenty-six, was a real-world exploration of his business school thesis—that Japanese-made sporting
goods were ready to take on the world.

• • •

The idea of "stepping out and growing up" is not new. The Peace
Corps, Fulbright Scholarships, and Teach America organizations have
exposed several generations of young adults to the world. Nor are the

maturity gains experienced during military service a new idea. In fact, many countries, including Israel, Switzerland, Norway, Denmark, and Singapore, require mandatory military service, for reasons that go beyond national defense. These countries enjoy lower rates of unemployment among their young adults than do similarly affluent countries such as the United States, Britain, France, and Germany, which have no mandatory service.

What is new—dramatically so—is how popular culture and even slow-to-embrace university thinking have come to embrace the benefits of gap years. Consider Kyle DeNuccio, who at eighteen was struggling in his freshman year in college. He told his parents he would be leaving school after his spring semester. His dad warned him, "If you leave now, you'll never go back." DeNuccio dropped out anyway. "Although my grades were not poor enough to be asked to leave school," he later wrote, "I had lost the motivation to do anything but fulfill the minimum course requirements. I felt guilty for wasting so much money and I couldn't see doing the same thing for three more years."

DeNuccio's reaction to his freshman year is not uncommon. Fortunately for him, his father gave his blessing—but with a caveat. Young DeNuccio would be on his own financially. The tough love was crucial (and all too rare from affluent parents) but just what the son needed. He found an internship at *Surf* magazine, slept in his car, and bathed in the ocean. He quickly saw that being at the bottom of the hierarchy of a financially struggling magazine was not what he wanted for his future. But roughing it on his own in California and later in Puerto Rico as a kitchen dishwasher rekindled a genuine desire to return to college, older and wiser.

DeNuccio's story of his adventurous gap year is inspiring. And new research supports the benefits of taking a gap year.

Andrew J. Martin, researching 338 students, discovered that young adults who take gap years tend to be less motivated than their peers *before* the gap year, much like Kyle DeNuccio. But *after* their gap year, most of them find new motivation. In Martin's words: "They had higher performance outcomes, career choice formation, improved employability, and a variety of life skills. . . . The gap year can be seen as an educational process in which skills and critical reflection contribute to an individual's development."

Martin goes on to suggest that taking a gap year enhances a person's "economic, social and cultural capital," offering competitive advantages in the job market and higher education. Gap years can reinvigorate unmotivated young adults—but only if they are prepared to take responsibility. The fact that Kyle DeNuccio's father refused to fund his son's year of adventure may have been the best thing for him. Kyle was forced to take responsibility for his finances and his decisions, sleeping in his car and washing dishes to make money.

Students who are already motivated probably won't become any more motivated by taking a gap year. But those arguing for gap years for everyone make a different argument. Mormon missions, the Peace Corps, and mandatory national services believe that such career or educational "detours" create more mature, better rounded, more responsible individuals.

And research suggests they're right. Young adults who take gap years devoted to service, whether voluntary or mandatory, work harder, drink less, and commit fewer crimes than their peers. According to the 2015 American Gap Association National Survey, 97 percent of respondents reported that taking a gap year increased their maturity, and 96 percent claimed that it increased their self-confidence. Eighty-four percent reported that it helped them acquire skills that led them to be more successful in their careers. Seventy-five percent reported that it helped them land a job. Former U.K. foreign secretary Jack Straw, who has publicly promoted the idea of students taking gap years, put it this way: "Taking a gap year is a great opportunity for young people to broaden their horizons, making them more mature and responsible citizens. Our society can only benefit from travel which promotes character, confidence, and decision-making skills."

The case for gap years has become so strong that even the slowest-to-change of our major institutions—higher education—has come around to embrace them. In the United States, no fewer than 160 colleges and universities have embraced the idea of a gap year, including Harvard, Yale, Princeton, Tufts, Middlebury, and Skidmore.

President Barack Obama's daughter, Malia, took a gap year before entering Harvard, working for the independent movie company Miramax. News of Malia's gap year created a Twitterstorm of attention.

Some gap years can be highly profitable. Mark Mills, a software industry venture capitalist and a senior fellow with New York's Manhattan Institute, grew up near Winnipeg, Canada. His father thought Mark should acquire a skilled trade so that if his fancy education failed him, he could still earn a living. Mills learned to be a welder. He told me, "Getting a skilled trade job after high school still makes a lot of sense. In North America, there is a shortage of 500,000 or more skilled trade jobs—job openings but no one to fill them. Thus the wages have gone up and up. It's not unusual at all for a skilled electrician, welder, and plumber to make $100,000 a year with a bit of overtime. You can make this kind of money at twenty, with two years of training that will cost maybe ten or fifteen thousand dollars. That's a great return on investment. And you can quit and go to college any time you want."

A kinder human development clock would allow for a period in which young adults have the chance to do something challenging and different: an exploratory period to open up paths of discovery both in the outside world and to their inner capabilities. In today's rush for early success, though, many students and young graduates hesitate to slow down or take a break that they will have to explain to graduate school admissions offices or employers. They fear they may fall behind or hurt their long-term earning potential. For those fearful of jumping off the career treadmill, some good news may help to assuage this concern.

• • •

We get smarter and more creative as we age, research shows. Our brain's anatomy, neural networks, and cognitive abilities can actually improve with age and increased life experiences. Contrary to the mythology of Silicon Valley, older employees may be even more productive, innovative, and collaborative than younger ones. The idea that we achieve an early cognitive peak, followed by a gradual decline of cognitive ability—or what Saul Bellow described as a "long dusty slide to the grave" in *Humboldt's Gift*—is simply untrue.

Most people, in fact, have multiple cognitive peaks throughout their lives.

This was the radical discovery of Laura Germine (a postdoctoral fellow at Massachusetts General Hospital) and Joshua Hartshorne (a postdoctoral fellow at MIT). Their 2015 study measured the cognitive abilities of nearly fifty thousand subjects on website brain tests, including testmybrain.org and gameswithwords.org. They found that different parts of our intelligence peak at different ages: "At any given age, you're getting better at some things, you're getting worse at some other things, and you're at a plateau at some other things. There's probably not one age at which you're peak on most things, much less all of them," said Hartshorne.

The data showed that each cognitive skill peaked at a different age. For example, the speed of information processing appeared to peak early, around eighteen or nineteen. Short-term memory continued to improve until around twenty-five, then leveled off for another decade. The ability to evaluate complex patterns, including other people's emotional states, on the other hand, peaked much later, when participants were in their forties or fifties.

The researchers used a vocabulary test to measure crystallized intelligence—the lifetime accumulation of facts and knowledge. Crystallized intelligence peaks later in life, just as psychologists thought. But the new data indicated that the peak occurred when participants were in their late sixties or early seventies, much later than anyone had speculated. Laura Germine summed up their findings in the chart that follows:

Ages at which cognitive skills peak

late teens	Cognitive processing speed
early 20s	Learning and remembering names
25-35	Short-term memory
early 30s	Face recognition memory
45-55	Social understanding
65+	Verbal knowledge

The Germine-Hartshorne study "paints a different picture of the way we change over our lifespan," said Germine. Other studies have confirmed that the human brain is remarkably adaptable throughout the life course.

In the early 1950s, University of California at Berkeley undergrad K. Warner Schaie began a study of adult development. Now ninety, Schaie says he embarked on his study because he could do it while holding a nighttime job in a print shop across the bay in San Francisco, and because his family doctor had a geriatric practice. Whatever caused young Schaie to become interested in the human brain and aging, he chose the right field. While barely twenty-one, he was already giving lectures at international geriatric conferences. Later as a graduate student at the University of Washington, he launched the project that would define his long career—the Seattle Longitudinal Study.

A longitudinal study is one that follows test subjects throughout their lives. Schaie and his research team looked at how life events, such as the death of a spouse or recovery from a physical setback, affected the cognitive abilities of people at different ages. He discovered that many factors can speed up decline, but decline can also be slowed, or even reversed, such as by coming to terms with a spouse's death. Continuing education, and a restless curiosity, will also slow the rate of decline. As Schaie told the *Seattle Times*:

> How you live your life makes a difference as to how you will
> move into old age. . . . You don't suddenly become a member of
> a different species when you grow old. It's clear that a person
> who is quick-minded and not rigid in his thinking has an ad-
> vantage. Things change, but if you're a good problem solver or
> successfully handled a personal crisis when you were younger
> you will likely continue to do so.

The Seattle Longitudinal Study continues to unearth new findings
about how adaptable our brains are. The current study leader, Sherry
Willis, discovered that while air-traffic controllers suffered a slow but
steady decline in mental processing speed and short-term memory as
they aged, their performance remained intact. How was that possible?
Because spatial reasoning and emotional calm—two skills critical for
air-traffic controllers—improve throughout middle age. As the American Psychological Association noted:

> It seems that the middle-aged mind not only maintains many
> of the abilities of youth but actually acquires some new ones.
> The adult brain seems to be capable of rewiring itself well into
> middle age, incorporating decades of experiences and behav-
> iors. Research suggests, for example, the middle-aged mind
> is calmer, less neurotic and better able to sort through social
> situations. Some middle-agers even have improved cognitive
> abilities.

Says cognitive neuroscientist Patricia Reuter-Lorenz of the University of Michigan, "There is an enduring potential for plasticity, reorga-
nization, and preservation of capacities."

This is good news for all late bloomers. The hitch is that we have
to be willing participants. We have to invest in our health, in our curiosity about the world around us, and in our learning. When we do,
we can enjoy multiple brain peaks in our lives and multiple personal
bloomings.

• • •

Cognitive research has revealed that each of us has two types of intelligence: *fluid intelligence* (abbreviated as G*f*) and *crystallized intelligence* (abbreviated as G*c*). Fluid intelligence is our capacity to reason and solve novel problems, independent of knowledge from the past. It's the ability to identify abstract patterns, use logic, and apply inductive and deductive reasoning. G*f* peaks earlier in life. Crystallized intelligence, on the other hand, is the ability to use skills, knowledge, and experience. For most adults, G*c* includes both occupational (job) and avocational knowledge (hobbies, music, art, popular culture, etc.). Unlike G*f*, measures of G*c* show rising levels of performance well into middle age and beyond.

Georgia Tech psychology professor Phillip Ackerman and his colleagues have shown a strong link between adult age and levels of knowledge. Older adults, frankly, are more knowledgeable than younger adults. According to Ackerman, the best way for older adults to compensate for declines in youthful G*f* is to select jobs and goals that optimize their G*c*—their existing knowledge and skills.

Consider that job of air-traffic controller. One might assume that youthful quick G*f* is helpful in that occupation. Yet oddly, by congressional mandate, one can't even train to become an air-traffic controller after reaching age thirty-one, when our G*f* is already in decline. As the Seattle study showed, air-traffic controllers in their thirties through their fifties compensate for declining G*f* with improved spatial reasoning and mental calm. The Federal Aviation Administration forces controllers to retire at fifty-six, when these skills decline. However, high-knowledge, G*c*-dependent jobs, such as teaching, practicing law, politics, writing, or consulting, remain stable across an entire career.

Most jobs, of course, require a balance of G*f* and G*c* for peak performance, such as surgery and financial analysis. Although G*f* declines with age, increases in job knowledge—or G*c*—more than compensate, resulting in superior performance into middle age and beyond. Different tasks might require a different balance of G*f*-G*c* skills. In the medical field, liver transplants are notoriously more complex than other organ transplants because of the many small blood vessels that connect to the liver. A Mayo Clinic liver transplant specialist admitted to me that his best days as a technically skilled surgeon peaked in his early fifties. "Liver transplants are like Whack-A-Mole," he said. "Bleeding pops up everywhere. You have to be quick." Yet even as his quick hand-eye coordination skills (Gf) declined, his diagnostic abilities (Gc) improved and should keep improving into his seventies. How, then, should a hospital manage his shifting balance of skills? The Mayo Clinic believes the solution is to pair an older, experienced surgeon, bristling with Gc knowledge, with a younger surgeon who is at his or her Gf technical-skill peak.

Jobs like software coding tend to favor fluid or Gf intelligence and thus younger coders. That's a key reason so many young employees populate the likes of Google and Amazon. But *managing* software projects and software businesses shifts the balance of desired skills from Gf to Gc. That is why you saw Diane Greene, in her early sixties, leading one of Google's most important businesses, Google Cloud. And why billionaire Tom Siebel, in his mid-sixties, is leading his latest software company, C3, in the hotly competitive space of artificial intelligence and the Internet of Things.

In a sense, our brains are constantly forming neural networks and pattern-recognition capabilities that we didn't have in our youth when we had blazing synaptic horsepower. As we get older, we develop new skills and refine others, including social awareness, emotional regulation, empathy, humor, listening, risk-reward calibration, and adaptive intelligence. All these skills enhance our potential to bloom and rebloom.

What about our creativity, our ability to land upon the unexpected insight? Once again, we retain that capability for much longer than previously thought.

In 2008, Hector Zenil, who coleads the Algorithmic Dynamics Lab at the Karolinska Institute in Sweden, studied 3,400 people between the ages of four and ninety-one on their ability to behave randomly.

The idea is that random thinking—seeing beyond the obvious—is connected to creative thinking. When an apple falls from a tree, the creative person doesn't simply think that apple must have been ripe; like Isaac Newton, she sees the apple fall and pictures the invisible force of gravity.

How did Hector Zenil and researchers test for random thinking? They developed five short "random item generation" tasks performed on a computer, including twelve simulated coin flips, ten simulated rolls of a die, and arranging boxes on a grid. The test taker's job was to make their sequence of answers appear as unpredictable as possible to a logical computer program. The researchers discovered that peak randomness (and implied creativity) occurs at twenty-five, as expected. To their surprise, however, they found the drop in random thinking ability (and implied creativity) very slight all the way through the sixties.

Elkhonon Goldberg, a neuropsychologist and cognitive neuroscientist at New York University and author of the 2018 book *Creativity*, says our creative *yield* increases with age. Dr. Goldberg thinks the brain's right and left hemispheres are connected by a "salience network" that helps us evaluate novel perceptions from the right side by comparing them to the stored images and patterns on our left side. Thus a child will have more novel perceptions than a middle-aged adult but will lack the context that turns novel perceptions into useful creative insights, or creative yield.

But do such findings translate to the real world? Are people still innovative as they age? Well, here's another surprise, at least for me. At a time when youth is unabashedly celebrated, most award-winning scientists, inventors, and entrepreneurs are getting older.

A century ago Albert Einstein and Paul Dirac were in their mid-twenties when they did the work that resulted in each winning a Nobel Prize. William Lawrence Bragg won his Nobel Prize in physics in 1915 at twenty-five for work he did at only twenty-two. (He pioneered the use of X-rays to study the atomic structure of a crystal.) Such was the presumed superiority of young scientists that Dirac wrote this poem:

Age is, of course, a fever chill
that every physicist must fear.
He is better dead than living still
when once he is past his thirtieth year.

Today, however, those who do work that leads to Nobel Prizes for science and other major science-based innovations are steadily advancing in age. A 2008 study by Northwestern University's Benjamin Jones and Bruce Weinberg showed that the average age of discovery leading to a Nobel Prize is thirty-nine. Today someone who is fifty-five is as likely to produce a major scientific breakthrough as someone who is twenty-five (i.e., roughly the ages of Einstein, Dirac, and Bragg). Researcher Jones speculates that the extended timeline of today's major innovations may have to do with the depth of every science field today. One simply has more to learn, which takes more time, before one can be productive. In neuroscience terms, it takes *both* early-blooming Gf intelligence and later-blooming Gc to perform Nobel-level work.

The Information Technology and Innovation Foundation published a study recently that claims that peak innovation age is, in fact, even later—in our late forties, almost a decade older than the Northwestern study suggests. A late-forties peak period of innovation is supported by the average age of U.S. patent applicants, which is forty-seven.

For those of us who are not scientists or innovators, a more important question is how long we can stay on a high plateau after we hit our cognitive peaks. New research and anecdotal evidence on this topic are encouraging, too. The Hector Zenil random-thinking test found that near-peak creativity lasts through one's sixties, a finding that runs parallel both to the Harvard–MIT–Massachusetts General multiple-peak study and to the Seattle Longitudinal Study. For some outliers, a high plateau may well last through our eighties. For a select few, a high creative plateau can last longer than that, as the amazing story below illustrates.

One indispensable component in both smartphones and the

electric car is the lithium-ion battery that stores electricity. While you've heard of Steve Jobs and Elon Musk, you probably have not heard of John Goodenough. At the relatively late age of fifty-seven, the University of Chicago–trained physicist co-invented the lithium-ion battery. Decades later, in 2017, Goodenough filed for a patent on a new battery that the *New York Times* reported was "so cheap, lightweight and safe, it would revolutionize electric cars and kill off petroleum-fueled vehicles." Goodenough was ninety-four when he filed the patent! And he didn't conduct his innovative work from a senior retirement center—he was working with a team from the University of Texas at Austin.

The Kauffman Foundation in Kansas City is dedicated to the study of entrepreneurship—what causes people to take a leap and start their own businesses. Kauffman says the average age of entrepreneurship is forty-seven. For the fastest-growing industries, such as medical and information technology, the age is lower, but even in those classically youthful fields, the average age is forty, not the twenty-something of popular lore. Amazingly, there are twice as many entrepreneurs over fifty as there are under twenty-five.

The idea that one's forties are a peak age of entrepreneurship is supported by the work of the twentieth-century developmental psychologist Erik Erikson. Erikson believed that ages forty to sixty-four constitute a unique period where creativity and experience combine with a universal human longing to make our lives matter. Starting a company is how many people pursue what Erikson called "generativity," building something that has the potential to make a positive contribution beyond our mortal lives.

• • •

Everything we know about the human brain and aging tells us that we have a remarkable capacity to stay creative and innovative deep into our lives. But this increased understanding speaks to a need for more enlightened career pathways. We need ways to start a career later, to have more flexibility in mid-career, and to taper off gently at our own pace near the end of our careers.

Sadly, the typical career today reflects the assembly-line thinking of the early twentieth century. We take a job, move up to greater responsibility and pay levels, then are abruptly forced to retire or are laid off around sixty. Law and accounting firms have a term for this: *up-and-out*. A kinder clock for human development would set aside up-and-out and picture a person's career as an arc. While we decline in some ways (synaptic speed, short-term memory), we gain in others (real-life pattern recognition, emotional IQ, wisdom). Our creative and innovative capacities remain strong in different ways as we age.

I believe enlightened employers have a grand opportunity to be more creative about career paths. I've spent time with thousands of executives in my career in journalism, and they all tell me the same thing: Talent recruitment and retention is a priority. A company that fails at it, that pushes its employees out the door when they reach a certain age, is not tapping their full capacities. If you want your company to have the best employees doing the best work, it's time to rethink up-and-out.

The problem for older employees is not themselves but the typical career path inside most organizations. Companies reward good employees with fancier titles, more authority, and bigger paychecks, until the day comes—and it always comes—when this practice no longer makes sense. Athletes, surgeons, software specialists, airline pilots, teachers—we all peak at some point: in our capability, in the size of our paycheck, or in our willingness to work long hours. It's unfair to our employer to have to keep raising the salary of those who have peaked in effectiveness or productivity. It costs too much money and blocks the rise of younger employees into positions of greater responsibility. That's what motivates employers to get rid of people who have peaked.

But this is a tragic loss for both the employer and the employee. The employer is losing a talented and experienced employee whom they've educated over the years and who knows how to get things done. Such employees still have a lot to contribute. It's a waste of human capital to get rid of them if they're still doing good work and want to continue working.

The practice of up-and-out is a foe of human blossoming on many levels. That leads to a radical idea: Instead of single-direction up-and-out career paths, why not see careers as an *arc* (or series of arcs)?

For the sake of argument, let's say that people in industry X peak in their forties or fifties. By peak, I mean the acme of a person's technical skills, team building and managerial skills, and productivity and communications skills, along with their willingness to work long hours, hop on airplanes for a week of sales meetings, and so on.

The traditional up-and-out career path would dictate: *You're gone after fifty-five. We, your employers, can't afford to keep you, a fifty-five-plus employee, on the payroll.* A kinder career arc would acknowledge that nearly all employees peak at some point, but even "past peak" senior employees can make valuable contributions. So why not fashion a career path in which at some point the pay raises stop and salaries may even decline, and the titles stop accruing, evolving from "group vice president" to "senior consultant."

Such a career arc includes no forced retirement age. Why should a sixty-five-year-old or a seventy-two-year-old not work if they want to and their employer finds their contribution to be valuable, at the right level of pay? (Note to CEOs: If your human resources and legal departments can't figure this out, replace them with ones that can.)

Another good reason for a career arc replacing up-and-out is age diversity. A valuable older employee on the arc's downslope has no need to defend his or her turf. They are now free to offer counterintuitive advice or words of caution: "This is a brilliant idea, but let's be sure to identify your base assumptions about sales, and talk them through, so we don't make any costly missteps." That's a different conversation from one that begins with an older employee defending his or her turf. The worst thing a company can do is kill off the creative energy of its young and talented people. The second-worst thing is to allow young people to blindly walk into avoidable traps that a wise senior employee can help them foresee.

. . .

Each of us deserves the opportunity to bloom in our own way. Again, I believe it is time to consider a kinder clock for human development, one that doesn't overemphasize standardized tests and that allows each of us to achieve our full potential.

We need to give ourselves a break. We need to recognize and celebrate the fact that we're all different, with different skill sets, developmental profiles, and backgrounds, and that each of us will forge a different path toward blooming. But today we do the opposite. Our society is grossly lopsided toward individuals who show themselves to be cognitively exceptional and precociously focused at an early age. We ask teenagers and young adults whose brains are still developing to "prove" themselves by gaining admission to the right schools, taking the right classes, and getting the right job. We hold up those who are exceptional in select and tragically limited ways.

So where does that leave the rest of us who were slower to physically, cognitively, and emotionally develop, who didn't excel early and weren't early bloomers? Rejoice, for we late bloomers have our own unique strengths, as the next chapter explains.

CHAPTER 4

Worth the Wait: The Six Strengths of Late Bloomers

The in spot on campus was called Ugly, and it was where my friends gathered on Monday through Thursday nights. Ugly was short for Undergraduate Library, and the building was as unattractive as its name, one of those 1960s-era blocks of steel and glass that looked suitable for a state government bureaucracy, not for books. But Ugly was where Stanford students went to study night after night. We went not so much for the stacks of books as to escape our dormitories and roommates, sex squeals and gossip, loud boozy busts on the side lawn, and leftover cookies in the parlor. We went to Ugly for quiet and concentration. At Stanford we had to put in four to six hours of study most nights. We went to Ugly to do it.

My roommate, Bob, went to Ugly most nights when he wasn't playing collegiate volleyball. He had a routine. He would stash a couple of Pepsi bottles in his backpack along with his books, pens, yellow highlighters, and notebooks. Fueled by sugar and caffeine, Ironbutt Bob would sit at a study carrel for hours at a time, oblivious to his bladder, and consume dozens of pages of psychology, economics, and legal textbooks. Nothing seem to rattle his attention to his studies. When he had to write a paper, he could handwrite forty pages on yellow lined paper in a single sitting, then go pee, hike back to our room, drink another Pepsi, and type the whole thing up.

Bob made Phi Beta Kappa in his junior year. He took his intellect and study habits to Stanford Law School and graduated near the top of his class. He's since had an impressively successful career as a corporate securities lawyer.

I tried to ape Bob's study habits, and on the surface I succeeded. I bought a backpack like his and packed it with textbooks, reading assignments, pens, notebooks, and yellow highlighters. Sometimes he and I would walk to Ugly together after dinner, talking about sports and women. Then he would slip over to his favorite carrel and get down to business. I would find a carrel and attempt to do the same.

But my Ugly routine was a bit different from Bob's. Well, maybe a lot different. While Ironbutt Bob would park for hours with his books and Pepsis and rapt attention, I couldn't sit still for fifteen minutes. For an hour, or maybe thirty minutes, I'd try my best to study Japanese prefectures or the early Industrial Age's effect on English novels, but it was futile.

Sooner or later I'd leave my carrel and head to the stacks where the hardbound archives of magazines were kept. I'd dive into back issues of *Sports Illustrated*. I'd spend hours with *SI*, which in those days devoted many pages to track and field and other Olympic sports. I would immerse myself in stories of the indoor pole vault at Madison Square Garden and four-man bobsled racing in St. Moritz. *Sports Illustrated* could make curling seem cool. I took it all in.

Needless to say, my nightly study in the Ugly magazine stacks did nothing for my grades. My grasp of Japanese prefectures remained weak. I managed to graduate with a political science degree on time, with precisely the minimum number of credits that I needed. I earned a 3.1 grade point average, all B's except for one A minus in film aesthetics. The B's I earned were more like gentleman's C's. At Stanford one was allowed to drop a class up to two weeks before the final test. Naturally, if you were headed for a C or worse, you dropped the class, and nothing bad went on your record.

With his straight A's, Bob went to Stanford Law, and with my phony B's I went off to be an editorial assistant (soon departed) at *Runner's World*, a security guard, and a dishwasher. Clearly, I'd wasted my time in the Ugly magazine stacks and squandered a golden opportunity. Right?

Fast-forward a dozen years. By then my prefrontal cortex had finally matured, my executive functioning capability was clicking, and though both had blossomed quite late, I was doing okay as a responsible adult. I was a technical writer at a Palo Alto research institute and copywriting for a Silicon Valley ad agency. I was married, and I owned a condo, a new Volkswagen Jetta, a Macintosh computer, and a laser printer. Not bad. I was on my way.

My friend Tony thirsted for far more. He was much more ambitious than me, openly so. He worked as a loan officer at Silicon Valley Bank and was frustrated with his slow career progress. He wanted to be a bank vice president, then a successful venture capitalist or rich entrepreneur. He wanted fame and power, and he was in a hurry. He confided many times that he wanted to be a Silicon Valley *player*. One day Tony, looking at the newsletters I was producing on my Mac for various Silicon Valley clients, asked if it was possible to design a magazine on a Mac, using a page layout program like Quark Xpress, a few type fonts from Adobe, and a laser printer. Yes, I said. Possible.

"Let's do a Silicon Valley business magazine," Tony said. "People will have to pay attention to us." He was serious. He had me design some layouts, and he took them to his boyhood friend, a young venture capitalist named Tim Draper. Tony raised $60,000 from Tim, enough to quit his Silicon Valley Bank job, and a year later we launched Silicon Valley's first business magazine, *Upside*.

Tony was the businessman who raised money and sold ads, and I was the editor and designer. Our first priority was to decide what *Upside* should be. My hunch was that business magazines needed a jolt. They needed to be more exciting, to capture the risk, the guts, the extremely competitive nature of startups, venture capital, investment banks, going public, the whole frenzied fight for glory and riches. *Aha,* I thought one day. Business magazines should be more like sports magazines. *Upside*, I decided then and there, should read and look like *Sports Illustrated*.

In those Ugly stacks, a dozen years before, I had read every back issue of *SI* from its birth year of 1954 onward, and I'd continued to be a fan. In fact, I'd read many *SI* issues repeatedly, and I'd noticed things. I'd noticed good writing by George Plimpton, Dan Jenkins, Anita Verschoth, and Frank Deford. I'd noticed type fonts and *SI*'s clever captions. I'd noticed great photography and illustration. One of my favorite *SI* design tricks was its use of caricature art by illustrators like Arnold Roth and Ronald Searle. No photographer could convey the nervous sweat of a golfer trying to make a six-foot curvy downhill putt to win a major tournament like a good caricaturist could. I loved caricature, and I sensed it would solve a huge problem for me at *Upside*. A major reason business magazines aren't as fun as sports magazines is that business action does not occur in a stadium, in front of loud fans and television cameras. In sports, the pivotal moment when a ballgame or match play is won or lost is right there for fans to see. It is observed by sportswriters and recorded by cameras for posterity. But what does a pivot look like in a business? Is it when a big sale is won or lost? When a key employee walks out the door with all the best ideas in his head and starts a competitive company?

The only way to show such pivotal moments, I thought, was to let a caricaturist re-create them. And so I decided *Upside* would read and look like *Sports Illustrated*, without the game photos of course, but with everything else, including storytelling cartoons and caricatures. I knew exactly what I wanted, because I had seen it years before in the Ugly stacks.

My hunch about *Upside* was correct. Within a year of launching, I had the boyish-looking CEO of Sun Microsystems on the cover, caricatured as Michelangelo's anatomically detailed sculpture *David*. I commissioned a long investigative article on Oracle, with founder Larry Ellison as Genghis Khan, plotting with his warlords, severed heads at their feet. I had Apple CEO John Sculley as Little Lord Fauntleroy in a sandbox, getting sand kicked on him. Within two years of launching *Upside*, everybody in technology and venture capital was paying attention to it. Bill Gates of Microsoft gave me four hours of interviews. *Forbes* looked into buying us. Steve Forbes hired me instead and gave me a wonderful career.

It turns out that my many hours in the Ugly magazine stacks were not wasted at all. They might have wrecked my grades, but curiosity made my career.

• • •

So far, I've focused on the problems facing late bloomers—namely, the growing tendency by schools and employers to overvalue early achievement and to regard late blooming as an afterthought or a deficiency. This bias can have lifetime consequences for late bloomers. When so many people believe they are inferior based on a few narrow measurements made when they were children, society as a whole suffers. So let's pivot to the bountiful world of late bloomer strengths, which don't get the attention they deserve.

Curiosity is the first late bloomer strength. All healthy children have curiosity in buckets, but America's early-blooming conveyor belt isn't impressed. It wants us to grow up fast and trade in our youthful curiosity for a determined focus. It does not want us to get off the conveyor belt and take wasteful side trips into, say, a library's magazine stacks, when the cost of doing so is a B instead of an A. It wants us to winnow our extracurricular pursuits from enjoyable recreation into activities that will demonstrate leadership on a college or job application.

Do late bloomers have more curiosity than early bloomers? Research can't tell us, but observationally late bloomers seem to retain more of their childhood curiosity, just as they retain more of every childish attribute. Childish retention doesn't help late bloomers in the early going, and as the early-success conveyor belt picks up speed and primacy as a sorting mechanism, youthful curiosity becomes a liability in the eyes of school administrators and employers. We are coached to walk away from the magazine stacks and return to the study carrel. We are urged to tamp our curiosity down to the practical essentials and get serious.

But a funny thing happens during one's twenties. The brain's prefrontal cortex completes its development (see Chapter 3), and executive functioning begins to assert itself. Impulsivity fades, and we think more about longer-term consequences. In short, somewhere in our mid-twenties—earlier for some, later for others—we become recognizable adults ready to handle adult responsibilities.

At that point, who is in a better position for success, fulfillment, happiness, and health? The conveyor belt's early-blooming superstar who learned to suppress childhood curiosity in favor of focus? Or the late bloomer who retained more childhood curiosity and now finally has executive functioning to give it a direction?

In the 2017 edition of its annual "100 Best Companies to Work For" list, *Fortune* asked several CEOs what employee attributes they want most. Bill Anderson of biotech leader Genentech led with "curiosity, a passion for the field, and a desire and drive to accomplish something great." Brad Smith, CEO of Intuit, said: "People who live our company values, who treat failures as learning opportunities, and who lead with their emotional quotient and their curiosity quotient, rather than their intelligence quotient." Business consultants Michael Hvisdos and Janet Gerhard claim that curiosity is the "overlooked key to business innovation." In *Inc.*, the global marketing consultant Don Peppers went further:

> People should consider it a moral obligation to be curious about things. Not being curious is not only intellectually lazy, but it shows a willful contempt for the facts. If you don't want to know the truth about something, then how moral can you claim to be?
>
> Curiosity, however, is also an act of rebellion, and as such it requires moral courage.
>
> Innovation cannot occur in any field without curiosity, and without innovation your company might as well close its doors now. But being curious about things represents nothing less than a rejection of whatever inadequate explanation existed before, and a search for a better one. By its very nature, curiosity demonstrates an independence of mind.

An entire chapter, or book, could be written about the key role curiosity plays in innovation. But curiosity has other life-enhancing attributes as well, including motivation. The London-based science journal the *Cube* writes that "curiosity is a cognitive process which leads to the behavior perceived as motivation. From the human perspective the relationship between curiosity and motivation creates a feedback; the more curious one becomes about something, the more motivated one will be, and the more motivated one is the more one learns and the more curious one will become." Curiosity is a dopamine hit, says the *Cube*.

But unlike drugs we swallow or inject, curiosity is the dopamine hit that keeps on giving—and getting better throughout our lives. According to the National Institutes of Health, curiosity has long-term health benefits, playing "an important role in maintaining cognitive function, mental health, and physical health in older adults."

Our childish curiosity, then, turns out to be one enormously valuable gift, a key to just about everything worth having in a long, continually blooming life, including the ability to bloom itself. So to return to the question I posed earlier: Is it better to be the early bloomer who was taught to trade in curiosity for focus, then in their mid-twenties and beyond finds they (and their employer, and everyone else) wish they were less of a grind? Or is it better to be a late bloomer, initially overlooked but holding on to childish curiosity, then grateful to have such a powerful X factor for the rest of their life?

• • •

Compassion is a second late bloomer strength, the ability to put ourselves in others' shoes and in doing so understand their challenges and how best to help them. Compassion includes tolerating difficult feelings. Empathy is the ability to feel the emotions that another person experiences, but compassion goes beyond empathy to generate action to help the other person. (Jeff Weiner, the CEO of LinkedIn, makes a similar distinction.) With empathy, we feel another's pain, and we both hurt as a result. With compassion, we engage, express, and act. Few would doubt the importance of compassion in our public and personal lives, especially in areas like health care, education, and justice.

Yet too often compassion has been sacrificed in our race to early success. In the cutthroat battle for higher test scores or greater wealth, many of us have lost sight of the importance of kindness and compassion. Among college students, concern for the well-being of others has been tumbling since the early 1990s and is now at the lowest point in thirty years. The conveyor belt to early success has created a crisis of compassion.

In facing the ups and downs of life, many late bloomers gain a greater sense of compassion. They show greater reflective thinking, diminished ego-centeredness, and a deeper appreciation of others' challenges—what psychologists call greater prosocial behavior. Prosocial behavior leads to a profounder comprehension of the contradictions, imperfections, and negative aspects of human nature, making many of us more forgiving, understanding, and compassionate. Late bloomers, by taking the "more scenic route" and experiencing the missteps, bumps, and bruises of life, gain connective insights and perspectives. And they're driven to use these insights to understand and help others. Compassion offers benefits to both themselves and the people around them.

One researcher characterizes this experience-based evolution as a "reduction in self-centeredness." Daniel Goleman, author of *Emotional Intelligence*, calls it "having a wide horizon." Regardless of how you define it, increased compassion affords us the ability to better understand the people we interact with, work with, and even lead.

Compassion sounds altruistic, but it also offers great gains for the giver. Daniel J. Brown, in his 2013 book, *The Boys in the Boat*, tells the story of the eight-man American rowing team in the 1936 Olympics: Eight Depression-era young men at the University of Washington, not a traditional rowing power, come together around an unconventional coach. (The book resembles the 1981 movie *Chariots of Fire*, about an English track sprinter at Cambridge University who hires his own professional coach, violating an unwritten code of amateur sports in the 1920s.) In researching the book, Brown discovered that one of the rowers, Joe Rantz, grew up in a family so poor that he was kicked out of the family at twelve—there wasn't enough food for everyone. The twelve-year-old was left to fend for himself. Brown learned about it by talking to Joe Rantz's surviving sister. More than seventy years after Joe was kicked out of the house, his sister would break into sobs describing the pain of watching him walk out the door with only a cloth sack of belongings.

The story of Joe Rantz's pain became the deeper current in *The Boys in the Boat*. How did the young man survive? What emotional scars did he suffer? How could he learn to trust again and become part of a rowing team whose necessary skill was built on trust, on learning to row together as one unit?

Brown began work on *The Boys in the Boat* in his late fifties and was sixty-two when the book was published. It made the *New York Times* bestseller list, where it remained for two straight years. "I could not have written this book in my thirties or forties," he said. "It would have been a different book. It would have lacked the layers." Those rich emotional layers grew out of his compassion for the suffering of young Joe Rantz.

Some mistakenly believe having compassion for others implies that we're weak or overly emotional. It may offer a tangible benefit for artists and writers like Brown, they say dismissively—people who make their living re-creating the human experience—but not in the bare-knuckle world of business. But the reality is that compassion is hard. It takes courage. Demonstrating true compassion often requires making difficult decisions and facing tough realities.

Many of our most effective leaders—in business, in the military, in politics—have the type of heightened compassion that comes from following an unconventional pathway. Shimul Melwani, of the University of North Carolina, has found that compassionate managers and executives are perceived as better leaders. Compassionate leaders appear to be stronger, have greater levels of engagement, and have more people willing to follow them.

A management style that combines compassion, authenticity, and integrity improves employee retention and employee performance—factors that directly improve the bottom line. One 2012 study found that compassionate leadership correlated with a 27 percent reduction in sick leave and a 46 percent reduction in disability pensions. Another research team, reviewing numerous case studies, concluded that "farsighted, tolerant, humane and practical CEOs returned 758 percent over 10 years, versus 128 percent for the S&P 500." University of Michigan professor Kim Cameron explains that compassionate leaders "achieve significantly higher levels of organizational effectiveness—including financial performance, customer satisfaction, and productivity."

Compassion offers very real returns. One benefit of being a late bloomer is that we earn a deeper sense of compassion—through years of trial and error, through mistakes and restarts—that improves our critical thinking. It allows us to see the bigger picture and make better decisions. It makes us keener artists, better leaders, and more effective business owners. This is something that deserves celebration—and something that more corporations, human resources departments, and organizations would do well to heed. Emma Seppälä, author of *The Happiness Track*, professes that "compassion is good for the bottom line, it's great for your relationships, and it inspires lasting loyalty. In addition, compassion significantly boosts your health."

• • •

At age eight, Michael Maddaus suffered a trauma that is not uncommon in poorer households. When he was a child in Minneapolis, his mother worked two jobs as a waitress while his grandmother took care of him. The three lived in a second-floor walk-up in an old brick apartment building. That was challenging enough, "but then the lid came off," says Maddaus. "My grandmother died and left us in a void. Then my stepfather came in, and that's when the alcoholism reared its head."

His mother began drinking at all hours, lying in bed for weeks at a time, summoning her young son to bring food and another drink. His stepfather sat in the kitchen with a cocktail, looking out the window. "I had lost my mother to this alcoholic life. That's when I began living on the streets and began to get in trouble." As a teenager, Maddaus ran with a group that robbed stores and stole cars. He was arrested twenty-four times before the age of eighteen.

Rick Ankiel, by contrast, led a charmed life as a teenager. As a high school senior in St. Lucie, Florida, he was the baseball team's star pitcher. He won eleven games and lost only one, with an earned run average of 0.47. Almost unimaginably, he struck out an average of 2.2 batters per inning, or twenty strikeouts for every nine innings. In 1997 he was named high school player of the year by *USA Today*. Upon graduating from high school, the St. Louis Cardinals signed him for $2.5 million. In the minor leagues, he was an immediate sensation, voted the top minor league player in 1999. At twenty, he made the leap to the majors and became a starting pitcher for St. Louis. He helped lead the Cardinals to a National League Central Division title in 2000 and finished second in the league's Rookie of the Year voting.

Then his baseball career fell apart. It wasn't an injury, illness, or drug use that wrecked him. What destroyed his brilliant young career as a major league pitcher was the most mysterious ailment of all. Suddenly he couldn't throw the ball where he wanted it to go.

The downward spiral began in the 2000 playoffs. Cardinals manager Tony La Russa chose Ankiel to start game one against the Atlanta Braves. For two innings, he pitched masterfully. But in the third inning he walked four batters, threw five wild pitches, and allowed four runs. Ankiel was the first major league pitcher to throw five wild pitches in one inning since 1890.

In the off-season, team doctors examined Ankiel but discovered no physical malady. He began the 2001 season with renewed hopes, but those hopes were soon dashed. He continued to walk batters and throw wild pitches. He was sent down to the Cardinals' AAA team in the minor leagues, where his troubles worsened. In only 4⅓ innings, he walked seventeen batters and threw twelve wild pitches. The Cardinals booted their millionaire prodigy all the way down to the rookie league, the bottom rung of professional baseball. Rick Ankiel had become a punch line on ESPN television and sports talk radio.

Janet Schneider was born into a blue-collar family in South River, New Jersey, and was the first in her family to attend college. She graduated with a degree in art but soon got married, had two children, and devoted herself to raising them. In her thirties, she decided to write the great American novel, but after finishing three manuscripts, she was discouraged to find that no publisher wanted them. A friend suggested she try romance novels. Her first two could not find a buyer. She then got a job as a temporary typist and worked there for seven months, when she learned that a publisher had bought her second romance novel for $2,000. She gave herself the pen name of Steffie Hall because, well, it sounded like a romance author's name. Janet wrote eleven more romance novels and began to enjoy some success.

But just as it seemed she was succeeding, she became bored with the genre. Writing clichéd sex scenes no longer interested her; she wanted to write action thrillers. Her publisher disagreed, and so Janet, now in her forties, took the next eighteen months off to figure out how to write action thrillers.

A Taiwanese teenager failed his college entrance exams twice, which bitterly disappointed his father, a college professor. The teenager was more interested in art. After completing his mandatory military service, he moved to the United States and studied drama and film at the University of Illinois at Champaign. He wanted to be an actor. But since he struggled with English diction, he turned his attention to directing, where he showed a spark of promise.

After the University of Illinois, he followed his future wife, who was doing postdoc graduate work in molecular biology, to New York

University. There he enrolled at NYU's Tisch School of the Arts. His film directing talents began to be recognized, and he won awards for two of his short films, *Shades of the Lake* and *Fine Line*. Then the William Morris Agency signed him. The new film director seemed to be on his way. And then . . . nothing. Hollywood, it seemed, was not interested in the man from Taiwan, who was not young anymore. At thirty-six, he was a stay-at-home dad and frustrated filmmaker while his wife supported the family with her work as a molecular biologist.

Now the good news. These stories of failure and seeming despair have happier endings. Michael Maddaus, the Minneapolis juvenile delinquent, is today the head of thoracic surgery at the University of Minnesota. Rick Ankiel, after toiling as a comedic punch line in baseball's minor leagues for several years, reemerged in his late twenties as a star outfielder and power hitter for the St. Louis Cardinals. Janet Evanovich mastered the ability to write action novels during her eighteen months away from romance writing and became the most successful female thriller writer in U.S. history, with her bestselling Stephanie Plum series. Taiwan-born Ang Lee finally got his chance at thirty-six, and as a celebrated film director, his credits include *The Wedding Banquet*; *Crouching Tiger, Hidden Dragon*; *Hulk*; and *Brokeback Mountain*.

The third strength that late bloomers tend to have in spades is *resilience*. As defined in *Psychology Today*, "resilience is that ineffable quality that allows some people to be knocked down by life and come back stronger than ever." Morton Shaevitz, a clinical psychologist at the University of California at San Diego, adds that resilience is not a passive quality but "an ongoing process of responding to adversity with concerted action."

Do late bloomers possess more resilience than early bloomers? They are certainly more familiar with adversity. And with age, one acquires more tools and perspective to respond to adversity and move forward. Adam Grant, a management and psychology professor at the Wharton School, believes that when it comes to developing resilience, the regulation of emotions gives mature people an advantage over the young: "There is a naturally learnable set of behaviors that contribute to resilience. Those are the behaviors that we gravitate to more and more as we age."

Reframing adversity in the life stories we tell ourselves is another key strategy that people tend to learn over time. A Harvard study showed that students who acknowledged the adversity they faced and reframed their challenges as growth opportunities performed better and kept their physical stress levels lower than students who were trained to ignore their adversity.

Early bloomers enjoy many advantages in affluent societies. But one huge disadvantage they face is that by dint of their youth and accomplishments, they give themselves credit for their success, more than the rest of us do. That's understandable: adolescents and young adults tend to be self-centered; it is a necessary waypoint in the evolution from a parent-centered childhood to an independent and mature adulthood. The problem arises when early bloomers have a setback: Either they put all the blame on themselves and fall into self-condemnation and paralysis, or they blame everyone else. Late bloomers tend to be more circumspect; they are able to see their own role in the adversity they face, without succumbing to self-condemnation or blame shifting. Stanford psychology professor Carol Dweck told me that her freshman students at Stanford, in 2018, are more "brittle" than those in 2008. They are youthful early achievers, and true to their age and exalted station, they are often quite full of themselves. But they are the opposite of resilient. Any chip in their self-image threatens to shatter the whole wunderkind mirage.

Late bloomers, in terms of resilience, have greater support networks outside their own circle. Adolescents tend to take direction from their peers, competing with them for social status and measuring themselves against them. A loss of status can be intolerable and perhaps permanent within their social circle, limiting their ability or desire to reach out to experts for help in the face of adversity. Late bloomers, in the same situation, tend to have already suffered plenty of social rejections and so build bridges to supportive communities, obtaining tools that early achievers have not had to develop.

• • •

Among the early bloomers on the conveyor belt to stratospheric SAT scores, to summer projects in the Galápagos Islands, to college acceptances to MIT and Princeton, and to internships at Goldman Sachs, one does not find people with names like Tammie Jo.

This Tammie Jo grew up on a ranch outside Tularosa, New Mexico, about fifty miles from the Trinity Site, where the first atomic bomb was exploded in July 1945. Tularosa, a dry windswept town, has a population of 2,900, and its tallest structure is a thirty-foot-high stucco pistachio nut. Tammie Jo Bonnell attended high school in Tularosa, then went off to a small college in Kansas, MidAmerica Nazarene University. The 2018 *U.S. News & World Report* ranked MANU as the seventy-fifth-best regional university in the American Midwest. It is not part of the conveyor belt to early success. After graduating from MANU, Tammie Jo attended graduate school at Western New Mexico University, tucked in obscurity on the southern end of the Gila National Forest. In the most recent *U.S. News & World Report* ranking of 141 western regional universities, WNMU was unranked.

Tammi Jo Bonnell's first attempt to step out met with failure. While still an undergraduate at NAMU, she applied to the air force and was turned down. At WNMU she tried the navy and was accepted at the officer candidate school at the Naval Air Station Pensacola. She went into flight training, where she discovered her gift and passion. And she began to bloom.

In *The Right Stuff*, Tom Wolfe's landmark 1979 book about fighter pilots and the original Project Mercury astronauts, Wolfe described the ascending "ziggurat" of skill and nerve it took to reach the pinnacle of military flying, of being a fighter pilot. Tammie Jo had that skill, nerve, and will, and she eventually became one of the first women to fly the F/A-18 Hornet fighter jet. During the Gulf War in 1991, women were not allowed to fly in combat, so Tammie Jo had to be satisfied with flying training missions as an aggressor pilot, engaging in mock dogfights with the boys.

By now, perhaps you've guessed that Tammie Jo Shults, her married name, is the Southwest Airlines pilot who became famous in 2018 for landing a 737 commercial airliner full of passengers with a demolished left engine, a blasted-out hole in a passenger window, and a mortally injured passenger. The Southwest jet, its pressurization compromised by the shattered window, dived from 31,000 feet to 10,000 feet in less than five minutes; passengers were screaming and throwing up. When Captain Shults safely landed the plane, the world's press hailed her for her calm demeanor and "nerves of steel" throughout the midair emergency. She was compared to Chesley "Sully" Sullenberger, the US Airways pilot who landed a packed commercial jet on the Hudson River after hitting a flock of birds, disabling both engines.

Captain Shults was fifty-six when she managed her feat of calm bravado. Sully was fifty-eight. Their stories illustrate another late bloomer strength. The best descriptor I can think of is *equanimity*. Equanimity means a "mental calmness, composure, and evenness of temper, especially in a difficult situation." How is equanimity a late bloomer strength? Is it genuinely an attribute that improves with age?

Our brains are driven to seek calmness as we age. Columbia University social psychologist Heidi Grant Halvorson claims that calmness is central to happiness. As we age, she says, "happiness becomes less the high-energy, totally-psyched experience of a teenager partying while his parents are out of town, and more the peaceful, relaxing experience of an overworked mom who's been dreaming of that hot bath all day. The latter isn't less 'happy' than the former—it's a different way of understanding what happiness is."

UCLA and Stanford psychologists Cassie Mogilner, Sepandar Kamvar, and Jennifer Aaker report that excitement and elation are emotions that move the happiness needle for younger people, while peacefulness, calm, and relief drive it for those who are older.

Research has long established that calm leaders are more effective. Elizabeth Kirby, a postdoctoral fellow in neuroscience at the University of California at Berkeley, created the following chart to show how optimal performance quickly degrades when emotions run too strong.

Performance Versus Emotion

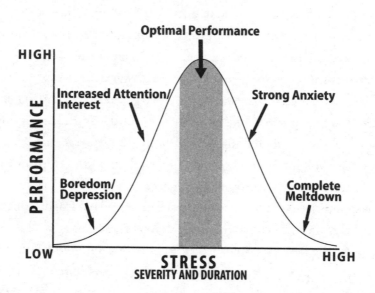

Travis Bradberry, bestselling author of *Emotional Intelligence 2.0*, notes that we're better problem solvers when we're calm—and better listeners, too. Former Navy SEAL Brent Gleeson says that under stress, people gravitate toward the calm leader. These benefits are hardly surprising. Equanimity equates to mental calmness, to composure, and to evenness of temper. It's a mind in balance. This is an advantage for any leader, pilot, Navy SEAL, or person under extreme pressure—and it's one that we late bloomers naturally develop.

• • •

By conventional standards, the thirty-six-year-old football coach had made a stupid career choice. The year before, he had been the Oakland Raiders running backs' coach, but he always wanted to be a head coach. And now at last he was a head coach, but his team was not in the National Football League. Rather, it was in a semipro league filled with high school stars who peaked early and never excelled in college. Most of the San Jose Apaches played for fifty dollars a game, and most supplemented their meager paychecks as physical education teachers, insurance salesmen, construction laborers, and bar bouncers. The Apaches played their games on a junior college field against teams like the Sacramento Buccaneers, the Eugene Bombers, and the Victoria B.C. Steelers. The West Coast league in which they played had the smell of used kneepads and discarded wannabes.

The Apaches practiced on a lumpy field in San Jose, next to a high school gym. At the conclusion of practice one day, the Apaches coach sauntered by the gym, heard shouts and a whistle, and stepped in. The high school basketball team was practicing a full-court press drill. The Apaches coach, mildly intrigued, took a seat in the bleachers.

In basketball, a full-court press is an aggressive ploy where the team on defense tries to prevent the opposing team from inbounding the ball and getting it past the half-court line. The press starts with the arm-waving harassment of the inbounds passer. But if the inbounds pass is successful, the press continues with defenders trying to trap the ball handler behind the half-court line. Full-court presses are physically and mentally exhausting. Generally, only teams that are behind late in a game will try a full-court press as a means of forcing turnovers.

It sometimes works by causing panic. But an offense that is prepared for a full-court press will usually defeat it by using blocks and screens to create an open player to pass to. The Apaches football coach sitting in the bleachers watched the full-court press practice with interest, perceiving something novel yet familiar. An insight jumped out at him: What if you could design a *football* passing game that operated like a basketball team trying to move the ball against a full-court press?

That was how Bill Walsh hatched the idea for the greatest revolution in professional football in the last fifty years—the so-called West Coast offense of high-percentage, short passes that spread out the offense across the field. Fifteen years after that high school insight, Walsh employed it to win the Super Bowl behind a tall and skinny quarterback who had achieved sports excellence first as a basketball player. His name was Joe Montana, and the winning team was the San Francisco 49ers.

Bill Walsh was a late bloomer, perhaps the greatest example in the history of professional sports coaching. His great strength—one that is available to late bloomers in particular—was *insight*.

What's insight? In popular lore, insight arrives in a sudden flash of perception, as seemingly it did for Walsh in that high school gym. But insight is more than a novel perception, arrived at in a moment of genius. In fact, our insights are the result of us drawing on our full mental library of experience, patterns, and context, yielding an idea of extraordinary value. For a fuller explanation, let's turn to seventy-two-year-old Elkhonon Goldberg, the NYU neuroscientist and neuropsychologist.

In his 2018 book *Creativity*, Goldberg debunked the popular notion that creativity resides in the brain's right hemisphere (while the left hemisphere is a repository for reasoning). The real story is more complicated and interwoven. The right hemisphere matures in childhood; the development of the left is consistent with the development of the prefrontal cortex, which is not fully mature until the mid-twenties, by the estimates of some scientists, and "early to mid-thirties" in Goldberg's experience. The right hemisphere is home to visual recognition and the ability to process novelty; the left hemisphere stores memories, patterns, and language. The left is also "generative"—it can create what Goldberg calls "memories of the future" by imagining new things from existing patterns. Language itself is generative. A writer can create a story out of letters, words, and grammatical structure even if no memory of the story exists in the brain.

But while the generative left side can make new things out of existing memories and patterns, novelty can be comprehended only by the right side. How, then, does the brain process and prioritize novelty? What happens to a novel perception after it is perceived by the right hemisphere? Goldberg believes that an interbrain network intermediates the right and left hemispheres; he calls it the "salience network." What salience does is help the left brain assign importance to incoming novel perceptions. (To understand how this happens, it is worth reading the findings Goldberg presents in *Creativity*.)

The implications of Goldberg's work are clear. As we age, our brains become more astute judges of what novel perceptions are actually useful to us, as they are prioritized by our salience network in the back-and-forth communication between right and left hemispheres. Our brains draw on everything we know—our mental library of memories and patterns—to help us prioritize such perceptions. Put another way, children, teenagers, and young adults may have more novel perceptions than they will later in life, but their ability to discern which novel perceptions are useful or salient, and which are just ephemeral and fun, is not fully developed. Turn a six-year-old loose at Disneyland to see how that works; meanwhile Mom and Dad are looking at the Disneyland map, calculating the most efficient trek through the park, and judging what rides and theme areas are most likely to interest their kids.

Back when I was reading back issues of *Sports Illustrated* in the Ugly stacks, the immersion did me more harm than good, since it pulled me away from my studies. And my grades suffered accordingly. It wasn't until a dozen years later that I derived a valuable insight from my cherished memories of time "wasted" in the stacks. Why did it take so long? In the interim years, I learned something about Silicon Valley and the rough-and-tumble world of startups, venture capital rounds, and paths to initial public offerings. I also learned something about business magazines. In fact, I concluded that most of them were boring.

That insight—of designing a business magazine to look and read like a sports magazine—occurred to me only when a long-ago memory of *Sports Illustrated* was stacked up against more recent perceptions and experiences. Like a storyteller, I was able to harness the left brain's generative powers and create a "future memory" of a business magazine that looked and read like *Sports Illustrated*.

So is insight a strength of late bloomers? While early bloomers, from Mozart to Mark Zuckerberg, can and do have valuable insights, the conversion of novel perceptions to useful insights tends to increase as our left hemisphere matures. In other words, our yield of useful insights improves as we age, giving a distinct advantage to late bloomers. That's why I believe insight is another fundamental strength of late bloomers.

• • •

Across time and cultures, *wisdom* has been considered the pinnacle of human attainment. Since ancient times, the elusive concept has figured prominently in philosophical and religious texts. In fact, the Greek word *philosophia* means "love of wisdom." Centuries before the ancient Greek culture, the religious traditions of India and China—Hinduism, Buddhism, and Taoism—contemplated the idea of wisdom, emphasizing the notion of emotional balance. And yet we continue to ask, What exactly is wisdom? And to that I would add, *How does wisdom manifest itself in late bloomers?*

Despite humanity's fascination with wisdom, it became a topic of empirical study only about forty years ago. As a graduate student in the 1970s, Vivian Clayton—a geriatric neuropsychologist in Orinda, California—began studying ancient and modern literature in an effort to quantify and define wisdom. Her study led her to think of wisdom as thoughtful behavior, usually involving social situations. She later refined this idea of wisdom to include behavior born of knowledge and instilled with thoughtfulness and compassion. Her early work has served as a foundation for subsequent research on the subject of wisdom.

By the 1980s, other psychologists started to tackle wisdom and its application in life. Many speculated that we attain wisdom through life experience, associating it with getting older. In the 1980s, German psychologist Paul Baltes, along with psychologist Ursula Staudinger, started the Berlin Wisdom Project, a pioneering effort to pin down the nature of wisdom. Staudinger, who today is the director of the Robert N. Butler Columbia Aging Center at Columbia University, said the project grew from "an interest in wisdom [as] an ideal endpoint of human development." It came to define wisdom as "an expert knowledge system concerning the fundamental pragmatics of life."

The recent trove of academic research on wisdom echoes what business leader Julie Sweet, CEO of Accenture North America, told me in 2018: "Great executives know how to manage ambiguity." That, to me, serves superbly as a definition of wisdom.

Wisdom, extensive research attests, isn't something that we're born with or that develops over a few years. It doesn't come with perfect SAT scores or a degree from an elite university. And much to the vexation of modern society, it doesn't come from an eight-figure bank account or a million followers on Instagram.

Instead, wisdom emerges through a complex pattern of personal characteristics and experiential features that coalesce as we weather the challenges of life. It comes with years of ups and downs. It accrues over a lifetime of meeting new challenges. It brings together the sum of our knowledge, experience, and intuition. As author Daniel J. Brown told me, wisdom is the ability to see the layers of life that were harder to see when one was younger.

Wisdom *increases* rather than declines with age and experience. Though our pure cognitive speed may deteriorate, asserts Staudinger, "what doesn't go down is reasoning and cognition that is based on knowledge and experience." And perhaps this is the perfect definition of wisdom: reasoning and cognition based on knowledge and experience.

Research on wisdom over the past several years has revealed that middle-aged people are much more expert at many social interactions—such as judging others' true intentions and moderating emotional reactions—than younger people. It peaks between ages forty and fifty, then stays on a high plateau until the final years of life. Such experience-induced expertise brings with it a number of proven benefits, including the ability to make better decisions, a heightened focus on the positive, better coping skills, an increased sense of equanimity, and the ability to more quickly and accurately interpret patterns.

It stands to reason that the more information we have stored in our brains, the more easily we can detect familiar patterns. Contrary to popular ideas about aging and creativity, many older adults discern patterns faster, determining what's important and what's trivial, then jumping to the logical solution. Elkhonon Goldberg, the NYU neuroscientist, has said that "cognitive templates" develop in older brains based on pattern recognition and form the basis for wise behavior and better decisions.

As he observed in *The Wisdom Paradox*, Goldberg began to realize that as he aged, he was increasingly adept at a kind of "mental magic." "Something rather intriguing is happening in my mind that did not happen in the past," he wrote. "Frequently, when I am faced with what would appear from the outside to be a challenging problem, the grinding mental computation is somehow circumvented, rendered, as if by magic, unnecessary. The solution comes effortlessly, seamlessly, and seemingly by itself. I seem to have gained in my capacity for instantaneous, almost unfairly easy insight. Is it perchance that coveted attribute . . . wisdom?"

Thomas Hess, a psychologist at North Carolina State University, has done a number of studies of "social expertise." Based on how we interpret events in the social world, social expertise appears to peak in midlife, when we're far better than younger people at judging the character of others and deciphering social experiences. Our brains, through years of building up connections, become exceptional at recognizing even vaguely similar patterns and drawing appropriate conclusions. "It's stunning how well a brain can recognize patterns," John Gabrieli, an MIT neuroscientist, has commented. "And particularly at middle age, we have small declines, but we have huge gains" in our ability to see connections.

As we age, we collect and store information. That, and not a "fuzzy memory," is part of the reason it takes us longer to recall certain facts. We simply have more things to remember. Older people have vastly more information in their brains than young people do, so retrieving it naturally takes longer. In addition, the quality of the information in older people's brains is more nuanced. While younger people excel in tests of cognitive speed, one study found, older people show "greater sensitivity to fine-grained differences."

Considering our wunderkind culture's celebration of early bloomer cognitive supremacy, it's fair to ask where these late-blooming advantages come from. As researchers have discovered, a specific neurocircuitry of wisdom may develop through years of experience. Dilip Jeste, director of the Sam and Rose Stein Institute for Research on Aging at the University of California at San Diego, has spent decades researching cognitive aging and the development of wisdom. The brain's prefrontal cortex, he speculates, may be part of a network of regions of the brain responsible for wisdom.

To understand wisdom and its possible neurological underpinnings, Jeste and his colleagues first did an extensive survey of the existing literature on wisdom and its definitions. Second, they gathered experts' opinions on a list of "wisdom" traits. Through this work, they identified six components of wisdom, including pragmatic knowledge of life; the ability to regulate emotion; prosocial behavior, which entails compassion, altruism, and empathy; and knowing one's strengths and limitations. Next, Jeste's team looked at studies on brain imaging, genetics, neurochemistry, and neuropathology that targeted the individual components of wisdom.

The evidence was compelling. "Based on all of those [brain imaging studies], we suggested there is a neurocircuitry of wisdom," said Jeste. The circuit involves different parts of the prefrontal cortex (which controls our higher functions), the anterior cingulate (which mediates conflicts between parts of the prefrontal cortex), and the striatum with amygdala (part of the reward circuitry). Wisdom, says Jeste, comes from a balance of activity in these regions. "In some way, wisdom is balance. If you are very prosocial, you give everything to other people, you won't survive. But of course, if you don't give anything to others, the species won't survive. You have to have balance."

Why does wisdom grow with age? Aging is associated with a shift in brain activity. Consider something called Hemispheric Asymmetry Reduction in Older Adults (HAROLD): the half of the prefrontal cortex that is less active in youth increases in activity as we age. In turn, this increases the overall activity in the prefrontal cortex. And older adults tend to use both brain hemispheres—called bilateralization— for tasks that activate only one hemisphere in younger adults. The best-performing older adults are most likely to show bilateralization. Additionally, during middle age activity shifts from the occipital lobes, which regulate sensory processing, to the prefrontal cortex, which controls higher brain functions like calculating probabilities, regulating emotion, and setting goals. Researchers have termed these changes and increased balance "brain integration."

One of the most passionate wisdom researchers, UCLA neuroscientist George Bartzokis, believes that brain integration—and its resulting increases in judgment, expertise, and wisdom—happens naturally as we move into middle age. As we age, we lose gray matter and gain white matter. Though gray matter—which makes up the basic cognitive networks—is crucial, the white matter—which holds the networks together—may be what gives us our true advantage. Many researchers, including Bartzokis, believe it's our amount of white matter that has allowed us to develop complex skills such as language. It is made up of myelin, the fatty outer coating of trillions of nerve fibers. The white matter acts like insulation on a wire, making neurological connections work more efficiently.

Myelin, Bartzokis believes, is what increases in middle age. After scanning the brains of seventy men ages nineteen to seventy-six, he found that in two areas of the brain, the frontal lobes and the temporal lobes, myelin continued to increase well into middle age. This insulation, according to Bartzokis, gives the brain "greater bandwidth." He added, "I'm fifty years old now myself, and I do find that I look at things with a much broader view. I see the whole big picture easier. That's the formidable—the amazing—maturity of the middle-aged brain. That's wisdom."

We've long suspected that age, neurological development, and wisdom are connected, but we're just now demonstrating it in science. There's a reason car rental companies are reluctant to rent to adults under twenty-five. There's a reason the U.S. Constitution dictates that you must be at least thirty-five to be president. Even two centuries ago, the founding fathers understood the value of an older, wiser brain.

A final piece of good research news for late bloomers: The development of wisdom has nothing to do with the early blooming so coveted by society. Wisdom researcher Monika Ardelt, of the University of Florida, hypothesized that mature personality characteristics in early adulthood would have a positive impact on a person's degree of wisdom in old age. Her longitudinal study showed she was wrong: Early maturity—or early blooming—in no way correlated to maturity and wisdom as an older adult. Wisdom, it turns out, isn't bequeathed. It's earned.

• • •

While today's wunderkind culture favors early bloomers and seems to create needless barriers for late bloomers, in fact, we late bloomers have our own amazing strengths that lead to success and fulfillment. And these qualities—curiosity, compassion, resilience, equanimity, insight, and wisdom—are conferred only with time.

By necessity, we late bloomers are on a different, more challenging trajectory. As we travel through life, we encounter obstacles like the push for conformity, the oppression of groupthink, and the pains of self-doubt. But, as we'll learn throughout the rest of this book, in all these challenges, we find our hidden treasure. We unearth our individuality. We see that a path to excellence, to reaching our true potential, is available to all of us. Within these challenges lies our true power, our covert talents and secret advantages as late bloomers.

We will discover all this—with a bit of patience.

. . . .

CHAPTER 5

Create Your Own Healthy Culture

The early-blooming mania, with its ever-narrowing definition of success, has roots in the IQ testing and scientific management eras of the early twentieth century (see Chapter 2). But our modern obsession with early blooming was born during the 1980s, with the personal computer boom and the arrival of heroes still in their twenties, like Bill Gates and Steve Jobs, who overthrew the old guard and got rich extremely fast.

While Jobs struck observers as a glamorous messiah, Gates looked like a nerd from central casting. The young Microsoft cofounder had grown up in the posh Seattle suburbs, was socially connected, and while attending the private school Lakeside Prep, scored 800 on his math SAT (and 790 on his written) and achieved top grades. For fun on nights and weekends, Gates spent thousands of hours at a University of Washington campus computer lab across the lake from his house. There he wrote software to collect traffic data and also hacked into Lakeside Prep's grade records. He was practically ordained to go to Harvard, and there he went. His sole act of rebellion as a young man was to leave Harvard a year early and cofound Microsoft in 1975. In two decades Gates would be among the world's richest people.

Steve Jobs gave the world magical products, but Gates left us with a road map that says, *Here's what you must do to become super-successful very early. Nail the SATs, ace the grades, and excel in an extracurricular project.* The algorithmic, hypermeritocratic culture we live in today is Bill Gates's culture. If Steve Jobs aspired to put a dent in the universe, Bill Gates really did succeed at bending the way society perceives success and milestones for young people. If we want to succeed big, and have our children succeed big, Gates showed us how to do it.

More than Jobs—more than any politician or pop figure—Gates helped shape today's zeitgeist, literally the spirit of our age. The obsession with early measurable achievement is a huge part of our culture. So let's now examine this culture, why it encourages us to conform, and how it affects our perceptions of late bloomers.

• • •

Our culture—the influence of our family, peers, and society—can build us up, knock us down, celebrate our efforts, or keep us stuck. Usually it does all of those. Our culture also transmits expectations to us. We may not perceive them at a conscious level, but they can shape our thinking and behavior for decades. These expectations are both spoken and unspoken, often communicated in subtle ways. They have an undeniable impact on how we see ourselves, and what we imagine is possible.

For late bloomers, culture is a big deal, and here's why. If we think we haven't yet fully bloomed—that is, discovered our destiny and fulfilled our potential—then we must examine our cultural influences to see if any of them are holding us back. I've already identified one missile aimed squarely at late bloomers: society's insistence on early achievement. Let's look at other cultural influences that help shape who we are now and what we might become.

Our cultural imprinting begins with our families. Even the best families can instill norms that do as much harm as good. That was the case for Erik Wahl, a globally renowned performance artist. As he tells it, the family and cultural values that pressured him to succeed at a young age eventually backfired. They brought him to the brink of disaster.

> I was raised in a system of meritocracy, and achievement and success. The message growing up: Get good grades. *Perfect*

grades. Get into a top college. Get a fantastic job. Make lots of money. Be a man of consequence.

Right out of college, I'd started working for an entertainment agency that booked entertainment and some keynote speakers. So if a trade show wanted Mariah Carey or the Beach Boys, I handled the brokerage. I became a partner in the firm within a year. I was young, fired up, and on a roll.

Then came the crash. Corporations stopped booking entertainers for trade shows. In the course of a few weeks, I lost everything that I had . . . everything that I'd worked my ass off for, and put my identity into. I was 30 and I had nothing to show for it.

I was humiliated. I was embarrassed. I felt worthless. I didn't want to go out in public. I didn't know what I wanted to do with the rest of my life. I just curled up in the corner of the bathroom crying.

I had to face facts. My old belief system was no longer working. I had to figure out another route. I was raised by my parents and culture to believe that, when the going gets tough, the tough get going. . . . But that wasn't working for me. And I was pissed. I was pissed at the business world. I was pissed at stock analysts who hadn't predicted this. I was pissed at everything around me that was associated with money. I'd put so much faith, and trust into this concept of money and wealth, and it had completely let me down.

I've since had a lot of conversations with people who've suffered setbacks. Mine happened to have been financial. Some people experience setbacks in their relationships. Others experience them through health, where they get jarred with something so substantial that they look for something to numb the pain. There were a lot of unhealthy avenues I could have taken to insulate the pain.

I get it. I understand why the pain is too overwhelming, and why we turn to distractions that numb us. I was lucky.

My solution happened to have been art. I went and hung out with artists.

I think I turned to art because it was the opposite of business. Artists, philosophers, and carefree thinkers are not attached to material possessions and things of this world. I just wanted to go and spend time with them. And as I did, I became fascinated with their viewpoints; I became fascinated with their talents. I discovered I had to do this.

At first my paintings sucked compared to these other artists who'd been doing it for a much longer period of time. But I learned very quickly elements of figure drawing, of shading, of balance, of value. It was like a whole new world had opened up for me. I began to see everything again for the first time.

All the things that I had glossed over in my life, because I was working to make another dollar, I suddenly began to see with open eyes. My new world was about beauty, sunsets, flowers, colors, the light. All of these things really opened up to me for the very first time, where I truly saw them.

The culture Erik grew up in oriented him toward early success and wealth. But the pressure to conform led him away from his higher gifts and eventually brought him to grief. After his crash, his reassessment of his cultural values took him through an emotional minefield, but it was something he had to do, and he made it to the other side. Amazingly enough, Erik makes more money as a performance artist than he did as a businessman and investor.

If we haven't yet bloomed into our full potential, or if we sense we're on a wrong path, it's natural to ask why. Natural, yet difficult. Who wants to cast a critical eye at societal norms to see what could be sabotaging our opportunities to bloom? Who wants to consider how our own parents, friends, and teachers might have put us in a box where it was impossible to bloom? Yet to avoid discussing culture in our lives is to sidestep one of the strongest forces that shape our beliefs, our natures, and our destinies. So let's try to identify and reflect on those cultural expectations that may be holding us back from blooming. My intent is to focus on how our culture—the sum of family, community, and society—shapes our individual paths.

• • •

The first level of culture we encounter is the family. While some unfortunate people suffer an impoverished, neglectful, or abusive home life, most of us grew up in families that were neither perfect nor awful. They were functional and supportive even as they nurtured at least some less helpful qualities: irrational thinking, petty biases, harmful belief systems, and parental missteps.

My own parents were college educated, but they had serious blind spots. My mother's strong suit was empathy but not reasoning. Though she was a valedictorian in high school, with a calculus teacher for a father, Mom was nonetheless attracted to wildly mystical explanations of things and events. When she heard hoofbeats, she thought zebras, not horses. My father was a terrific high school athlete who became a physical education teacher, a coach, and a high school athletic director. He was the king of high school sports in my town and state, but he knew nothing about business and was intimidated by the financially successful men in town. I could see his discomfort around doctors, lawyers, car dealers, oilmen, and people who belonged to the country club. I would process the meaning of this only later, but I can now see that Mom's irrational mysticism and Dad's status anxiety were forces of ignorance in an otherwise loving, nurturing family. My own late blooming is partially due to simply not knowing what I didn't know at the time—and, really, had no reason know in my family's house. Many of us grow up with similar knowledge gaps.

To fully bloom, we must declare our independence from our family. That doesn't mean we must reject their love, turn 180 degrees from their influence, or rebel against their expectations. It means only that we must reach our own conclusions about what does and does not support our blooming. Loyalty to family is one thing. Blindly conforming to family expectations is another and will likely hold us back from fulfilling our potential. That said, declaring a true independence from our family is not easy.

Our families are our first teachers of cultural norms. Our parents play a key role in teaching us about the broader world and how to relate to it. They help us form our identities both as individuals and as group members. They shape our expectations about the world and show us how to act. They influence our priorities and our decisions about college major, career, friends, and spouse. Some families encourage a wide range of possible futures; others don't.

The film director Robert Zemeckis, whose credits include *Back to the Future* and *Forrest Gump*, grew up in a working-class family on the South Side of Chicago. When he was twelve, he told his parents about his desire to be in the movies someday. One can imagine him as a boy pouring out his dreams. But his parents' response was, well, less than enthusiastic. "For my family and my friends and the world that I grew up in," he recalls, "this was the kind of dream that really was impossible. My parents would sit there and say, 'Don't you see where you come from? You can't be a movie director.'"

As young children, we observe and internalize our family values and expectations. What psychologists, sociologists, and social science researchers call "socialization" plays a major role in forming our identities—developing a sense of self. It instills in us the values and beliefs of the people who surround us. During childhood and into adulthood, we test and retest our socialized behavior. And we tend to behave like our family members—often without being aware of it.

Whether we like it or not, our families affect us in both positive and negative ways. They defined our first boundaries, many of them good for us: "Don't hang around with the kids who smoke and drink." But boundaries also can limit us: "You'll never be happy or successful if you go into business." Or, "Your father always wanted to go to medical school but couldn't afford it. We sacrificed so you could go."

• • •

As we grow up, we begin to shift from being socialized by our family to seeking acceptance and identity from the wider community. Aristotle first defined the word *community* (or *polis* in ancient Greek) as a group established by people with shared values.

One's community can include a social circle, a set, a clique, an ethnicity, or a tribe; it may strongly identify with a location, as New Englanders or Southerners do; a community may be like-minded people situated in a specific city, town, or neighborhood; and it may be an ethnic group with a distinct subculture. Community includes everything from a peer group in school, to colleagues at work, to members of a weekly knitting circle. Communities even form around certain products like motorcycles (think Harley-Davidson) and comic books (Comic-Cons); around college football games, Grateful Dead concerts, and Oprah Winfrey book clubs; around old TV shows like *Star Trek*, *Buffy the Vampire Slayer*, and *Dr. Who*; and around cable TV networks we find agreeable with our politics, such as Fox News for conservatives and MSNBC for liberals.

Do our communities shape us? Absolutely. They influence our achievement, health, income, behavior, and well-being. Everyone wants to feel like they belong. We're all influenced by friends, co-workers, and members of organizations in which we are members, from churches to book groups, from softball teams to gun clubs.

This yearning to fit in, to be part of something beyond our family and bigger than ourselves, begins in adolescence. Regardless of where or when we grew up, most of us can remember the peer pressure we felt as teens—to wear a certain brand of shoes, to listen to a specific kind of music, to conform in any number of ways. During this time, our peers—and their perceptions of us—assert greater power over our attitudes and behaviors than do our parents, as every parent knows and fears. Young adults often take part in risky behaviors such as binge drinking, illegal drug use, and reckless driving to impress their peers.

But peer pressure doesn't end with our teenage years. As we enter adulthood, we continue to be influenced by our peers, surrounding ourselves with people who are similar to us. If the majority of our friends earned advanced degrees, we're likely to consider doing the same in order to remain part of the group. If most people we know are buying houses, having children, and working their way up the career ladder, we're likely to integrate these activities into our own lives. Doing so allows our relationships to continue, with mutual understanding, shared stories, and conversations.

In truth, adults are just as subject to peer pressure as children and teens. Any time a group nudges us to conform to a behavior or dress, we are experiencing peer pressure. And when we follow an unfortunate fashion trend or we laugh at a joke we don't understand (or don't think is funny), we're signaling that we want to be a part of the group. Some of this influence can be healthy and positive, as when we join a hiking club or sign up for a program to quit smoking. But not every peer push leads us to a better version of ourselves; not all communities support growth and positive change.

As J. D. Vance wrote in *Hillbilly Elegy*, certain Rust Belt and Appalachian communities have become so dysfunctional, they've lost the ability to nurture individual success. "People talk about hard work all the time in Middleton," wrote Vance. "[But] you can walk through a town where 30 percent of the young men work fewer than twenty hours a week and not find a single person aware of his own laziness." To bloom despite such conditions, people in struggling communities—whether rural, inner city, or blighted suburb—have to run a gauntlet. To break free of those influences requires a willingness to declare independence from the community. That's not easy.

Childhood poverty is correlated with various measures of physical health, achievement, and behavior, as countless studies, books, and reports have shown. The consistency of these associations is remarkable. In terms of physical health, children who grow up in poor families have 1.7 times higher rates of low birth weight, 3.5 times higher rates of lead poisoning, 1.7 times higher rates of child mortality, and 2.0 times higher rates of requiring a short-stay hospitalization than their more privileged counterparts. In terms of achievement, the correlations are equally bleak. Children who grow up poor are twice as likely as their wealthier classmates to repeat a grade or to drop out of high school, and 1.4 times as likely to suffer from a learning disability. Youth of lower socioeconomic backgrounds have more emotional and behavioral problems, are more often abused and neglected, and more often experience violent crime than those who come from financial security.

It's tempting to say that poorer people are held back simply by lack of financial resources, especially today as the wealth gap between rich and poor is the highest it has been since the 1920s. But it's more complicated than that. As Vance notes, the problems in poor communities are also cultural. The few upwardly mobile people from the community often leave and thereby deprive the community of role models for success. Many of those left behind fall into a fatalism that leads to drugs and alcohol. As employers leave, citing lack of qualified employees, community trust collapses, and with it a hopeful sense of the future. Against this cultural gravity, it's hard for anyone to summon the effort to work and invest for the long term. Anger and defiance take over, so that a community may consider even showing up for work at a low-skill job to be a "sellout."

But even successful communities—including those in high-expectation, high-performance cities and suburbs—leave indelible imprints on us, not all of them good. In some ways, high-performance cultures can be a special kind of trap, pushing kids to a breaking point. They're raised to be ambitious and driven, verbally and mathematically quick, to get into elite schools and launch high-paying careers. But these kids often have little time or room for self-exploration. They are shuttled onto the conveyor belt, moving in one direction, with no encouragement of other interests or career choices. The conveyor belt moves them along a narrow path of success and starves them of opportunities for self-discovery.

Health psychologist Shilagh Mirgain notes, "Pressure from peers might cause us to feel like we have to keep up with the Joneses, pressured into a lifestyle that isn't authentically ours, or leading us to strive for 'success' that is someone else's definition." People on the receiving end of this kind of pressure are often "false-start" bloomers like Erik Wahl, whom we met in the chapter's beginning. They have all the markings of success but implode from having applied themselves to something that doesn't excite them or represent their true gifts, passions, and mission.

Beyond material circumstances—poverty or high-pressure affluence—a community's cultural norms can present obstacles. Even cultures that are mostly positive can have odd quirks.

Take my own culture, the Scandinavian Lutherans who live in Minnesota and North Dakota. Expressing emotions and asking for things are considered alien. When I went to California for college, I thought everybody was loud, a braggart, and shamelessly needy. But objectively, the Bay Area was a different culture with different means of expression. Only now, in looking back, do I see how the quiet stoicism of my regional culture, while inculcating many good values such as an appreciation for hard work and endurance, also worked against me. My midwestern modesty limited my possibilities in a California context and blocked my way forward. Contrary to my North Dakota experience, I learned that in California asking questions is normal and hugely useful. It is not pushy. Rather, it accelerates learning. I learned that self-promotion is not bragging, if done correctly.

In California, it would be hard to bloom if you didn't know what its culture considered normal and good.

One thing is clear: All communities pass along beliefs that can keep us from blooming. Whether we attended an elite prep school or grew up in a poverty- and crime-ridden inner city or a depressed town in the rural sticks, each community puts an imprint on its inhabitants, exerting pressure to conform to its expectations.

• • •

The third stratum of culture is society, that large social group that shares the same geographical or social territory and is subject to a common political heritage and dominant cultural expectations. Society has been defined as "the highest cultural grouping of people and the broadest level of cultural identity." The society we live in provides us with our most persistent set of cultural standards, mores, expectations, and behaviors. It determines our national identity. It creates tacit biases and implicit expectations that touch on nearly every dimension of life, including politics, gender, race, religion, sexuality, and health, as well as ideas of success and money. These are beliefs we internalize.

American society, for example, promotes both positive ideals (a belief in opportunity, the rule of law, and fair play) and less positive ideals (unrealistic body images, obsession with early success, and status materialism). Whether we know it or not, these standards and expectations exert tremendous influence over our choices and behaviors. Most people sense this to a degree, but they are often oblivious to how pervasive these influences are.

In the United States, according to the Nielsen media tracking company, we spend nearly eleven hours per day watching TV, surfing the Web, using an app on our phone, listening to the radio, and reading on various devices. That's right, nearly half of each day. These are all conduits for societal messages on what to believe, how to behave, and how to look. Of course, some people consciously defy this influence and try to go their own way, pursuing their own interests. But for most of us, this ubiquitous social pressure is surprisingly powerful. It affects our expectations, our hopes and dreams, and our self-image. It shapes our very sense of self.

Perhaps the most pervasive and insidious societal pressure comes from the mass media—newspapers, magazines, books, radio, video games, movies, and television. While the impact of social media is growing and is finally getting the critical attention it deserves, television still influences young children and their social development more than all other media. The fact that television is not interactive—we simply take in what it tells us, with no chance for rebuttal or debate (shouting at the screen doesn't count)—has an enormous impact on cognitive development. The average American high school student spends more time passively watching TV than sitting in classrooms or meeting socially with friends. Even infants between birth and age two average about an hour and a half of television a day. American homes have an average of two television sets, and nearly 40 percent have three or more.

While mass media may seem relatively benign—streams of content we choose and take in passively—they have the power to dictate how we learn about what's happening in the world. They show us how to appropriately interact with one another and shape the kind of people we become. They can have a strong impact on our outlook and aspirations, helping to construct our social reality.

What's more, mass media present their own kind of socialization, "by reinforcing existing values and attitudes, and by serving as a source of norms and values." Anyone watching cable TV news or late-night comedy quickly comes to see what values are considered good or bad. Most of the information people take in is now based on what they see and read in the media rather than personal experience.

Today the media increasingly push us to identify with certain group norms. Fox News fans bolster their self-esteem by comparing their social identity to the norms and attitudes of MSNBC viewers. Fans of Jimmy Kimmel's late-night show feel superior to fans of Jimmy Fallon's. Media offer viewers many such opportunities to develop and maintain their social identities. We use media to learn about in-groups and out-groups. For example, adolescents often watch dramas to learn social lessons about how to flirt or start and end relationships, or which types of humor are appropriate. The media provide users with what psychologists call "social identity gratifications."

But tips for flirting and frames of reference for acceptable jokes aren't the only things mass media can communicate. They also promote cultural, racial, or gender biases, either through stereotyping roles and behaviors, or the under- or overrepresentation of minorities. And repeated exposure to media content can lead viewers to begin to accept media portrayals as representations of reality. In what researchers call "cultivation," over time, heavy viewers of television may come to believe that the real world is similar to the television world. Heavy exposure to media cultivates this belief.

For example, someone who watches a lot of television might come away with the belief that more than one in ten males hold jobs in law enforcement. In reality only one in one hundred do. Media depictions of thin female body types can lead women to see them as ideal, as well as normal, expected, and the standard of attractiveness. Researchers are particularly concerned with the cultivation of racial, ethnic, and gender stereotypes, as well as attitudes about violence. Other research has shown that by familiarizing individuals with groups other than themselves, the media may also provide positive learning opportunities that help overcome stereotypes and prejudices. Ongoing racial bias during the civil rights era was helped greatly by the appearance of black lead actors on popular television shows such as *I Spy* and *Julia*. In the early 2000s, acceptance of gay people took giants leaps forward with shows like *Ellen* and *Will and Grace* that featured gay and lesbian stars.

To mass media's influence on us over the last three-quarters of a century, add social media, which have risen to near ubiquity. Social media have rapidly grown a new culture of comparison—a kind of mass self-media—in which people from all spheres present their curated best-of-all-possible selves. While these idealized selves are often far from reality, they fill up our ever-narrowing feeds and add to the barrage of media-driven norms and attitudes and beliefs that we consume in ever greater quantities with great regularity.

• • •

What does all this have to do with late blooming?

The problem for late bloomers is that many of the standards and expectations pushed through mass and social media can work against us. Even if we ourselves are immune to media influences—we don't own a TV, say—we live in a society where norms that affect us directly have been altered by media. Thus media affect how we define success, what types of careers or relationships are desirable or even acceptable, and when life milestones should be met. So the dominant social culture can create self-doubt, or even self-loathing, among those who do not conform. We feel we don't fit in. The twenty-year-old virgin is made to feel like he or she has something to hide from friends and peers. The twenty-five-year-old late bloomer working odd jobs while figuring out his or her career path is made to feel like a loser. Our value as a person can be thrown into question when we follow a slower or unconventional path. Today's media wildly overcelebrate youthful success. It is hard to overstate the influence this exerts on our children, our peers, and ourselves. Commenting on this darker side of society, the French psychologist Adolphe Quetelet famously said, "Society prepares the crime, and the guilty are only the instrument by which it is executed."

Mass media ask us to compare our body shape, sex life, marriage, house, car, family, and community to unattainable television versions of perfection. Social media ask us to compare our own commonplace or even boring reality against the curated accounts of how absolutely wonderful someone else's life is—people we know! Recovering addicts have a useful saying: Don't compare your inside to other people's outside. It's good advice. But social media make it almost impossible to follow.

Why should it be so hard? We have free will, don't we? To understand why pressure to conform makes keeping our own counsel so difficult, let's look at what sociologists call social norms.

• • •

Social norms are a society's unstated rules, without the legal standing. In every society norms exert a great deal of social control and help to regulate conduct. They are the foundation of everything from language to social interaction, cuisine, love, sex, marriage, prejudice, and material expectations. They underlie seemingly natural interactions like opening the door for an elderly person or giving up our seat for a disabled person. They even influence personal preferences, such as what music we like, what books we read, and what policies we support. In truth, it's difficult to see how human society could operate without social norms. We need norms to guide and direct our behavior, to provide order and predictability in social relationships, and to make sense of one another's actions.

The idea of norms is a key to understanding what researchers call "normative social influence," which explains a near-universal human trait, our tendency toward conformity.

The immense power of normative social influence stems from precisely our need to be accepted. We human beings, after all, are social beings with a strong need to belong to a group, to be accepted, and to have strong social bonds. This means we tend to act like and think like the people in our families, our communities, and our broader society.

How powerful is normative social influence? Let's take a look.

Imagine that you've been asked to take part in a psychological research study. On a specified date, you and seven other participants arrive at the research site. You're all seated at a table in a small room.

The researcher arrives and tells you that today's study is intended to explore people's visual judgments. She places two cards in front of you. The card on the left contains one vertical line. The card on the right displays three lines of varying length. Together the two cards look like this:

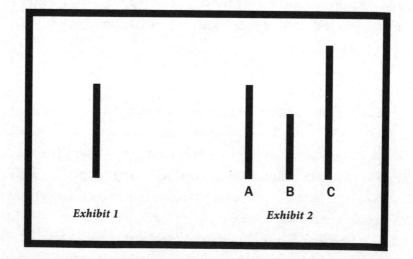

Exhibit 1   Exhibit 2

She then asks each of you, one at a time, to choose which of the three lines on the right card matches the length of the line on the left card. Although you don't know it, the other participants are actually in league with the researcher. In other words, they're confederates. Their behavior has been scripted. You're the only true research subject.

The task is repeated several times with different cards. On some occasions, the other participants, who vote first, unanimously choose the wrong line. It's obvious that they're wrong, yet they've all given the same answer. Do you go along with the majority opinion? Or do you trust your own judgment?

The answer might surprise you.

Social psychologist Solomon Asch devised this now classic experiment in 1951. If the participant gave a wrong answer, it would be clear that this was due to group pressure. Asch completed the test with fifty students from Swarthmore College, placing each of the subjects in a room with five to seven fake "participants." There were eighteen trials in total. The fake participants gave the wrong answer in twelve of the trials. Even Asch was surprised by the outcome. In the twelve "wrong answer" trials, 75 percent of the test subjects gave the wrong answer and conformed to the majority at least once.

Why did they conform so readily when the answer was clearly wrong? When interviewed, a few participants said that they really did believe the group's answers were correct. Most of them, though, admitted that they didn't believe their conforming answers but went along with the group for fear of being thought "peculiar." They were seeking acceptance and avoiding disapproval. A number of subsequent studies resulted in an even higher rate of conformity than Asch—as much as 80 percent.

That is the power of normative social influence.

Researchers next turned to questioning the extent to which people are able to detect the influence of social norms on their behavior. When we laugh at that joke that isn't funny, give an obviously wrong answer to show solidarity with a group, or decide that vegan is the right way to eat even though we love hamburgers, do we recognize how much of our behavior is due to social influence and how much is based on our own choice—on our own free will?

Study after study has shown that most of us are clueless when it comes to understanding why we so readily conform. People are more environmentally responsible—conserve energy and increase recycling—due to social normative influence more than any other factor. We put out our recycle bins because our neighbors do it. Yet in these same studies, participants rated normative social influence as the least important factor in evaluating why they changed their behavior. Normative messages increased towel reuse by almost 30 percent in hotels and have been successful in decreasing heavy drinking among college students.

The findings from dozens of studies on normative social influence are clear: Normative social influence is a powerful lever of persuasion. Yet we consistently do not acknowledge it or recognize it. Most people are unable to identify the true cause of their behavior. According to psychology professor Robert Cialdini, "Given the ubiquity and strength of normative social influence, it is surprising how little note people take of this potent form of influence when, as observers, they decide how to interpret the causes of their own actions."

This is what makes normative social influence so powerful—and possibly at war with our attempts to bloom later in life. It's invisible. It's a force we don't see, can't feel, and don't even want to believe in. Yet it influences nearly all our behavior, choices, and opinions.

Social norms have a huge influence on our expectations of ourselves, convincing many of us that there's only one single way to learn, grow, achieve, and succeed. And today that means succeeding early. Psychologists call this "normative thinking."

• • •

Normative thinking creates the belief that the right pathway is the one followed by the person we see as a normal member of our social group. There are, of course, good aspects to it. Life is complicated. It's often easier to observe and model our behavior on that of others in order to navigate the complex situations we encounter throughout life. But normative thinking also creates challenges. Many of us want to believe there's a road map to how our lives should unfold. The reality, however, is that there's no single "right" pathway for human development—physically, cognitively, morally, or professionally. This reality exposes a couple of clear drawbacks to normative thinking.

First, normative thinking creates informal social barriers that segregate us by income, class, race, religion, gender, and education. These barriers play on our normal human fear of exclusion. Think of groups that can be accessed only by those "in the know," those with the right information, in the right social group, or who have enough money. To feel comfortable, you have to understand the right cues or signals, know the proper people, and share the same convictions. If you don't, the message is, *You're not one of us. You don't fit in.*

The second drawback is that normative thinking leads to a seemingly endless—and destructive—process of comparison. We compare the progression of our lives against what we view as normal benchmarks. Whether for ourselves or for our children, we measure our growth and success by normal milestones. Those milestones could involve walking, reading, grades, testing, graduation, college admissions, a first paycheck, the right career, marriage, or that first house. We compare ourselves to our parents—Where were they at forty? At fifty?—to our friends and siblings. We compare our kids to our friends' kids. When we miss milestones, we worry, Are we slow? Are our children behind in their development? Am I a failure? We fear that deviation from the norm might indicate a serious problem.

It's a self-defeating process. In every aspect of our lives, there are many, equally valid ways to reach a positive outcome. There are always many ways to achieve a goal, gain expertise, or find success. In sports or music, this is easy to see. A hard rocker, country singer, rapper, and opera diva can all achieve success in music. So can an undersize soccer player and a giant NBA center in sports. But it's not as easy to see multiple paths for success in most endeavors. How can I get a first job at Google? How should I explain to an employer that dropping out of work to be a full-time parent has made me a better manager? What's the best way to invest in apartments if I haven't done so? Confused, we default to following norms and take the road everyone else is taking. But the problem for late bloomers is this: That road is crowded with early bloomers up ahead! By the time we late bloomers get there, the paths to opportunity are closed off. Late again, our life story! This can make us feel marginalized—or even ashamed.

• • •

So why don't more of us rebel against those cultural expectations? Why don't we skip the "normal," disregard the conventional, and happily take the road less traveled? Because the fact is, when it comes to cultural norms, breaking up is hard to do.

We are social creatures. It's the single most culturally significant thing about our species. Our sense of ourselves is grounded and shaped by our social connections and affiliations. Evolutionarily speaking, we are, as a species, "a people." As Jane Howard, biographer of the anthropologist Margaret Mead, put it, "Call it a clan, call it a network, call it a tribe, call it a family: Whatever you call it, whoever you are, you need one."

In one of the most influential studies on the neuroscience behind group conformity, scientist Gregory Berns and his team of researchers at Emory University examined the physiological effects of deviation from a norm by using fMRI to scan participants' brains. The researchers were interested in examining their brain activity when they were under pressure to conform to the group majority. The amygdala, which is associated with negative emotions, was activated when participants sought to break off from the influence of the majority. In other words, resisting normative social influence—even when the majority opinion is clearly wrong—can lead to negative physiological consequences. Put another way, it shows that we're cognitively hardwired to conform to group opinion, no matter how erroneous that opinion may be.

Almost nothing rivals the intense hatred that is directed toward people who turn their backs on a group. We call them turncoats and traitors, deserters and backstabbers. In American politics today, the really vicious fights often are not between Republicans and Democrats, but among Republicans and among Democrats to decide what constitutes normal correct thinking within their parties. The idea of what's normal can fuel a tyrant or a dictator. All cultures and social groups have engineered consequences for dissenters. These range from shrugs and eye-rolls to derogatory names to physical persecution and even imprisonment and death. One of the most pervasive punishments is social ostracism—identifying nonconformity as a perversion, originality as weirdness, and uniqueness as deviant behavior

This is the hidden, iron grip of culture. It's the overwhelming tide of the norms created by family, community, and society. It's the pressure to conform that's demanded through normative social influence, normative thinking, and cultural cognition. What, then, are those who are differently gifted, who operate on their own timetable of development—we late bloomers, in other words—to do? How can the curious and creative, the searchers and explorers, jump off the dominant culture's conveyor belt and begin shaping our own fates?

To find the answer, read on.

CHAPTER 6

Quit! Subversive Advice for Late Bloomers

Quit.

That's right. Just quit.

I ended the previous chapter by asking, "How can the curious and creative, the searchers and explorers, jump off the dominant culture's conveyor belt and begin shaping our own fates?" We do it by quitting. Quit the path we're on. Quit the lousy job. Quit the class we hate. Quit the friends and associates who hurt us more than help. Quit the life we regret.

As we saw in the last chapter, our culture and social norms create powerful unwritten laws about what's correct thinking and acceptable behavior. Dissenting from our culture and its social norms isn't easy. But we late bloomers must step up and do it anyway. Why? For the simple reason that as late bloomers, we haven't been served very well by our culture and social norms. Our unwritten laws, at this moment in history, are tilted in favor of the early achiever.

Consider our culture's opinion on quitting. The unwritten laws around it are as follows: *Quitting shows you can't take the heat; you can't handle the stress. You lack internal fortitude, you lack willpower. Quitters never win, and winners never quit. If you're a quitter, you'll never succeed.*

Our culture inundates us with the idea that sticking with something, persevering through all challenges, overcoming the odds, and above all, never quitting is the secret to success. And yes, relentlessness is unquestionably a virtue. We've been told an endless number of stories about people who doggedly achieved ultimate success. The notion that tenacity is essential for success and happiness is deeply embedded in popular *and* scientific writings. If we want to be successful, we need to work as hard as possible. We need to be willing to sacrifice, even suffer. We should be ferociously determined.

A slew of books extol the benefits of determination and glorify the advantages of perseverance, from *The Power of Habit* by journalist Charles Duhigg, to *Discipline Equals Freedom* by former Navy SEAL Jocko Willink, to *The Willpower Instinct* by Kelly McGonigal, to *Make Your Bed* by William H. McRaven, to the wildly popular *12 Rules for Life* by Jordan Peterson. Each of these books, in its own way, applauds the primacy of discipline, fortitude, and determination. Many of these authors' theories are surely valid in certain situations. But today tenacity and determination are as touted as *the* way to succeed.

Tenacity is invaluable, without question. As Samuel Johnson wrote, "Great works are performed not by strength but by perseverance." And as we'll see later in the book, persistence has its place in the late bloomer arsenal, as long as it's applied correctly, with patience and purpose. But I believe our current obsession with unyielding determination overshoots the mark.

While perseverance can and does produce success, there's another side to the story: Sometimes quitting is the right decision. In fact, giving up, for the right reasons, can make us enormously successful. Daniel J. Brown wrote his breakthrough international bestseller *The Boys in the Boat* in his sixties. Early in his life, he had to make some tough decisions about which path to follow—decisions that upset the people closest and most important to him.

Brown's first major act of quitting was high school. He explained:

> Even before I was seventeen, I had issues with anxiety. I would have panic attacks at school and a great deal of anxiety about going to school. In those days, they really didn't understand anxiety disorders very well. I was just expected to tough it out.

I suffered like this for a number of years. I was really miserable. Then came a day. I was in my junior year in high school, and I was in biology lab. I don't remember what precipitated the moment, but I was just *consumed* by anxiety.

It wasn't about the academics. It was about social things at the school and fitting in. I just got up and walked across the street and got in my 1963 Chevy Impala. I drove home. I told my mother I was not going back, ever. That precipitated a lot of emotion. She was very upset. Not angry, but just very upset. My father was stunned when he came home and I told him this. But I was absolutely determined that I was going to take control of my life.

I didn't know what to do. I just knew I couldn't keep enduring things. And so my mother, bless her heart, talked to the school. They arranged for me to take correspondence courses. The deal was that I was to spend eight hours a day at the library at Cal Berkeley completing these correspondence courses. Those credits would be applied to the high school. I would eventually earn my high school diploma that way. It was a huge change in my life because I started going to the Cal campus every day, and going to the library. The correspondence courses weren't very challenging. I would typically finish them in a couple of hours. But it put me on a university campus, you see. That's what changed my life. I was among books, in a world-class library.

Was Daniel J. Brown a quitter in the normal sense? Did he lack courage? Did he lack ambition? Should he have stuck it out in high school, miserable and ostracized and perhaps doomed to a mental breakdown? I would argue that quitting was the best possible option for young Dan Brown. By saying no to the expectations of others, including his parents, he set his life on a much healthier track.

Later in life, Brown performed another defiant act of quitting. In doing so, he had to abandon his father's expectations:

My brother had been a captain in the Air Force. Then he went to law school, became a law professor. I was teaching part-time composition classes at San Jose State—barely able to pay my rent. That's when my father died. He must have gone to his death wondering, *Is Dan ever going to amount to anything?* Not that my father was a person who really measured people that way. He wasn't. But he never saw me married with children and reasonably successful. So that's unfortunate.

My father had had to drop out of law school because of the Depression. I don't know if my brother Rick felt pressured by this, but I think he knew it would win Dad's approval. I actually tried to do the same thing—go to law school and win Dad's approval. That's another false start I made. I applied to law school and went for a grand total of three days. That anxiety issue that caused me to drop out of high school came right back. I realized after my third day in law school that I was in the wrong place.

I called my parents and told them. I was twenty-six years old. I said I felt I was going to disappoint them. I had moved to go to law school. I said, "I'm not going to do this. I just don't really want to do this."

I felt bad. But later I realized I had done the right thing. I had started down a path and quickly [realized] no, it's not the right path. I'm going to find another path.

I will be honest about it. It's not like part of me felt liberated. Part of me also felt guilty. "Wow, you're quitting something again. . . ." And so it felt like, "Oh, God. I'm just going to quit again. What's Dad going to think of this?"

No one wants to become a serial quitter, the kind of person who gives up at the first sign of adversity. But there's a case for quitting that gets little attention, and it may serve late bloomers especially well. In today's age of the Wunderkind Ideal, the overachieving teenager, we've neglected, or culturally outlawed, the idea of giving up. And yet it's a strategy that we late bloomers successfully bring to business, to innovation, to nearly every facet of our lives. The results will not only be liberating—quitting with intention can be a way to leap toward our goals.

• • •

Despite our cultural enthusiasm for determination, there are situations in which perseverance is actually maladaptive. Research points to three awkward truths about our determination not to quit: (1) tenacity, or willpower, is a limited resource; (2) quitting can be healthy; and (3) quitting, not doggedness, often produces better results.

The first problem with our cultural obsession with determination is that applying single-minded resolve to something that you don't really believe in actually makes you less effective. Tenacity misapplied erodes our ability to summon willpower or persistence when we really need it. This thinking lies behind the psychological concept of ego depletion, a term popularized in the 1990s with a hugely influential series of experiments led by Roy F. Baumeister, a pioneer in the field of social psychology. In 1996, together with his former Case Western Reserve University colleagues Ellen Bratslavsky, Mark Muraven, and Dianne Tice, Baumeister examined the effects of resisting a tempting food on participants' willpower.

To start the trial, Baumeister kept the study participants in a room that smelled of freshly baked chocolate cookies. Then he showed them the actual cookies, along with other chocolate treats. Some of the participants were allowed to eat these sugary snacks. The rest of the participants, however, were forced to eat raw radishes instead. These were the participants whose willpower and resolve were being tested.

Surprise—the radish-eaters weren't exactly happy about the switch. As Baumeister wrote, many of the radish-eating participants "exhibit[ed] clear interest in the chocolates, to the point of looking longingly at the chocolate display and in a few cases even picking up the cookies to sniff at them."

After everyone had finished their assigned snacks, Baumeister gave all the participants a puzzle to solve to test their persistence. How long would they persevere in trying to solve the puzzle after their willpower had already been tested by being denied the cookies? The results were striking: Those who were forced to eat only radishes devoted less than half the time to trying to solve the puzzle compared to the participants who were allowed to eat chocolate (as well as a control group that participated only in the puzzle-solving phase of the experiment). Apparently, those who had to resist the sweets could no longer summon the willpower to fully engage in a second task that required persistence.

They'd run out of determination. They'd used up their resolve.

The breakthrough finding of Baumeister's study was that self-control—and its analogs like willpower, determination, and perseverance—can be depleted. Determination is not simply a skill to be mastered or a habit to be developed. Instead, like overexercising a muscle to the point of injury, tenacity can fatigue us and break us down. Our determination "appears to be quite surprisingly limited," Baumeister wrote. In summarizing the results of his famous study, he called willpower "a scarce and precious resource." Ego depletion represented "a potentially serious constraint on the human capacity for control."

The notion that self-control depends on the expenditure of a limited resource was actually anticipated by Sigmund Freud as far back as the 1920s. Freud believed the ego (the controlled self) needed some form of mental or psychological energy to resist the urgings of the id (the instinctual self) and the superego (the internalization of cultural rules). Freud used the analogy of a horse and rider to depict this relationship. The rider (the ego) is generally in charge of steering, but sometimes the rider can't prevent the horse (the id and superego) from going where it wants to go. This early recognition created the basis of Baumeister's finding: When the rider gets tired, the horse takes over.

• • •

The story of Bill Bowerman's amazing coaching career illustrates a key point about the limits of human resolve. Excessive tenacity can exhaust us, even make us sick. Bowerman was the track and cross-country coach at the University of Oregon from the 1950s to the 1970s, and a cofounder of the giant shoe and apparel company Nike. As Bowerman's bio reads, "Over his career, he trained thirty-one Olympic athletes, fifty-one All-Americans, twelve American record-holders, twenty-two NCAA champions and sixteen sub–4 minute milers," among them the legendary runner Steve Prefontaine.

That Bill Bowerman became famous for training middle- and long-distance runners is itself remarkable, because Bowerman had no firsthand knowledge of distance running. He had been a football player and track sprinter in college. In sports, perhaps no greater divide exists, both physically and mentally, than between muscular and aggressive football-sprinter types (fast-twitch athletes) and those starved-looking stoics that make up the ranks of middle- and long-distance runners (slow-twitch athletes). Bowerman made his mark by coaching his physical and mental opposites, the skinny stoics.

How was he able to cross the divide? On a 1962 trip to New Zealand, he met a self-taught late-blooming coach, Arthur Lydiard, who had developed highly unorthodox ideas about training middle- and long-distance runners. Lydiard directly challenged the then-popular idea that high-intensity interval training, done every day, was the foundation for success. In his observation, interval track workouts, such as running 400 meters very hard, followed by a two-minute rest, followed by another hard 400 meters—repeated ten or twenty times— produced quick success, but then the runners would plateau after a few months. Raising the intensity of the interval training even more, the accepted method for getting runners off the plateau, would work for a few runners, but most would become injured or ill. Lydiard thought the culprit was a low blood pH factor. High-intensity interval training, performed daily, would leave the runner with excess lactic acid, Lydiard suspected, which would lower the runner's blood pH and overall immunity. Interval-saturated runners, Lydiard noted, would be exhausted from their day's training session, yet be unable to sleep well that night.

What's remarkable is that Lydiard had no formal training, either as a coach or as a scientist. He simply experimented, observed, took notes, took pulses, watched the trend lines, and made adjustments. No organization paid him to do this. To support his amateur coaching career in the beginning, he took a job as a milk deliveryman.

But the milkman was getting extraordinary results from his unorthodox methods. He put all his runners, from half-milers like Peter Snell to marathoners like Barry McGee, on aerobic long-distance training for several months. The goal was to get up to one hundred miles a week, including a Sunday run of twenty miles or greater, but at a slow enough pace that conversation could be sustained throughout the run.

Having established an aerobic base, Lydiard would move his runners to alternate days of hill training for strength and easy long-distance runs to flush out the lactic acid from the hill workouts and restore a healthy blood pH. Finally, just prior to and during the racing season, he would "sharpen" his runners with sprints and some high-intensity intervals, but always balance the speed work with slow easy runs on alternate days. His method worked spectacularly. At the 1960 Olympics in Rome, his runners won the men's 800 meters and 5,000 meters and took second in the marathon. New Zealand, with a population of 2.4 million in 1960, dominated men's distance running for the next twenty years. That's not quite true. It was a former milkman who was dominating: Arthur Lydiard.

America's Bill Bowerman was stunned by Lydiard's success, and he returned to America with filled notebooks.

As Kenny Moore, Bowerman's biographer, notes: "Bowerman began exhorting his Oregon runners to finish workouts 'exhilarated, not exhausted.' . . . He would scrutinize their form, grabbing a runner's throat and taking his pulse. He'd check the glint in their eye, sending the tight and dull to the showers, and especially those whose pulses weren't quick to return to 120 beats per minute. His credo was that it was better to underdo than overdo."

Moore notes that Bowerman's rebellion from the church of pain did not go over well in the coaching fraternity. "When Bowerman first articulated the 'hard-easy' method, he was despised for it. The anthem for most coaches then was, 'the more you put in, the more you get out.' When Bowerman chided them—'Come on, the greatest improvement is by the man who works most intelligently'—they were morally affronted. His easy days were derided. The intentional tailoring of stress to the individual was called coddling."

My point in bringing up Bowerman's story is this: Saluting the benefits of tenacity only makes sense to a point, because each of us only has a certain amount of resolve, both mental and physical. If social norms encourage us to apply our determination in excess, or to the wrong endeavor, we'll only run out of it. Perseverance applied in meeting others' expectations—whether family, community, or society—will deplete our reserves of willpower. We'll finish our days exhausted, yet be unable to sleep. And then when we really need determination and resolve, we may not have enough left to pursue a new pathway or a genuine passion.

• • •

The notion that we can somehow strengthen our willpower "muscle" is misleading at best, and detrimental at worst. Conventional wisdom suggests that if we do certain exercises or practice certain habits, we can strengthen this muscle. But science and research tell us that this isn't true. We can't simply apply determination like a jelly spread to everything we do in our lives—we'll burn out. When we force ourselves to do things we're not naturally inclined to do, or that don't fit our passion or purpose in life, we pay for it with reduced motivation and drive.

In their book *Designing Your Life*, authors Bill Burnett and Dave

Evans write of a woman who'd just made partner at her high-powered law firm. Let's pause for a minute and examine what that means. The woman had performed exceptionally enough in college—straight A's and summa cum laude—to get into one of the ten top law schools that her powerful law firm considers when recruiting newly minted lawyers. At law school she had to finish near the top. Then as an associate lawyer at her firm, she had to work eighty hours a week or more for at least five years before she was eligible for partnership in the firm. That's many consecutive years of work, stress, and minimal sleep. One hopes she liked it. But she didn't. After making partner—after climbing many mountains of grit to get there—she was exhausted. Rather than enjoy her new partnership status and seven-figure income, she cried herself to sleep each night in a state of exhaustion and despair. Her grit reservoir was empty.

When it comes to our willpower "account," we can make some withdrawals, but we can't make unlimited withdrawals. We have to choose wisely.

The second problem with the cult of tenacity is that quitting is actually a healthy thing to do at times. Many of the things we desire—thanks in large part to culture—are unattainable. Research shows that when we quit pursuing unattainable goals, we're happier, less stressed, and even get sick less often. That's right, quitting is actually physically good for you.

A number of studies tracking subjects ranging from adolescence to young adulthood to older adulthood have shown that goal disengagement—quitting—strongly and positively affects physical health. Three studies found that people who were able to quit pursuing unreachable goals had healthier hormonal patterns and greater sleep efficiency. *Not* quitting was associated with higher levels of depression, stress, and emotional upset. These symptoms can modify biological processes in our endocrine and immune systems in ways that increase our vulnerability to health problems like asthma and make us more susceptible to disease. In other words, misplaced tenacity can actually make us sick.

The third problem with our obsession with determination is, simply, that quitting often works. One of my favorite examples is the great CEO of the late twentieth century Andy Grove and his company, Intel.

I knew Grove personally. He was as gritty as they came. Born Andras Grof in Hungary, he escaped Communist rule under a barbed-wired fence after the Soviet tanks crushed a democratic rebellion in 1956. Arriving in New York at twenty without money or connections, he aced his classes at the City College of New York (CCNY then had free tuition) and won a scholarship to study chemical engineering at the University of California at Berkeley. Grove quickly distinguished himself and caught the eye of a Berkeley grad and famous Silicon Valley technologist, Gordon Moore, who offered him a job at Fairchild Semiconductor.

In 1968 Moore and his colleague Robert Noyce left Fairchild to start Intel, and they took young Andy Grove with them as Intel's employee number three. Throughout the 1970s, Intel made most of its revenue and nearly all its profits selling memory chips. In 1971 it released a promising new product, the microprocessor, but as revolutionary as it was, its financial contribution to Intel's bottom line throughout the 1970s was small. Memory chips were Intel's bread and butter.

But in the late 1970s, Japanese and then South Korean companies entered the memory chip market and undercut Intel on price. By the early 1980s, Intel was in a financial crisis. Grove suggested a radical solution: Intel should quit the memory chip business and bet its future on the microprocessor. There was heated disagreement. Bob Noyce thought quitting the memory business was the same as losing. But Grove persisted. As he recounted years later, "I asked Gordon [Moore], you know, what would happen if somebody took us over? What would the new guy do? To which Gordon said, 'The new owner would get rid of us (laughter) and get out of the memory business.'" Intel did just that. It quit a fading and futile business to focus on its future.

Any experienced tech startup founder will tell you how critical it is to know when to quit. Successful businesses like Intel quit projects and businesses all the time. Entrepreneur and billionaire Richard Branson is a serial quitter. Think of the businesses he exited when they didn't work as hoped. Virgin Cola. Virgin Digital. Virgin Cars. Virgin Brides.

In Silicon Valley there's a mantra: "Fail often to succeed faster." But to fail, you have to try. Then you try harder. At some point, however, seeing that the situation is hopeless, or that there are better uses of time, talent, and treasure, you move on to the next opportunity. It's really counterproductive to label an individual who walks away from a hopeless task a quitter when entrepreneurs are celebrated for the exact same thing. A general who did the same would be lauded for strategic retreat or flexible tactics.

• • •

Of course, quitting isn't easy. It's hard. When we quit, we're saddled with guilt. We feel shame. Quitting means overcoming cultural expectations and ignoring social pressures. But the popularity of unflagging tenacity as a cultural norm—one that our society has created, supported, and emphasized—sometimes results in exhausted people who are unhappy with their current direction in life. We're bombarded with stories of relentlessness leading to success, but we hear little about the positives of abandoning a project or a pathway that no longer makes sense.

As part of our obsession with early achievement, we've turned quitting into a pejorative, an insult that cuts straight to our sense of self-worth. And that's not just unfair, it's destructive. In a drive to suppress individuality and reinforce cultural norms, society has turned one of the most effective tools for self-discovery into a proverbial four-letter word. It's Taylorism at its worst, reinforcing the message: Stay on the culturally accepted conveyor belt to success at all costs.

Cultural resistance to quitting is a very real problem, but it is not the only source of flawed thinking. We all possess cognitive biases that hinder our ability to abandon a miserable job or fruitless activity. These biases can best be defined through two economic concepts:

the *sunk-cost fallacy* and *opportunity cost*. The first, sunk cost, deals with the past. Sunk cost is the money, time, or effort we've already put into a project or direction in life. The more and the longer we invest in something, the more difficult it is to let it go. The sunk-cost fallacy is when we tell ourselves that we can't quit because of all the time or money we've already spent.

The second economic concept is opportunity cost. Unlike sunk cost, this concept deals with the future. It means that for every hour or dollar we spend on one task or direction, we're giving up the opportunity to spend that hour or dollar on a different, better task or direction. In other words, instead of focusing our efforts on something that isn't working or fails to make us happy, we could be directing our energies toward something that might make us happier, better suit our lifestyle, or help us make more money—if only we weren't so worried about the sunk cost.

And that's the catch: we adult humans have a hard time breaking free of the sunk-cost fallacy. We shouldn't fall for it, but we do all the time. Hal Arkes, a psychologist at Ohio State University, along with his colleague Catherine Blumer, discovered just how bad we are at weighing sunk costs. Most adults, they found, are (embarrassingly) worse at considering sunk costs than children and dogs. Yes, dogs. That's how beholden we are to the sunk-cost fallacy.

Why? Apparently, according to Arkes and Blumer, we take a rule we learned growing up—don't be wasteful—and overapply it. When we quit something, we feel as if we've wasted all that time and effort put into learning the piano, preparing for medical school, or chasing a dream to please our parents. To better understand this dynamic, consider a scenario from Arkes and Blumer's study:

> Assume that you have spent $100 on a ticket for a weekend ski trip to Michigan. Several weeks later you buy a $50 ticket for a weekend ski trip to Wisconsin. You think you will enjoy the Wisconsin ski trip more than the Michigan ski trip. As you are putting your just-purchased Wisconsin ski trip ticket in

your wallet you notice that the Michigan ski trip and the Wisconsin ski trip are for the same weekend. It's too late to sell either ticket, and you cannot return either one. You must use one ticket and not the other. Which ski trip will you go on?

Which trip would *you* go on? The trip that cost more or the one that you believe will bring greater enjoyment?

Over half of the participants said they would rather go on the ski trip they would enjoy less—the Michigan trip. Why? Because the investment was greater (sunk cost), and therefore skipping it seemed more wasteful. A number of other experiments have supported the notion that the avoidance of waste is a huge factor in people's decisions to honor sunk costs by not abandoning a failing course of action.

In the context of the sunk-cost fallacy, abandoning a failing pathway seems to waste the resources we've already expended. For late bloomers, this would be the feeling that all those years pursuing a Ph.D., a law firm partnership, or that career in fashion would be a waste of time, money, sweat, and tears if we gave up now.

The sunk-cost fallacy is a major impediment to making positive changes and subsequently living a better life. There are additional psychological factors, however, that hold us back from quitting things in order to be happier or more successful. According Dan Ariely, author of the bestselling 2008 book *Predictably Irrational*, we're hindered in quitting by a mental state called "cognitive dissonance." Ariely says that if we've acted in a certain way, over time, we'll overly justify our behavior. If we've put ten years into a job—even though we despise that job on a daily basis—we'll convince ourselves that we love it. In addition, Ariely suggests that we actually like suffering for things we love. In fact, we like it so much that if we suffer for something, we'll decide we must love it! Ariely points out that fraternities and sororities, the military, and sports teams leverage this psychological tendency when they make participants suffer through hazing or extreme hardship. By turning indignity into commitment, these processes combine our intense desire to belong with our intense desire to justify our actions.

Yet refusing to abandon our investment in a college major, a job, or a path that's not right for us can be costly. For every moment we double down on something that's not working, we're forgoing other potentially valuable opportunities. As behavioral economics and psychology show us, the real waste is not in sacrificing our past by quitting a failing endeavor. It is in sacrificing our future by not pursuing something better.

• • •

Call it a strategic retreat. Think of it as a pivot or a rebirth. For those who are cardplayers, think of it as "knowing when to fold 'em." The fact is, it's just as important to know when to drop something and shift direction as it is to know when to stick with something. We've all regretted not quitting a dead-end job, or not ending a toxic or unhappy relationship sooner. When we quit the things that aren't working for us, we free up our willpower and perseverance for the things that really do matter. We all have a limited amount of time and attention.

Quitting doesn't necessarily mean we're weak or lazy. Quitting can also mean we're being honest with ourselves. Quitting is really the process of saying no. Often saying no can be the best thing we can do to improve our lives, whether it's saying no to late-night email, to a job, to a city, or to an unattainable goal. If we really think about it, every successful person or extraordinary person was a quitter. Seth Godin, in *The Dip: A Little Book That Teaches You When to Quit (and When to Stick)*, maintains that truly successful people are "smart quitters" who change direction when they realize that their current path won't get them any closer to their ultimate goals. Cutting their losses allows these successful people to reallocate their time and energy to the things that do continue to move them forward. Knowing when to quit those actions that don't work "gives you a sense of empowerment," says Godin.

Is there a catch to quitting? Yes. Quitting that is an affirmation of our true selves and talents inherently requires us to take personal responsibility. It recognizes that we are aware of our own limits as well as our potential. For most of us, this type of personal agency is a powerful level of awareness. When we need the strength to change course—when we find ourselves going down the wrong road—the ability to quit is the power necessary to turn around our lives.

And that's the key: Quitting is power.

Quitting, done for the right reason, is not giving up. It's not submitting or throwing in the towel. It is saying that a job just doesn't suit us. It is trying something and not liking it. In this way, quitting is actually part of the process of discovery. We define who we are by quitting, whether it's a club, school, job, or hobby. Forced adherence or unquestioned devotion leads to atrophy—to slowly dying. But quitting is the process of growing, the process of living.

As Steven Levitt, coauthor of *Freakonomics*, explains:

> If I were to say one of the single most important explanations for how I managed to succeed against all odds in the field of economics, it was by being a quitter. That ever since the beginning, my mantra has been "fail quickly." If I started with a hundred ideas, I'm lucky if two or three of those ideas will ever turn into academic papers. One of my great skills as an economist has been to recognize the need to fail quickly and the willingness to jettison a project as soon as I realize it's likely to fail.

Keep in mind, quitting, for many of us late bloomers, isn't necessarily forever. Many of us quit school, then return. This is why gap years (see Chapter 3) have become so popular. In this way, quitting is a form of patience. It's our bodies or our minds telling us—and we as late bloomers listening—that we're not quite ready for a challenge or a certain phase of life. This type of patience shows that quitting is often a progression or a stage, not an end result. Through quitting, an inkling of fervor morphs into a true passion: Photography leads to filmmaking, poetry becomes copywriting, law school becomes law enforcement, a miserable time in medical school turns into a long career in nursing.

How can we find our true passions if we don't try—and subsequently quit—things?

We can't.

This reality raises an important question: How do we know the right time to quit something? This is a question without an easy answer. Quitting is a personal decision, but a few worthwhile tips are floating around the research sphere. Steven Levitt, of *Freakonomics* fame, once said, "I've pretty much quit everything that I'm bad at." According to Hal Arkes, the expert on sunk costs, "The first thing is you've got to pull that Band-Aid off, and do it quickly." Arkes believes that people who are truly successful in leaving a job or making a major pivot are those who make the decision quickly and act immediately. "I think this idea of not looking back," he said—"I know it's a clichéd expression, but so many of the people that are able to move on, just go forward." And personally, I believe you should quit when you have a clear idea of your plan B, when you have a picture of your rebirth. Like quitting a bad habit, quitting an unsuccessful path in life is easier if you have something to replace it with.

But the single most important lesson in quitting—and I hope an idea that will stick with you—is that it is a strength, not a failing. We need to overcome our natural tendency toward the sunk-cost fallacy. We need to see quitting for what it really is, a virtue—the ability to "fail quickly" and to pivot nimbly.

The fact is, everybody quits. Successful late bloomers are just better at it.

CHAPTER 7

The Superpower That Is Self-Doubt

Most of us allow far too much self-doubt into our lives. That's true of late bloomers and early bloomers alike. But for hopeful late bloomers, self-doubt can seem a heavier load. As today's conveyor belt to success sorts us into categories of early bloomers and also-rans, the more self-doubt has risen. In our age of ubiquitous data and analytics, we all know the score, whether in grades, salaries, or Facebook likes. Transparency has its virtues, but it's also a wind that blows more of us toward bad feelings about ourselves.

In addition, culture (examined in Chapter 5) has created boxes we must fit into. We may have come from a family scarred by conflict and anger, one that was overly critical or had unrealistic expectations. Maybe we had mediocre test scores, attended the "wrong" college, or got the "wrong" degree. Today's culture warns us that if we break off the fast track, we'll pay a price. If we do something that goes against the norm, we'll face judgment. Fall off the conveyor belt to early success, and the first thing we'll see are the bruises.

Finally, many of us late bloomers find ourselves going through unwelcome life transitions, whether divorce, illness, or the death of a spouse. As a result, our mindset can be shaken. We had child-care responsibilities, an elder-care issue, an unexpected health problem. Or maybe life just hammered us, and we had to take a time-out from our career. These forces can be paralyzing. Many women struggle with self-doubt because of what researchers call "competing urgencies"— pregnancy, child care, and other family responsibilities. These urgencies tend to delay career preparation and advancement, may require an unusual approach to education, and result in professional success at a later age than expected. Self-doubt can grow as we see our friends from school or former colleagues advance in their careers while we, due to these factors, feel like we're stuck.

Let's pause here. As late bloomers, our paths to success are necessarily unconventional. By failing to accept this truth, we often start out in a hole by undervaluing our abilities and contributions. This type of self-doubt inflicts many different kinds of pain, from embarrassment to panic to paralysis. But the long-term damage from self-doubt is even worse than the initial pain. Left to fester, self-doubt leads to lifelong passivity and self-sabotage. Unmanaged self-doubt prevents us from realizing our full potential.

That's the bad news.

The good news?

The good news is that self-doubt, odd as it may sound, is actually a secret weapon for blooming. When properly managed, it is a source of information and motivation. As a result, it can help combat complacency and improve our preparation and performance. It drives us to question results, experiment with new strategies, and be open to alternate ways to solve problems—all tactics that correlate with late bloomer strengths such as curiosity and resilience. But self-doubt isn't only a performance enhancer; it's also a recipe for being a wiser leader, teacher, parent, and friend. Coming to terms with self-doubt makes us more compassionate and gives us greater insight into ourselves and others.

The ability to turn self-doubt into information and motivation is key. Such alchemy doesn't happen by chance. Late bloomers must learn to utilize a few different techniques to transform this perceived weakness into a wellspring of strength. They must learn to manage the random inevitable feelings of self-doubt. The best strategy for managing self-doubt is compassionate honesty. We must learn to acknowledge our self-doubt and to reframe it in a healthier, more constructive way. We must learn to see self-doubt for what it truly is: information—no more, no less.

Seen as information, pure and simple, self-doubt can change from a lifelong enemy into a trusted adviser that can help us reach our goals and, ultimately, bloom.

· · ·

What exactly is self-doubt? The word *doubt* comes from the Latin *dubitare*, "to waver, hesitate, and be uncertain." From an evolutionary standpoint, doubt is a good thing. It's bred into every human as a survival trait. Our ancestors "wavered and hesitated" before deciding to cross a raging river. Their doubt helped them survive. In our own day, we may feel "uncertain" about wiring money to possible scam artists. That's a good thing. Doubt about dangerous situations and sketchy propositions is a survival trait. Doubt is essential to our progress as a species.

Self-doubt, therefore, means wavering, hesitation, and uncertainty about our own capabilities. It's lack of confidence in ourselves, our abilities, and our decisions. This can be good—it can be helpful to question our capabilities. But if taken to an extreme, this sort of insecurity can rob us of opportunity or waste our potential. Our insane cultural obsession with comparing and ranking causes many hopeful late bloomers to struggle with self-doubt. Being held to standards that we're unable to meet—or choose not to meet—makes us susceptible to disregarding our unique capabilities.

How do most people deal with self-doubt? Not always so well. Many of us self-handicap, or sabotage our chances of success. We imaginatively create an obstacle right before any true test of our ability. That way if we fail, we have a perfectly acceptable justification and can protect our internal beliefs about our talent and ability: *I drank too much the night before the big test, so of course I didn't do as well as I could have.* Procrastination is one of the most prevalent forms of self-handicapping for late bloomers: *I didn't get around to writing my résumé until the last minute—that's why I didn't get the job.* Or, *All my time was taken up with busywork—thanks to my boss—so I couldn't get to that big presentation. That's why it bombed. If only I'd had another day or two.*

To be clear, self-handicapping isn't just simple excuse making. Instead, people who self-handicap purposely shoot themselves in the foot in order to protect themselves from having to confront their possible shortcomings. Many self-handicapping behaviors are those small, subtle bad habits like being late, gossiping, micromanaging, behaving passive-aggressively, or being a perfectionist. We may not recognize these self-defeating—and self-handicapping—traits for what they are. Or we may even wrongly perceive them as strengths. But in truth, they often get in the way of us blooming.

Additionally, many self-handicappers rely on what psychologists call the "tomorrow fantasy." This fantasy is that we'll give our full effort tomorrow, down the road, when it suits us. When the time is right, we'll give our genuine best—which, of course, will produce success. *I don't care that much about this project, so whatever. But when it's something I'm passionate about, I'll work hard at it. Then people will see what I can really do.* This illusion allows us to avoid putting our ability to a true test. Self-handicapping works as a security blanket for fragile egos, but it carries with it the cost of never experiencing true success.

Some late bloomers cope with self-doubt through a strategy researchers call "other enhancement," another form of self-defeating rationalization. Those early bloomers succeed because they're more gifted, better-looking, and more together. With their glaringly obvious talents, they were born to succeed. *She got perfect SATs and is so confident. What chance do I have? I can never be like that.* Or, *He only got the job because he's young and handsome. They only promote good-looking salespeople.* We enhance others by attributing their success to some preordained superiority, while underestimating our own talents and capabilities, in the belief that other people are inherently superior and therefore live better lives. Society's obsession with early achievement only feeds this belief. When society so overtly favors early bloomers, it's difficult for the rest of us to see ourselves as worthy.

Finally, another common—and maybe the most pernicious—late

bloomer strategy for dealing with self-doubt is "stereotype threat." We internalize negative stereotypes about our own capabilities in a way that convinces us that we can never be good at certain activities, no matter how hard we try. Many late bloomers fall short of mandated educational objectives, leading to negative messages about our learning abilities. *You'll never be great at school,* we're told. Or, *You're just not a go-getter.*

Exposed to these types of negative stereotypes, we come to believe them and use them as pretexts to avoid certain topics, challenges, or even careers. For instance, we may view ourselves as "not a math person" or as a bad leader. And rather than working to disprove the stereotype, we avoid any situation that involves math or requires managing people. We give up on ourselves before we have a chance to develop a skill or test our true capabilities. In this way, stereotype threats act as both a self-protecting and a limiting strategy.

Do you identify with any of these unhelpful, self-defeating coping strategies? I do. And I have a strong suspicion that some late bloomers are being held back by them. These aren't the only psychological approaches people use to cope with self-doubt, but they're the ones that most of us who feel marginalized by society's love affair with early blooming use in order to protect ourselves from the consequences of disappointment or failure. Take heart, though. They are mere bumps in the road toward unlocking the true value of self-doubt.

• • •

Imagine for a minute that you're a world-renowned physicist, a real-world Sheldon or Leonard from *The Big Bang Theory*. You've scrutinized atomic particles, unraveled string theory, and studied the mysteries of the universe. You've published hundreds of peer-reviewed papers. You're a tenured professor at a major university and considered brilliant by your students, your colleagues, and your family and friends. You're truly one of the most respected intellects in the world.

You wouldn't have much to doubt about yourself, right?

Wrong.

In 2005 the sociologist Joseph Hermanowicz found the opposite to be true. It turns out that the smartest and most accomplished physicists—the real-world Sheldons and Leonards—have loads of self-doubt. In fact, the more accomplished they were, the more self-doubt they admitted to.

Hermanowicz investigated top scientists and their appraisals of their own success. These physicists had published more than one hundred peer-reviewed papers in prestigious journals, been cited thousands of times, and reached the level of full, tenured professor at major universities. He initially assumed that self-doubt would decrease for these successful scientists. These were some of the most successful physicists in the world, after all. But that's not what he discovered.

"When you get a series of two or three rejections on proposals, you worry about whether you can actually cut the mustard anymore or maybe your ideas really are wrong after all," one physicist admitted. "I always have doubts about myself," another confessed. "I'm always plunged into a situation that I feel totally unqualified, unprepared to do, and somehow you have to rise to the occasion," she added. "Insecurities . . . drive a lot of us," a different physicist acknowledged. "[Insecurities about] how good you are. How well you are doing. Whether you measure up."

Stop and reflect on this. Even the world's top physicists routinely ask themselves, *Am I good enough?* or *Will I succeed?* or *Do I have what it takes to be successful?* You might assume that their achievement and high recognition would bring a strong sense of affirmation. Yet the passages convey a different reality.

This is one of the first important points to understand: *All of us* experience self-doubt.

This is true no matter how successful we are. Feelings of self-doubt may be more acute in those of us who haven't yet bloomed, but it doesn't mean we're damaged, dysfunctional, or even unusual. Self-doubt is normal. It's a mistake to believe that you, me, or any of us are alone in facing this problem. With multiple Academy Awards, one would think that Meryl Streep was free from self-doubt. Yet she has readily admitted to struggles with insecurity. "I say to myself, 'I don't know how to act—and why does anybody want to look at me on-screen anymore?'" she once lamented in *O: The Oprah Magazine*. From Pulitzer Prize–winning author Maya Angelou, to popular musicians, to world-renowned brain surgeons, even the brightest and most creative aren't immune to this nagging sense of dread—a feeling that, eventually, someone will pull back the curtain and reveal just how untalented and unworthy they truly are. Maya Angelou once confessed, "I have written eleven books, but each time I think, 'Uh-oh, they're going to find out now. I've run a game on everybody, and they're going to find me out.'"

All healthy people have self-doubt. Some late bloomers may feel it's our own peculiar burden, but it's a universal trait that people in all walks of life experience. And from an evolutionary viewpoint, self-doubt is actually useful. Self-doubt alerts us and can motivate us. It becomes harmful only if we let it run amok and resort to coping strategies like self-handicapping and other enhancement. Furthermore, as many studies have shown, a little self-doubt can actually improve performance and increase achievement. That's right, self-doubt benefits performance. Several studies involving tasks and challenges ranging from golfing, rope skipping, and pistol shooting to taking academic exams and performing analytical tasks show, definitively, that when it comes to high performance, a healthy dose of self-doubt improves results. This is true because participants who experience self-doubt put in more effort, both in their preparation and during their performance. In both sports and academic pursuits, self-doubting participants pay more attention to their practice routine and invest more cognitive effort. Self-doubt, properly harnessed, combats complacency.

This is very encouraging for those of us who are late bloomers. Throughout our lives, society has compared us unfavorably to early bloomers. This has fed our self-doubt, and now many of us have too much of it. A major difference between people who bloom and those still waiting to bloom is this: The bloomers don't let self-doubt hold them back. Rather, they use self-doubt to help them improve. It sounds somewhat counterintuitive, I know.

But it can be done.

. . .

In Chapter 4, I praised the insight of famous football coach and late bloomer Bill Walsh. Early in my career at *Forbes* magazine, I asked Walsh to write a column for *Forbes ASAP*. He had just returned to coaching football at Stanford. Prior to that, he'd taken the San Francisco 49ers from the worst record in the NFL to a Super Bowl win in just three years. He won two more Super Bowls and left the 49ers franchise in a position to win two more. He was arguably the most brilliant football coach of his era. Even his detractors had to concede that Walsh, creator of the West Coast offense, was a premier innovator in the field of football. I visited him at his Stanford office, where we would talk for an hour at a time, with me taking notes.

Before meeting Bill Walsh for the first time, I would have expected a supremely self-confident man with a military general's demeanor— the very picture of a successful big-time coach. But on the surface, he was just the opposite. He wore his self-doubt like an open wound. He constantly shifted in his seat, corrected his own sentences, and jumped up to his well-stocked bookshelf to check a fact. Walsh, the great football coach, came off like a neurotic professor.

Our conversations reinforced this surprising view of the great man. Walsh described his evolution as a coach in humble ways. He was always learning, always experimenting, and always coping with his own doubts.

One day I asked him about the role of confidence in a successful career. He snorted. "Confidence," he said. "In my whole career I've been passing men with greater bravado and confidence. Confidence gets you off to a fast start. Confidence gets you that first job and maybe the next two promotions. But confidence stops you from learning. Confidence becomes a caricature after a while. I can't tell you how many confident blowhards I've seen in my coaching career who never get better after the age of forty."

Walsh did not get his first serious head coaching job until he was forty-six, and his first professional job until forty-eight. Even with this late start, he went on to become one of the greatest coaches of all time. Walsh never tried to repress his self-doubt about whether to draft a certain player or make a risky play call with a game on the line. He used his doubts to experiment and reassess, experiment and reassess.

To me, Walsh epitomizes how one should deal with self-doubt: to use it as a means to drive performance, to constantly get better. And that's my point. To bloom, we all must learn not to fear self-doubt but to embrace it as a normally occurring opportunity for growth and improved performance.

But how?

The key to harnessing self-doubt starts at the very core of our individual beliefs about ourselves, with something psychologists call "self-efficacy." And understanding self-efficacy begins with Albert Bandura.

• • •

In the field of psychology, Albert Bandura is a giant. But unless you follow the field closely, you might not know his name. In 2002 Bandura was ranked the fourth most important psychologist in history by the *Review of General Psychology*. Only such pillars as B. F. Skinner, Jean Piaget, and Sigmund Freud ranked higher than Bandura, who achieved his exalted status for his theories on self-efficacy—an individual's confidence in their ability to accomplish what they set out to do.

Bandura was born in 1925, in a small town on the windswept northwestern plains of Alberta, Canada, the last of six children. His early education occurred at a small school with only two teachers. Because of limited educational resources, he says, "the students had to take charge of their own education."

The self-sufficient young Bandura realized that while "the content of most textbooks is perishable . . . the tools of self-directedness serve one well over time." Taking charge of his own education beyond the raw basics in rural Canada undoubtedly contributed to his later emphasis on the importance of self-direction and personal agency.

Bandura attended the University of British Columbia, intending to major in biological sciences. He worked nights and commuted to school in the early morning with other students. During one term, they all arrived at school before his classes started. He had to pass the time somehow. "One morning, I was wasting time in the library," he explained. "Someone had forgotten to return a course catalog, and I thumbed through it attempting to find a filler course to occupy the early time slot. I noticed a course in psychology that would serve as excellent filler. It sparked my interest, and I found my career."

Bandura earned his degree in only three years, then went on to graduate school at the University of Iowa. After earning his Ph.D., he was offered a position at Stanford and began working there in 1953. He is still there to this day.

His 1977 paper "Self-Efficacy: Toward a Unifying Theory of Behavioral Change" caught the world's attention and caused a huge shift in psychology. Self-efficacy has since become one of the field's most studied topics. But what, exactly, is self-efficacy?

Bandura has defined self-efficacy as confidence in one's own ability to develop strategies and complete tasks necessary to succeed in various endeavors. More simply put, it is an individual's belief about their own capabilities, like their ability to perform specific tasks: Take a test. Launch a business. Close a sale. Give a speech. Complete a marathon. High self-efficacy is good because unless we truly believe we can produce the result we want, we have little incentive to try stuff in the first place or persevere in the face of challenges.

Over the past few decades, dozens of studies have examined the importance of self-efficacy in academics, occupational development, and career success. Multiple cross-sectional and longitudinal studies prove that high self-efficacy has a positive influence on salary, job satisfaction, and career success. Self-efficacy has been studied, and verified, in a variety of areas, including phobias, depression, social skills, assertiveness, smoking addiction, pain control, health, and athletic performance.

Why is self-efficacy such a big deal?

Virtually all of us can identify goals that we want to accomplish or habits we'd like to change. Most of us, however, realize that putting these plans into action is not quite so simple. Bandura and others have found that our self-efficacy plays a major role in how we approach goals and challenges. This is particularly true for late bloomers. Because of society's obsession with early achievement, late bloomers are often denied the two primary sources of a strong sense of self-efficacy: *mastery experiences* and *social modeling*.

Mastery experiences are instances of mastering a task or achieving a goal. Acing a class or a test, dominating a sport, nailing a job interview—these are all mastery experiences that increase self-efficacy. But many late bloomers have fewer of these types of experiences. Because we don't fit the mold created by society, we often fail to meet typical milestones. We may not score as high on tests, get the anticipated promotions, or meet cultural expectations. And so we don't experience the socially applauded outcomes that bolster self-efficacy as often as early bloomers may.

The other source of self-efficacy, social modeling, refers to seeing people similar to ourselves succeed, which raises our belief that we too possess the capabilities to excel in life. Unfortunately late bloomer success stories garner little attention in our world, which focuses excessive attention on early achievers—the precociously talented and youthfully ambitious. Late bloomers are largely excluded from our social models. For many of us, this dearth of role models puts another ding in our sense of self-efficacy.

Here is a crucial distinction: Self-doubt and self-efficacy are not the same thing. People with a strong sense of self-efficacy view challenging problems simply as tasks to be mastered. Like Meryl Streep, they may feel a general sense of self-doubt. But they proceed anyway. They develop a deeper interest in the activities in which they participate and form a stronger commitment to developing their interests. They recover more quickly from setbacks and disappointment. People with a weak self-efficacy, on the other hand, avoid challenging tasks, believing they are beyond their capabilities. They tend to focus on personal failings and negative outcomes, which causes them to lose confidence in their personal abilities.

Put another way, self-doubt is okay. Lack of self-efficacy is not. It's a spectacular understatement to say that low self-efficacy is detrimental. Self-efficacy affects nearly every aspect of life: how well we learn, work, love, and live. For late bloomers, a strong—or at least stronger—sense of self-efficacy gives us the confidence to defy social norms, maintain a different pathway to success, and root for the success of those around us. As such, we must acquire and develop high self-efficacy if we're to bloom. Yes, even with high self-efficacy, we'll still feel self-doubt (sometimes a lot of it), but we'll be able to maintain a sense of personal agency nonetheless, a belief in the face of self-doubt that we can take meaningful action. This belief is the very foundation of translating self-doubt into motivation and information.

Fortunately, we can improve our self-efficacy through something that we all already do: talk.

• • •

Language is the hallmark of humanity. It allows us to form deep relationships and complex societies. It lets us teach and learn from others. But we also use it when we're alone. We all talk ourselves through situations, good and bad. It's the little voice in our heads. It's our inner cheerleader—or our inner critic. Psychologists and researchers call this little voice self-talk. Self-talk shapes our relationships with ourselves. We can use it as a tool to gain distance from our experiences—to reflect on our lives. In a sense, when we talk to ourselves, we're trying to see things more objectively. In a world that so overtly favors early bloomers, this level of objectivity can be enormously beneficial for late bloomers. It can help us overcome the negative cultural messages we receive from family, friends, and society.

Self-talk is often looked at as just an eccentric quirk, but research has found that it can influence cognition, behavior, and performance. Positive self-talk can improve our performance by helping us regulate our emotions, thoughts, and energy. It can increase our confidence, improve coordination, and enhance focus. As in the children's book *The Little Engine That Could*, phrases like "I think I can, I think I can," actually work to decrease self-doubt, increase our self-efficacy, and improve our real-world performance. It might sound corny, but motivating ourselves through positive self-talk works.

Positive self-talk and its relationship to self-efficacy has been a topic of intense study for sports psychology researchers. Researcher Antonis Hatzigeorgiadis and his team at the University of Thessaly in Greece studied water polo players and how self-talk affected their performance in throwing a ball for accuracy and distance. The players using motivational self-talk significantly improved at both tasks versus the others. The following charts illustrate their findings.

Overall, the study showed that motivational self-talk dramatically increases both self-efficacy and performance. It also confirmed Bandura's premise that increases in self-efficacy are related to improvements in performance.

Whatever our skill level at a particular task, self-talk can help all of us increase our self-efficacy and perform better. The power of self-talk has been conclusively demonstrated in a host of fields beyond sports, including management, counseling, psychology, education, and communication. It improves our self-efficacy and performance in tasks ranging from throwing darts and softballs to playing handball to increasing vertical leaps. It's helped struggling young writers and budding entrepreneurs gain confidence and persevere in the face of challenges.

I can attest personally to the power of self-talk. When I was learning to fly an airplane, I performed much better when I talked myself

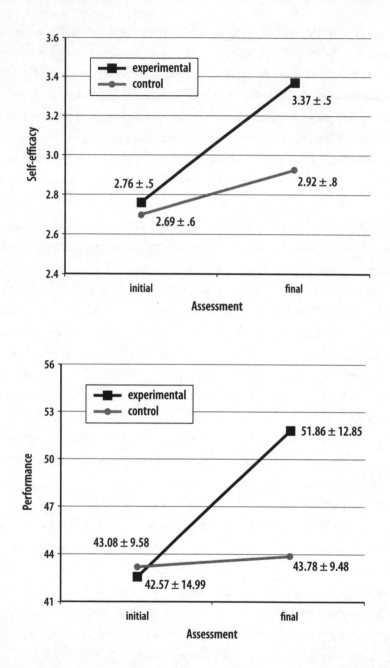

through various maneuvers, such as making forty-five-degree turns while maintaining altitude, and landing in a crosswind. When I took my private pilot's flight test, the examiner commended me for using self-talk, saying it demonstrated "situational awareness." It certainly kept my mind focused.

Even how we refer to ourselves can make a difference. Ethan Kross, director of the Self-Control and Emotion Laboratory at the University of Michigan, has found that people who speak to themselves as another person—using their own name or the pronoun *you*—perform better in stressful situations than people who use the first-person *I*. In a study, Kross triggered stress in participants by telling them that with just five minutes to prepare they had to give a speech to a panel of judges. Half the participants were told to try to temper their anxiety using the first-person pronoun: *Why am I so scared?* The other half were told to address themselves by name or the pronoun *you*: *Why is Kathy so scared?* or *Why are you so scared?* After they each spoke, the participants were asked to estimate how much shame they experienced. People who used their names or *you* not only reported significantly less shame than those who used *I*, their performances were also consistently judged to be more confident and persuasive.

According to Kross, when people think of themselves as another person, "it allows them to give themselves objective, helpful feedback." This is because they self-distance—they focus on themselves from the distanced perspective of a third person. "One of the key reasons why we're able to advise others on a problem is because we're not sucked into those problems," explained Kross. "We can think more clearly because we have distance from the experience." By using external pronouns for ourselves, we view ourselves as a separate person, enabling us to give ourselves more objective advice.

Lesson: If you're frazzled and need a motivational pep talk, consider giving it to yourself in the second or third person. This can help you look at the situation from a logical, objective perspective rather than an emotional, biased one.

When it comes to increasing self-efficacy in late bloomers, the motivational power of language isn't limited to self-talk. It also applies to how we speak to others, especially as a parent, partner, or colleague of someone with low self-efficacy. Verbal suggestion can lead us to believe that we can cope successfully with a task or challenge that has overwhelmed us in the past. When we're persuaded that we possess the capabilities to master difficult situations, we apply greater effort than we would otherwise. "Persuasive boosts in perceived self-efficacy," according to Bandura, "lead people to try hard enough to succeed; they promote development of skills and a sense of personal efficacy."

On the flipside, negative feedback can exacerbate fragile self-efficacy. To break what he called "exacerbation cycles" of people with low self-efficacy, Bandura suggests we avoid the negative reinforcement of a skill deficiency or promotion of the idea that a particular task is easy.

This just reaffirms a point we all already know: words matter.

Instead of telling a late bloomer, "This isn't brain surgery," try saying, "This is a challenge, but you can figure it out." Or instead of telling yourself, "I feel terribly overwhelmed right now," try, "Alex, you have the capability to do this, and here's how." These simple linguistic tweaks can help late bloomers—as well as everyone else—make significant strides toward greater self-efficacy.

One caveat: Verbal encouragement of this kind isn't about being a relentlessly optimistic cheerleader. It's one thing to put a positive or constructive spin on a situation. It's another thing to create unrealistic beliefs and expectations. Setbacks and mistakes are not to be brushed aside with a glib cliché. Instead, they're moments for reflection and opportunities for learning. To get the greatest benefits from self-talk—or any sort of verbal encouragement—we need to develop statements that support a realistic self-image. Ludicrously positive statements can be disheartening and actually reduce self-efficacy. So how do we find the right balance between inspiration and reality?

When helping ourselves—or a late bloomer we care about—manage self-doubt or overcome setbacks, finding the right words and tone begins with a process that psychologists call "framing."

• • •

A frame around a painting subtly directs attention to the painting's features, shaping how we see the colors and lines. Similarly, we can use cognitive frames to shape our behavior. For example, what is our frame for handling criticism? For handling a setback? For meeting a new kind of challenge?

Most of the time we frame situations automatically. More than we realize, our frames are shaped by past experiences, good and bad. Many late bloomers fall into the habit of bringing negative or self-defeating assumptions to our challenges, especially if we have a low self-efficacy. In our minds, we've failed at a task before we've even started. Such negative framing hurts our chances to bloom. So the key question is, Can we change our habit of negative framing and learn to frame our challenges in a more positive light? The answer is yes.

Alison Wood Brooks of Harvard Business School recently studied the influence of framing on our emotions, looking at anxiety in karaoke singing, public speaking, and math performance. When confronted with performance anxiety, most people try to suppress their emotions. Brooks investigated an alternative strategy: framing anxiety as excitement. Compared to those who attempted to calm down, individuals who instead framed their anxious energy as excitement actually felt more genuine enthusiasm and performed significantly better.

Brooks found that we can frame anxiety as excitement by using simple strategies like self-talk (saying "You are excited!" out loud) or simple messages ("Get excited!"). These framing messages allow us to channel our anxious energy into an opportunity mindset rather than a threat mindset. Brooks's findings demonstrate that we all have remarkable control over our perceptions and our resulting feelings. The way we frame—and verbalize—our feelings helps us construct the way we actually feel.

This should be encouraging news to late bloomers. In many cases, our cognitive frames have been shaped through years of negative feedback and input, causing us to default to a detrimental frame. But we can change our frames.

Most models of framing in psychological research consist of

two contrasting alternatives: learning versus performance, promotion versus prevention, healthy versus unhealthy, or in the case of the previous study, excited versus anxious. The positive frames—learning, promotion, healthy, excited—lead to greater perseverance, greater innovation, and increased learning. By contrast, the negative frames—performance, prevention, unhealthy, anxious—lead to worse outcomes, promoting a sense of risk aversion and a bias for framing new situations as chances to lose ground.

If we have the power to choose our frames, then why would we frame events in a way that undermines our efforts? In general, researchers believe that many spontaneous frames like the ones late bloomers use are about self-protection. But self-protective frames dramatically inhibit our opportunities to learn, improve, and bloom: They are the "I'm not good enough" and "I'm going to blow it" thoughts. As late bloomers, accepting our limiting frames rather than challenging them has grave consequences: We end up not achieving our goals, discovering our passions, or living our destinies.

Successful late bloomers don't let themselves default to self-protective framing. Instead, they learn to reframe. The idea is, we're all free to reframe literally any thought into something more positive, just like the nervous performers who reframed their anxiety as excitement. Reframing doesn't mean ignoring facts. It means changing our perspective on the facts to give them a more beneficial meaning.

At its simplest, reframing involves two steps: acknowledging a negative frame, then replacing it with a positive one. Suppose that you just failed a job interview and feel terrible (who wouldn't?). Well, the question you must ask yourself is, *How long do you want to feel terrible?* Long enough to get on social media and trash the job recruiter's reputation? The most challenging part of reframing is to acknowledge that you have a choice in how you frame a difficult situation. A healthy choice for reframing the job rejection would be, *Wow, that stung. What did I just learn? Maybe I wasn't prepared, or maybe I sensed that the job was a lousy fit for me, and the recruiter picked up that vibe.* In other words, frame the defeat as you would for a good friend you're trying to help. Just realizing the existence of your default frames—*Woe is me, a late bloomer who never seems to bloom*—can be liberating. If you know good framing choices exist even for bad situations, you can break the chain of self-protection and train your mind to bloom.

The second reframing step is to link a challenge to a larger goal: *This big presentation is not only exciting, it will give me visibility and lead to more opportunities.* The larger goal should be clear and compelling in your mind. It should capture the excitement of doing something new that can substantially improve your life.

Framing also matters after the fact. If you blow an opportunity, don't beat yourself up or make excuses. Frame your mistake as an opportunity to learn. Instead of saying, *I bombed that presentation,* or *They gave me a terrible time slot,* ask yourself, *Where did you start losing people?* Then admit, *That wasn't your best effort, Lisa. Next time, you prepare smarter.* Post facto framing is an incredibly powerful tool for late bloomers, as well as everyone else.

Smart framing is good for you and your organization. Cognitive psychologists have shown that effectively reframing challenges is a key to organizational success, in settings ranging from automotive manufacturing on the Toyota Production System (TPS), to pet adoption in shelters in Los Angeles, to hospital operating rooms across the country. People who learn to reframe are better able to solve problems, face challenges, and effect significant change, making them better team members. Even more, skilled reframers make better leaders. Leaders are spokespeople: They create shared awareness, build consensus, focus attention, and motivate action. Leaders who are able to reframe challenges as learning opportunities, who can reframe change initiatives as chances to help others, are consistently more successful. This means we late bloomers who learn to manage self-doubt, who learn to frame challenges and obstacles as opportunities, are positioned to be not only better team members but better team leaders.

Is reframing just a fancy way of putting a positive spin on events? Again, no. It's not pretending that everything is perfect or wonderful. Rather, it's about positively interpreting the challenges we face. It's about expanding our possibilities to find better, more fruitful paths for moving forward. Reframing isn't about turning off our negative thoughts. It isn't about suppressing concerns or fears. It's not about turning untrue negative thoughts into untrue positive thoughts. Rather, it's about stepping back and grounding our thoughts in a more positive framing of reality—both for ourselves and for the people around us.

Self-talk and reframing work together, and both work better when we put a bit of distance between ourselves and our challenge. As we have seen, referring to ourselves in the third person is a proven technique for doing so. Still, it's a challenge—even for the most successful late bloomers—to avoid getting wrapped up in our flaws or beating ourselves up over our mistakes. This is especially true when those around us are determined to stereotype us as different, slow, or disengaged. And realistically, our personalities and perspectives don't change overnight just because research tells us they should.

There's one more tool to managing self-doubt that late bloomers can use to gain a healthier level of objectivity. Pay attention. It might be the most important tool in your kit. That tool is self-compassion.

. . .

When discussing self-doubt, the popular advice is that we just need more of the opposite—more confidence, more assurance, more chutzpah. But the issue with confidence is how we try to achieve it. Too often we try to win high self-regard in cheap ways. We undermine others, or we compare our achievements to those of the weakest around us. We conform to cultural norms, believing that what society values is what we value and that how society defines success is how we must define success. These cheap self-confidence tricks are unsustainable and can lead to narcissism during good times and depression during hard times.

Late bloomers have a far better way to manage self-doubt and increase self-efficacy. Just as we need a kinder clock for development, we also need a kinder way to see ourselves. We can do this through increased self-compassion, a form of self-acceptance and internal empathy. Self-compassion encourages us to acknowledge our flaws and limitations, to see them from a more objective and realistic point of view. In this way, self-compassion is integral to helping us create motivational self-talk and reframing anxiety-inducing situations as exciting opportunities.

How does self-compassion work? A key is to acknowledge that we are good enough, no matter what society tells us. We're humans with flaws and imperfections, but we have an innate right to pursue our destinies. And when we make mistakes, we also have an obligation to learn from them. Then once we've learned what we can from a situation, it's time to move on and let go. Self-acceptance for late bloomers is the cornerstone of self-compassion.

When we stop pressuring ourselves to act like an early bloomer or live up to the Wunderkind Ideal, we can accept feedback and criticism more easily. When we allow ourselves a bit of kindness, it's easier to reframe challenges and missteps as learning opportunities. Psychologist Mark Leary of Duke University and his team investigated how self-compassionate people deal with unpleasant life events. They found that self-compassion buffered people against negative self-feelings, moderated negative feelings when people received negative feedback, and helped people acknowledge their roles in negative events without feeling overwhelmed by negative emotions. "In general, these studies suggest that self-compassion attenuates people's reactions to negative events in ways that are distinct from and, in some cases, more beneficial than self-esteem," the researchers concluded.

Self-compassion is closely associated with emotional resilience—a late bloomer strength—including the ability to soothe ourselves, recognize our mistakes, learn from them, and motivate ourselves to succeed. Self-compassion is also consistently correlated with measures of emotional well-being, such as optimism, life satisfaction, and autonomy, and with reduced levels of anxiety, depression, stress, and shame. Understandably, self-compassionate people can improve on mistakes, failures, or shortcomings more easily than others because they view them more objectively. And the sense of self-worth that comes from being kind to ourselves is much more stable over time than self-worth that comes from a seemingly boundless abundance of confidence.

Finally, self-compassion enhances motivation. People who are more self-compassionate are less afraid of failure. One study found that when participants failed a test, the ones who showed high levels of self-compassion actually studied longer and harder for the makeup test. Because self-compassion helps create the sense that it's okay to fail, it motivates us to try again—and try harder.

Nonetheless some people still think self-compassion is soft or weak. It's just the opposite. As Dr. Kristin Neff, a leading researcher of self-compassion, remarked, "When you're in the trenches, do you want an enemy or an ally?" Whereas confidence is aimed at making us feel adequate and powerful regardless of how adequate and powerful we actually are, self-compassion encourages us to accept a more objective reality. Therefore if we have self-compassion, and we fail at something, the frame is not *Poor me, poor me,* but *Well, everyone fails at something. Everyone has struggles. This is what it means to be human.* That type of mental frame can radically alter how we relate to self-doubt and, ultimately, failure. Being able to say, *Oh, this is normal, this is part of what it means to be human,* opens the door to growing from the experience. On the other hand, if we feel like self-doubt and failure are abnormal, then when we fail—and we will, especially when we choose to take a unique pathway to success and happiness—we fall into the trap of blaming ourselves or others.

How do late bloomers cultivate self-compassion if it doesn't come naturally? The first and most important step is to notice that voice in our head—the self-talk we use to guide ourselves through life. Often that voice is too critical. Many of us beat ourselves up for every perceived mistake. To be more self-compassionate, we need to notice that voice, acknowledge the criticism, and reframe it in a more self-compassionate way.

"Self-compassion is treating yourself with the same kindness, care and concern you show a loved one," explains Dr. Neff. "We need to frame it in terms of humanity. That's what makes self-compassion so different: 'I'm an imperfect human being living an imperfect life.'"

Most of us have a lot more experience being compassionate to others than to ourselves. If a good friend tells us about an ordeal they've been through or a mistake they've made, we most likely respond by offering kindness and comfort. When our friend recovers and the conversation continues, chances are we'll encourage them to learn from the mistake, plan next steps, and persevere in the face of difficulty.

In this sense, adopting a self-compassionate frame is about treating ourselves as we would a close friend or loved one, even when they (we) make a mistake. Understand, this doesn't mean lying to ourselves. It means changing the way we talk to ourselves. The harsh critic in our head is not our enemy. Self-compassion is about learning to make friends with that critic, gaining some objective distance from it, and making it into a motivational tool.

We all make mistakes. None of us are perfect. Successful late bloomers have become experts at quickly moving on from their slip-ups without beating themselves up. They accept that they're human, recognize their failures and frustrations, and avoid dwelling on them. We all need to do this if we're to break free from the misconceptions and social forces that can bury us in insecurity and self-doubt.

• • •

To sum up: All healthy people have self-doubt, but we late bloomers often have too much of it. We make our situation worse by adopting unhelpful coping mechanisms, such as self-handicapping, to protect our self-image. But these coping mechanisms only take us further away from blooming. Self-efficacy is what thriving late bloomers seek in order to convert self-doubt into a friend. Self-efficacy is our belief that we can accomplish a specific task with a reasonably positive attitude, make a plan based on facts, and bloom by cultivating self-talk, framing/reframing, and self-compassion. These techniques are foundational to late bloomer success, leveraging many of the traits—curiosity, compassion, resilience, equanimity—that make us exceptional.

As important as these late bloomer traits may seem right now, they'll likely be even more important in the future. Millions of us will soon discover software can do our jobs. Many "rules-based" careers are being taken over by artificial intelligence (see Chapter 2). Those who work in more complex jobs will become more numerous, while less complex work will be increasingly automated. Simultaneously, the time it takes for our skills to become irrelevant will shrink.

You can probably see where I'm going with this. As work at every level gets more complex and collaborative, late bloomer traits like curiosity, compassion, and insight will become even more important. The skills that come with facing self-doubt—the ability to acknowledge mistakes, to support self-efficacy, to reframe challenges, and to show compassion—all support our future need for innovation, continued learning, and improved teamwork. These late bloomer talents are future-proof skills that set us apart from many early bloomers.

This doesn't necessarily mean that late bloomers are destined only to be great employees. Many of these traits and skills translate to more effective leadership. Leaders who show compassion, support self-efficacy, and are able to reframe tasks are better at creating trust and promoting innovation. Leaders willing to embrace reality and invite others to help solve problems are better able to overcome challenges. These types of leaders are more selfless and more present, more in tune with their team members and coworkers. Leaders who embrace self-doubt—like the late Bill Walsh—are more adept at improving performance and increasing commitment. I'm not alone in understanding this reality. Global consultancies like McKinsey & Company, Deloitte, and Mercer are currently promoting curiosity, compassion, and equanimity—all late bloomer strengths—as critical capacities for tomorrow's leader.

Self-doubt, properly used, is not a handicap. It's a superpower for late bloomers.

CHAPTER 8

Slow to Grow? Repot Yourself in a Better Garden

Maybe your old friends won't stop using an embarrassing nickname from your past. Or maybe your boss refuses to promote you, despite years of great work, because your degree is from a relatively unknown university, and it wouldn't look good on the company website. These kinds of situations can make you feel trapped or pigeonholed. It seems like you just can't break away from an older, outdated version of yourself.

This happens far too often to those of us who didn't bloom early, whose credentials don't impress, or who stumbled out of the gate. If you were "Bob in the mailroom" but then got an accounting degree through professional courses, you're probably still "Bob in the mailroom" to people at work. To be "Bob the respected financial officer," you might have to change companies. Likewise, if you were "Katy the band nerd" in high school, you may still be "Katy the band nerd" two decades later to your high school friends. To be fully accepted as "Katy the driven professional and mom of two," you might need to leave some of these old friends behind—or even change your zip code.

It's often difficult to acknowledge that other people have a stake in our blooming—or *not* blooming. And just like the flowering rosebush that's grown too big for its container, you might need to change jobs, or companies, or even cities, in order to reach your full potential. Otherwise some people may define and treat you as that outdated and lesser version of yourself.

When you make a concerted effort to improve yourself, to move beyond your current limitations, your act of self-assertion risks upsetting the social status quo. Your growth threatens your social or professional hierarchy. If you somehow do better than the people around you, it makes them question their own achievements and lives. They start to feel like they're being left behind, so they try (consciously or not) to keep you in our place.

Why would people, even friends, try to keep you "in your place"? Animals and humans are wired to be status conscious. Groups of crabs will quite literally pull down any member who tries to escape a trap or a bucket, relegating the whole group to certain death. Psychologists and sociologists call this phenomenon the "crab pot syndrome." Among humans, members of a group will attempt to negate the importance of any member who achieves success beyond the success of others.

The late bloomer who blooms is suddenly "too big for your britches" or a "tall poppy" in need of pruning. You risk being seen as a traitor to your class, religion, or race. Sometimes the negative words are motivated by undisguised envy, spite, or unhealthy competitiveness. But more often, your critics may not be aware of their harmful negativity. They may sincerely couch their warnings in words of concern: "I don't know, Sarah. I just don't want you to get hurt." As the author Tom Wolfe once said in explaining the philosophy behind *The Electric Kool-Aid Acid Test* and *The Right Stuff*, "Status has more or less been my system for approaching any subject. For instance, *The Right Stuff* is not a book about space, it's a book about status competition among pilots." In Wolfe's work, the evolutionary truth that humans compete in extreme ways for status is endlessly entertaining. But to actually experience the blunt end of it—to be a late bloomer near the bottom of the status order—is not fun.

In these types of situations, the solution is clear: We need to pull up roots and transplant ourselves in a different pot. Repotting, the active process of personal reinvention, is rarely easy or smooth. It is inherently tense, which is why so much literature across different eras and cultures features the coming-of-age story. In this genre, the maturing young man or woman realizes they possess an independent mind and are not necessarily the person their family and culture want them to be. But leaving one's family and culture is never easy.

The change involved in repotting can be either modest or significant. It may involve spending time with a new group of like-minded people, getting a new job, or moving to a new state. The key is to make a change, to take a step, no matter how little, toward a more fertile environment for blooming.

• • •

When we try to improve or reinvent ourselves, we often encounter resistance not just from the outside but from within ourselves. Most of us resist change, even of things that cause us pain or hold us back. Communities, or "tribes," have appeal because they make us feel safe (see Chapter 5). But what if our tribe also causes us to stagnate? What happens when our tribe isn't good for us, but we don't know quite what to do about it because everything else looks scary?

Another belief that plagues many late bloomers springs from the limiting stories we tell ourselves. We hold these stories—*I was shy in high school, and I'll always be shy*—in our heads as if they're immutable facts. But these stories stem from the old us, the nonblooming us. They imply that we possess certain fixed behavioral traits and always will. Such a fixed belief about ourselves prevents us from repotting and trying alternative paths.

In *The End of Average*, Harvard's Todd Rose debunks the idea that behavioral traits are fixed:

> Are you an extrovert or an introvert? This deceptively simple question plunges us into one of the oldest and most contentious debates in psychology: the nature of your personality. On the one side of the question are *trait psychologists*, who argue that our behavior is determined by well-defined personality

traits, such as introversion and extroversion. . . . *Situation psychologists*, on the other hand, claim the environment drives our personality far more than personal traits.

For decades, trait psychologists and situation psychologists waged academic battles, but Rose believes the situation psychologists have won, have better evidence. This is great news for late bloomers. The way we acted in the past, however clueless, immature, dysfunctional, or incompetent, is not hardwired into our personalities. We can change our circumstances if we change our behavior and our situation—if we repot.

A late bloomer himself (he dropped out of high school with a D average), Rose explains how he repotted himself as a college student at Weber State University in Orem, Utah.

> I thought back to my experience when my school designated me an "aggressive child." I recalled that when my grandmother heard this verdict she refused to believe it, telling my parents, "He's always so nice at my house." This was not grandmotherly obliviousness. I really *was* nice when I was around her. My aggressiveness was triggered by very specific contexts, such as when I was being bullied. In the class where I got in trouble for shooting spitballs there were three bigger kids who liked to push me around. I tried to avoid them outside of class, but within class I often reacted to their presence by becoming the class clown, since I thought if I could make them laugh, they would be more likely to ignore me. It usually worked, though it earned me a trip to the counselor's office.
>
> Later, when I managed to attend Weber State University, I used my knowledge to change the way I approached my classes. One invaluable thing I did from the beginning was to avoid classes where I knew other students from my high school. I knew that particular context would lead me to be-

have like a class clown, and I knew I would never be successful
in college as a class clown.

The barriers to repotting go beyond just the psychological. Most
of us see the Internet and search tools as positive innovations. We
should, because they've increased our access to information. They've
democratized many previously gated processes, including publishing
and investing. And they've facilitated our ability to network. But the
Internet and search tools can also be a barrier to reinvention. By ar-
chiving the minutiae of our lives, they have chained us to every mistake, misstep, or poor choice we've ever made—making the possibility
of self-reinvention seem like an ideal from an older time. In a sense,
we've collectively lost our ability to forget. And with it, we've forfeited
a very American ideal—the right to a new beginning.

Another barrier to repotting is more pedestrian: We as a country
are experiencing a sharp decrease in geographic mobility. Domestic
migration within the United States is currently about half of what it
was in the early 1990s. No one is exactly sure why, but some theories point to a higher rate of homeownership, which anchors people
to hefty mortgages. In addition, because of our growing material
consumption, moving has become more expensive, in both real and
psychological terms. Americans used to be able to load up a U-Haul
trailer and move, but now most people seem to need six moving vans.
Another reason is the frequency of dual incomes: When two people
in a family work, it's a lot harder for both to leave their jobs and find
new ones in the same place, at the same time. Finally, wage stagnation
could play a part, as many workers may now have less to gain from
moving to a different company or job.

Aside from these practical challenges, there are also people challenges. It's simply painful to leave our community. It's hard to leave
our loved ones; they love us and will miss us.

But ultimately, genuine friends and family will want what's best for
us. They will want us to bloom, even if it means they'll miss us.

• • •

Kimberly Harrington is the late-blooming author of *Amateur Hour: Motherhood in Essays and Swear Words*, her first book, which she published at age fifty. Prior to that, she was a copywriter and creative director at ad agencies in Los Angeles and Portland. But she'd always wanted to write essays and books, and to do that, she realized she had to get away from the big-city advertising worlds. She chose rural Vermont as her new garden.

Could I have written a book while living in L.A.? I can answer that one very quickly. No. If you look at my earlier career in advertising, it's a big city industry. And even if you're not in the big city, the industry itself is all consuming. It's your whole life. You know everyone who works in advertising. That's who you hang out with. I hung out with cool people in cool cities but it costs too much money to be cool all the time. I didn't really understand this until I was laid off. All of a sudden, I had no professional bubble anymore.

Here in Vermont I'm surrounded by academics and environmentalists, and people who generally think, "Advertising is a crappy industry that's ruining the world."

It's humbling to realize that a job that you actually really enjoy and have spent your whole life doing is just not perceived as all that awesome by other people. I think that further widened my point of view. The world I'd left was intense, but I realized that it wasn't everything. It wasn't the whole game.

Leaving big, cool cities and the full-time world of advertising behind for the flexibility of freelancing in a smaller city provided the opening for me to think of doing something else. By running my own freelance business in Vermont, I suddenly felt like I had headspace. I could try new things like submitting pieces to *The New Yorker*, *McSweeney's*, and *Medium*. I felt this constant widening, and I had the mental space in my life to be able to take advantage of those thoughts, which I wouldn't have had if I was working my normal schedule in Los Angeles.

Kimberly's positive experience with moving from her "professional bubble" and to a more diverse (and less "cool") environment is supported by extensive research. Journeys like hers—journeys to new lives—involve embracing roles and jobs that are more congruent with one's true self. Studies have shown that "higher levels of satisfaction and mental and physical well-being will occur when there is a good fit between the person and the environment." This includes the work environment.

According to authors Daniel Cable and Timothy Judge, people who succeed in making a job or career change place less emphasis on person-to-job fit than on person-to-organization fit. In other words, the culture and environment of an organization are more important to success and satisfaction than the actual job tasks. This means job seekers should collect and evaluate information about an organization's culture in addition to the specific job. It also means that people who do find a working environment in which their individual values match the values of the organization have better "work attitudes" and are more likely to flourish. According to Cable and Judge, people who select environments that fulfill their needs are more likely to be committed, motivated, and loyal—attributes that lead to better job performance and satisfaction.

As Kimberly's story, supported by existing research, clearly shows, finding the right pot can make a big difference. Though it may be scary to think about it, moving to a different company or city can be a powerful catalyst for blooming.

• • •

The central question to ask yourself is, *Am I in the best possible pot to bloom?* And since finding a perfect pot might be impractical or take too long, you should also ask, *What is the range of pots that will support my talents, temperament and enthusiasms?*

In her magnificent book about introverts, *Quiet*, author Susan Cain cites research suggesting that some people are naturally hardy and will bloom in almost any pot, while others will bloom only in certain pots. Most of us fall somewhere in between, meaning that the chances of our thriving (or blooming) rise if we can match our talents and temperament to the most hospitable environment.

Jerome Kagan, the head of Harvard's Center for Child Development, established the link between "high-reactive" babies—those most sensitive to light and sound and who responded to it by crying—and a lifelong tendency to emotional sensitivity. These babies grew up to be introverts, preferring to spend most of their time in solitude and quiet. Meanwhile "low-reactive" babies were the opposite—light and sound didn't bother them so much. They grew up to be extroverts, craving human interaction and activity.

Jay Belsky, a child-care expert at the University of London, notes that high-reactive children—those who grew agitated by light and sound—were as adults more likely to suffer from depression, anxiety, and shyness as a result of stress. The wrong pot could damage these kids, but the same kids would thrive in a stable home environment with good parenting and child care.

Writer David Dobbs compares children, in their differing reactions to stress, to plants. Dandelions can thrive under almost any conditions. Likewise, low-reactive dandelion children and people—mostly extroverts—do well in a range of situations. Orchids—and high-reactive children—will thrive only in certain environments.

The orchid hypothesis provides great insight into late bloomers. If we are slow to bloom, perhaps we are more orchid-like in our temperament and live in a pot that's inhospitable to that temperament. That was certainly true for me. My native city of Bismarck, North Dakota, was not an ideal pot for me. Like many small cities, it was splendid for former high school sports stars (in football, basketball, and hockey), extroverts, go-getters, and people who excelled at spatial IQ—that is, people adept at developing, building, fixing, and assigning value to physical things like oil wells, waterways, bridges, and buildings. This kind of person, a dandelion, can succeed almost anywhere. But the introvert, with an interest in books and abstract ideas—the orchid—has fewer hospitable pots and will generally find them in larger cities and university towns.

Are you a dandelion or orchid? The answer is good to know as you contemplate your repotting options.

• • •

Suppose you have decided to repot to a new job as a means of changing your environment. I would caution against repotting to an entirely new vocation or career if your paycheck depends on it. Radical repotting is a luxury of the young and the retired. For late bloomers in midcareer—in their thirties through fifties—and with family and financial obligations, it's best to think in terms of repotting to "adjacent spaces," or similar work, the way Kimberly Harrington transitioned from writing advertising copy to writing essays and books. She built on her expertise of writing copy to professional standards, but she tweaked the product and the audience. She didn't toss away her talent and love of writing; she repotted it to an adjacent space.

Let me give you another example of adjacent repotting from a profession I know well: journalism.

Generally speaking, journalists aren't well paid. Probably only a few thousand in the entire United States, across all media, from print to television to Internet, earn an upper-middle-class income. It's therefore common to see journalists—often after they get married or have their second or third child—suddenly tire of being paid like journalists. They see they're not going to advance much further in their careers, so they repot into an adjacent space, public relations.

But here the journalist will experience a loss of status, if not pay. Journalists are a prideful tribe, and most have a negative view of public relations, even if it happens to pay more. "I could never do PR," many journalists think. "It would violate my principles." Then the financially strapped journalist repots into PR and realizes the job is more engaging than they thought. They investigate clients, frame their challenges, come up with an interesting set of promotional solutions, then execute them. PR, at senior levels, is more like management consulting. You get to play at a high level, dealing with senior people on the client side who respect your experience and listen to what you have to say. And since you aren't a junior staffer, you blessedly don't have to stay up until midnight cranking out press releases, or cold-calling journalists who don't want to talk to you.

I know several ex-journalists who couldn't have conceived of themselves in public relations jobs but now happily do them, and do them well. And guess what? They feel reborn. Quentin Hardy, a former colleague, was once the Silicon Valley bureau chief for *Forbes*, then a reporter for the *New York Times*. He did some really good work for the *Times* and was often ranked among the most influential journalists in the world in subjects such as artificial intelligence and big data.

Today Quentin is the top editor of all the content around Google's Cloud. He's gone to the client side and is having a ball. He bravely repotted out of a career with prestige and glamour but no prospect of further advancement and flat or declining paychecks. At Google, he gets paid well and works with some of the smartest people on the most important digital technologies of our day. His competitive juices are fired going to battle against Microsoft and Amazon.

This type of repotting made sense for Quentin. He moved to an adjacent space. He moved at a point in his career before he'd become cynical—an occupational hazard for journalists— and when he could leverage his success and professional contacts. This allowed him to keep blooming, rather than stagnate.

· · ·

One more kind of repotting is worth mentioning: repotting to a new set of friends and colleagues, when you suspect your old friends are holding you back. Here I suggest the same strategy as for job repotting. It's one thing to acknowledge that our current environment is harmful, and that we need a clean break. More commonly, however, we find ourselves simply stuck in an environment where we get along without blooming. The job is meh. Your colleagues at work are okay. Your friends save you from boredom but fail to feed and support your desire to bloom. What then? Throw everything overboard, the good and the bad, in a risky repotting?

A less risky way to repot in such circumstances is to join peer groups. Perhaps the granddaddy of peer groups is Toastmasters, formed in 1924 to help members become better public speakers and thereby gain professional confidence. (*Quiet* author Susan Cain advocates Toastmasters as particularly effective for introverts and the shy.) Another important peer group is Alcoholics Anonymous, formed in the 1930s by two problem drinkers with no professional training, as a way to help other problem drinkers, and thereby themselves, achieve recovery. The AA model has been copied successfully in one form or another by many organizations, not just by addiction recovery groups.

One of the more intriguing professional peer groups I've seen is Vistage International, whose paid members are owners of small businesses. Whom do small business owners talk to when they're faced with a major challenge? When they're out of ideas? When top employees leave for competitors? When they can't meet payroll? Or perhaps when their home life and health are in trouble? They probably shouldn't confess their worries to their employees, and their board of directors might interpret advice-seeking as weakness and pounce at their most vulnerable hour.

But confessing their problems to peers—owners of other small businesses not directly competitive with theirs—might feel safe if the peers were trusted, and if their advice and counsel had credibility and cost nothing except a promise to reciprocate when needed. The absence of emotional bonds can make it feel safer to admit a vulnerability, ask for help, and accept advice.

Churches and other faith-based organizations are another good source for peer groups. I once asked megachurch founder and pastor Rick Warren the secret behind the growth of Saddleback Community Church. "Small groups," he said. "The real work of Saddleback, and the thing that creates loyalty to Saddleback, is not what I preach on Sundays. It's what happens in small groups from Monday through Friday." My own church and many like it have weekday groups for recovery from divorce, raising small children, raising teenagers, recovery from job loss, starting a business, and many other challenges. Like AA and addiction recovery groups, small church groups are free, run by non-professionals, and observant of confidentiality. They ask only that you help others as you are helped. Small groups are a safe and low-risk way to explore your repotting options.

. . .

Once you've decided to move to a more suitable pot, the next step is to create a vision for the future. UCLA's Hal Hershfield has shown that people who can identify more closely with their future selves make decisions that are better for them. The future self you must identify with is your blooming self. You have to believe that that person can be you and *is* you. Psychologically, this is called "creating an identity goal." Researchers Peter Gollwitzer, Paschal Sheeran, Verena Michalski, and Andrea Siefert argue that achieving an important goal, like pursuing a new career path, is helped considerably by linking it to an identity goal. In other words, imagine the new you as you want to be. How will that new you dress, eat, and talk? How will that new you interact with others?

Our behavior can change when we repot, but be careful not to bend your fundamental temperament too far. Rather, work with it, stretch it, and leverage it to your advantage. When I was writing *Life 2.0*, I interviewed a man who had moved from the New York area to Des Moines, Iowa. He was in the insurance business, where one has to sell. In the New York area, he was constantly criticized for not being as aggressive in sales as he should be. He was told, "You gotta pick it up a notch." When he moved to Iowa, he was told the opposite: "Tamp it down a little bit." It was easier for him to tamp it down than to ramp it up. And he bloomed in Des Moines, which rewarded his lower-key temperament. When I last talked to him, he had a beautiful house in West Des Moines, a fifteen-minute commute to work, and he raved about how much he liked his neighbors. He loved the heck out of Des Moines. When he felt the need for a bigger city, it was easy to pop up to Chicago or Minneapolis.

The best way to ensure that you have a hospitable pot for blooming is to build it yourself. That's what millions of company founders have done through the ages. The popular idea is that founders start companies for financial reasons, to get rich. The reality is that founders start companies for a wide variety of personal reasons: to get rich, to prove a point, to overthrow the status quo, to exact revenge upon on an old employer, to "make a dent in the universe," to fill a gap in the market, to set their own hours, and so on. What all these reasons have in common is control. Entrepreneurs get to choose the products, the employees, and the culture as they see fit. They get to construct the pot.

What amazes me after writing and speaking about business for three decades is the sheer variety of successful companies. I don't mean variety in terms of products, industry, or location. I mean variety by organizational structure and culture—by the shape and soil of the pot. FedEx, started by Fred Smith in 1971, is a $65 billion global juggernaut that Smith chooses to run like the military. An ex-marine, he insists on a corporate dress code of white shirts and ties for men and a strict adherence to schedule. Being late for a meeting is a no-no. An employee will thrive in the FedEx culture or not, but there is great clarity to what that culture is and no employee should be confused. Richard Branson's companies, on the other hand, are structured more loosely, because those are the kinds of pots that long-haired social rebel Branson likes for himself.

Diane Greene, who cofounded and ran software giant VMware, constructed a pot that was family friendly, certainly by the workaholic standards of Silicon Valley. Until January 2019, the CEO of Google Cloud, she encouraged parents at Google to get home and have dinner with their families. Google Cloud's fierce competitor in the market is Amazon Web Services, run by Andy Jassy, who reports to Amazon founder and CEO Jeff Bezos, one of the most demanding bosses in the world. Amazon is a tough culture, especially for those reporting to Bezos. Certain kinds of people will bloom in Amazon's pot, but many will not. No one should be surprised by the shape and soil of a company's pot if they've done their research on Glassdoor and other free Web sources.

So finding the right pot—whether by location or by organizational culture—is crucial to our blooming. Some of us are more dandelion-like and can bloom in a variety of pots. But many late bloomers will identify with orchids of the kind Susan Cain and David Dobbs wrote about.

It's okay to begin repotting without fully realizing what the next pot will look like. We must commit ourselves to the process anyway, for what psychologists call "goal commitment." As dozens of studies have shown, goal commitment is the key to goal attainment. Goal commitment is correlated with significant improvements in health, academic performance, and job performance. In one study, students who committed to academic goals by writing them down actually achieved those goals more often and showed greater academic improvement than students who didn't articulate their goals. A separate 2002 study of goal commitment concluded that "commitment is one of the most important factors involved in change."

So if commitment is key to change, how do we do it? As late bloomers, how do we commit to something as disruptive as repotting ourselves?

By taking the first step.

That's right—just take one step forward. Don't worry if it's not the perfect step. Research an interest, a peer group, a place—a hope. Envision your next pot.

Be careful, however, that when you repot yourself, you're not running away from something. Recovery programs call endless repotting "doing a geographic." You blame all your problems on the people you're with, believing that if only you had a fresh start in another city, things would be different.

But aside from that type of rationale, if your current pot is not helping you bloom, it might truly be time to repot. Don't be deterred if you have second thoughts. Getting unstuck from your current life is hard. You'll face resistance. Though many of us dream of a future that's very different from our present, powerful psychological and social forces are aligned that obstruct our reinventing ourselves. That's something you'll have to accept as fact. Nothing changes in life without an opposite force resisting that change.

"We have to modify our identities as we go through life," says psychologist Ravenna Helson of the University of California at Berkeley. Helson followed 120 women over fifty years, examining personality traits, social influence, and personal development. In the process, she proved that it's never too late to reinvent yourself. "Even at sixty," she said, "people can resolve to make themselves more the people they would like to become. In my study, about a dozen women showed substantial positive personality change from ages sixty to seventy."

Remember, when it comes to repotting, late bloomers have a distinct advantage over early bloomers. We're naturally curious and resilient. We're not afraid to follow a different path or break free of convention. We genuinely want to see what's around the corner or over the hill. These late bloomer strengths enable—even propel—the change we need to find the right people and right place to help us thrive.

The real benefit of repotting is that we get to define our own life instead of having someone else define it for us. There will never be the perfect pot that can contain us. We will always be growing. We will always be learning. And we can use the experience we gain for our next challenge, our next pot. People who dare to leave their unhappy lives behind give themselves permission to pursue their passions and find a renewed zest for living. Our right to new beginnings, to self-definition and self-determination, has always been among the most foundational of human ideals.

Together let's keep it that way.

CHAPTER 9

Late Bloomers: The Long Run

Now ninety-two years old and retired, Geraldine Weiss knows what it means to persist. In her thirties, she financially struggled as a mother with children and the wife of a modestly paid naval officer. Then later in life, in true late bloomer fashion, she became the most successful female stock investor in history.

Born in San Francisco in 1926, Weiss attended local high schools and studied finance at the University of California at Berkeley. While at Cal, she spent her spare hours in the library reading every business and investment book she could find. She soon fell under the compelling logic of a 1934 book called *Security Analysis*. (It would also cast its spell on an unknown young man halfway across the country, Warren Buffett.) Authors Benjamin Graham and David Dodd argued that since company stocks represent a percentage ownership in a real company, they all have "intrinsic value." Moreover, this intrinsic value is always mispriced by the stock market. During stock booms like the 1920s, stocks were overpriced and ultimately, before the 1929 crash, insanely priced above their intrinsic values. After the stock crash and during the early 1930s, most stocks were trading far below their intrinsic values. The public was sick of stocks, which had lost most of their value since the 1929 peak. Graham and Dodd said the stock market rarely gets it right at any moment in time. In the short run, it acts like a voting machine, a popularity contest. But in the long run, it acts like a weighing machine and gets closer to the intrinsic truth of a stock's value.

In 1949 Graham and Dodd released their second and more famous book, *The Intelligent Investor.* Amazingly, this dense, 640-page tome has sold more than a million copies over the years. As I write in the summer of 2018, the book ranks as the number three bestseller on Amazon in the category of finance. But even when *The Intelligent Investor* first appeared and reinforced the intrinsic value philosophy of investing, Geraldine Weiss was already thinking beyond Graham and Dodd and developing her own ideas about stock investing.

Weiss had no quarrel with intrinsic value as a philosophy, but she harbored doubts about how value is determined. Graham and Dodd particularly liked using two ratios: price/earnings and price/book value. Investors still use these ratios today. Tune in to CNBC almost any given day, and you'll hear Jim Cramer talk about a stock's "P/E ratio" and its "price-to-book" number. And if you Google a company's stock, the price/earnings and price/book will pop up instantly. But Weiss was skeptical of these ratios. She felt, and continues to feel, that both ratios could be manipulated by company executives.

Weiss thought a stock's dividend payments, not its earnings, tell the true story of a company's financial health and momentum. Rising dividends, she saw, predict stock growth. A company's history of rising or falling dividends would establish a pattern that would show whether its stock, on any given day, was overpriced or underpriced.

Eager to test her new theory, Weiss began to apply for jobs at investment firms. But she immediately hit two walls: the anti-Semitism that still pervaded much of the investment world in the 1950s and 1960s, and the fact that she was female. Even with her degree in finance, her knowledge of Graham and Dodd and all the key investment textbooks, no firm offered her a job beyond secretary.

In 1962, living in San Diego "hand to mouth" by her own description, she asked her husband if she could buy one hundred shares in a stock that met her criteria of being "blue chip" yet was underpriced according to its dividend trend. The investment succeeded, as did Weiss's next four years of investments that tested her dividend theories in the stock market. Now convinced that she had a unique investing advantage to offer, she stopped applying for jobs at firms. Instead, at forty, she started an investment newsletter called *Investment Quality Trends*. The first issue recommended thirty-four stocks as "select blue chip" but nevertheless "undervalued," according to her analysis. Among her thirty-four picks in April 1966 were IBM, Kellogg's, and General Motors.

The newsletter, today called *IQ Trends* and run by Weiss's hand-picked successor, Kelley Wright, is still making money for its readers. But when Weiss started it, she had to overcome her slim finances. Though she had made money investing in stocks, starting in 1962 with those one hundred shares, her initial investments were necessarily tiny. When she started the newsletter in 1966, she was still cash-strapped and figured she could afford to put in only $2,000. Between 1966 and 1969, she hung on, barely, reinvesting every spare subscription penny. It took three years for the newsletter to turn a profit. "The thing that it taught me is to persevere," she said.

But Geraldine Weiss wasn't finished fighting gender bias. As a 2017 profile on her that ran in a London newspaper, the *Telegraph*, put it: "No one wanted investment advice from a woman. She kept a letter from a gentleman who refused to take advice from a woman unless he knew she had gotten it from a man. To get around this prejudice, she signed her name 'G Weiss' and everyone believed that the service was run by a man—until, that is, she appeared on *Wall Street Week*, a popular TV show, in 1977."

"By then I'd been in the business long enough that people were making money with my service," Weiss said. She was fifty-one years old, and the investing world was only beginning to pay attention to her.

Geraldine Weiss's late-blooming success can be attributed to persistence—the kind that's nourished by patience and augmented by deep passion. Patience is part and parcel of Weiss's investing philosophy (as it is for Warren Buffett, that other famous Graham and Dodd disciple). One doesn't get rich overnight investing in value dividend stocks. In fact, Weiss often lost money in late-bubble periods such as 1999, when investors turned their backs on value stocks and swung for the fences with dot-coms. But she trusted her own investment philosophy, tested it in the unforgiving stock market over many years and investment cycles. An occasional bad year doesn't ruffle her.

• • •

Geraldine Weiss is an exemplary late bloomer and a model for all of us. To succeed at anything worthwhile in life requires persistence, no matter how gifted, fortunate, or passionate you are. When I interviewed late bloomers for this book, nearly every one said that once you find your passion and your "pot," you need to hang in there—you need to persist.

Fortunately, if we patiently stick with a pursuit or a passion, if we persist, we all have an opportunity to make great breakthroughs at any point in our lives. Many "overnight successes" finally break through after twenty, thirty, or even fifty years of trying. Because of our obsession with early achievement, success from years of hard work is often mistaken for innate talent. But the many success stories presented in this book should be seen as an inspiration, as templates for learning, trying, persisting, and ultimately, succeeding.

No matter how self-possessed or prepared we may be, however, many of us still secretly wonder, *Do I have the inner strength, the persistence, to find and live my destiny?* It can mean quitting a safe job, leaving a circle of friends, or persevering even when your faith and conviction waver.

The simple answer: yes.

How can I say this with such certainty? Many of us can't even stick with a diet for more than a week, much less persevere through years of adversity and sacrifice. How can we persist during an unconventional journey of reinvention, especially in the face of inevitable setbacks, disapproving parents, and doubting friends?

I'm confident that late bloomers can persist for two reasons. First, we are natural storytellers. In our personal lives, we think in stories, talk in stories, communicate in stories, and even dream in stories. It's safe to say that the default mode of human cognition is narrative. We instinctively make reason out of chaos and assign causality to all the random events that make up our lives. Stories help us do that. Story-telling as a weapon of persistence may not seem obvious, but our ability to tell stories is much more powerful than many of us appreciate.

The second reason for optimism is that as we age, and as we gain experience and absorb life's lessons (often painfully), we exercise persistence. Like every aspect of our psychological character—as well as our neurological structure—persistence is more plastic than we know. Persistence, along with talent, emotional regulation, and all other psychological traits relevant to success in life, is influenced by experience. Our persistence has the ability to grow as we grow. Persistence won't grow automatically, of course. It can atrophy like any other human quality in the face of depression, discouragement, or neglect. Therefore we have to take an active role in growing our persistence. And, odd as it may seem, often we can feed our persistence more at the movies than at the gym.

To better understand the keys to late bloomer persistence, let's take a closer look at the power of stories, the plasticity of persistence, and how they're linked.

• • •

Stories don't just describe what's happened—they help determine what will happen. The stories we tell ourselves help shape our attitudes and enhance our well-being. For late bloomers, this is terrific news. Extensive research shows that stories can change the way we think, act, and feel. Put another way, if we late bloomers change our story, we can change our behavior and even our life. This may sound like self-help hype, but stories truly are the hidden catalyst for growth and success.

The power of narrative is the premise of a fairly new branch of medicine called *narrative psychology*. Proposed independently in the

1980s by psychologists Theodore Sarbin, Jerome Bruner, and Dan McAdams, it's a school of thought concerned with how people make meaning through the construction, telling, and recounting of stories. If neuroscience and some branches of psychology think of the mind as a container, a machine, or something akin to a computer's CPU, narrative psychology sees the mind as the "great narrator."

Of course, the mind as a storyteller isn't exactly new to psychology. Well before psychology began to borrow the tools of literary criticism, Sigmund Freud and his followers seemed to intuit the idea that a breakdown in mental health correlated with a breakdown in story.

While plenty of Freud's work has since been discounted, part of his genius was in his ability to work with individuals to make sense of their otherwise messy lives. The key insight that Freudian psychoanalysts came up with was that their patients somehow couldn't keep the story of themselves straight—or they had no story at all. They had the task of repairing essentially broken stories, like a script doctor. In other words, the real value in psychoanalysis was in working with patients to dissect or sift through random memories and events that on their own made little sense, to construct a coherent narrative. The story would be about how a patient got from point A somewhere in the past, to the present, then oriented themselves toward the future in a meaningful way.

In a sense, constructing a narrative did more than just help individuals see their life events in a new way. It shaped their reality by making it manageable.

Cold objective reality, after all, is chaotic. It's an assemblage of people and places and dates and times all jumbled together, constantly shifting and changing. It produces love and beauty but also bad luck, calamity, and tragic outcomes. And while random chance might be the basis of some cosmic or evolutionary beliefs, it usually doesn't make for a good story.

Thus we all do what novelists, historians, biographers, and obituary writers have always done: We impose a narrative structure on otherwise random sequences of events until they cohere in a way that makes sense to us and that we can manage. We put things in order, and in so doing, we give them meaning.

But stories are not just about events tumbling into order in a way that makes sense. Stories aren't just a list of times and dates and happenings in sequence. Stories are driven by very real choices—what we choose to include, what we choose to exclude, what we choose to amplify and diminish. The urge to narrate is so ingrained in us that we tend to see stories even where no stories exist. We see stories in the stars. We see stories in the clouds. We see stories in shapes and sounds.

Take, for instance, a classic experiment conducted by Fritz Heider and Marianne Simmel in 1944. Heider and Simmel showed participants a short animated film of a few different shapes (two triangles, one circle) moving in and around a box. When asked to describe what they had seen, participants responded by telling short stories as if the triangles and circles were people. They ascribed characteristics like "aggressive," "angry," "bad-tempered," and "quick to take offense" to one particularly ornery triangle. (To be fair, this triangle was ornery because another, smaller triangle ran off with his girlfriend, the circle.)

But the participants did more than simply assign human characteristics to nonhuman objects. They also saw those objects as having *agency*—the ability to act of their own accord, to make free choices, and to author their own destiny. Paul Ricoeur, a French philosopher who wrote extensively about narrative and identity, defined agency as the opposite of suffering. According to Ricoeur, when we lose the ability to act independently of our own free will, we suffer. We submit. We give up.

How can we regain agency when it's lost? By revising and rewriting our own role in our ever-changing narrative.

If narrative psychology teaches us one thing, it should be that, particularly in difficult times or setbacks, constructing a narrative can have a huge impact on our thoughts and behavior. It can change the direction of our lives. Dozens of studies—with undergraduates, maximum security prisoners, people suffering from arthritis or chronic pain, women who just gave birth to their first child, men who had just been laid off, across all social classes and ethnic groups from countries as far flung as the United States and New Zealand—have shown that the simple act of creating a personal narrative has positive effects on health and behavior.

The idea behind narrative psychology is not to delude ourselves that bad events or experiences are actually good. Instead, it's to find meaning—and hopefully, motivation—in the progression from one event to the next. Narrative psychology should help us recognize that circumstances constantly change. In our lives, we move from triumph to failure to boredom to ecstasy and back again, sometimes during a single day. How do we grapple with so many emotions and still soldier on? Quite simply, stories offer us a framework for enduring the vagaries of life.

This is good news for late bloomers. For most of our lives, we've suspected that our real story—of our destiny discovered and potential fulfilled—has yet to be written. So how can we write a plot that lets us bloom into our true potential?

• • •

Narrative psychology has shown us that when it comes to the stories we tell ourselves, the facts matter less than the narrative. In other words, a story doesn't have to be true to be effective. Our personal stories can help keep us moving forward. Our stories can be based on facts, adhering closely to reality, or they need not be true at all. Frequently, we sustain our determination and perseverance by telling ourselves optimistic stories about the future. Very often these stories are stronger than we are. Christian believers are inspired by a story of the disciple Peter in the New Testament. When Peter's life was threatened by Roman guards as Jesus was dying on the cross, Peter denied knowing Jesus three times. His courage failed him when it counted. How shameful that must have felt to Peter. How understandable it would have been to sneak off and return to his vocation, fishing. Yet in the days following, Peter was transformed by a new narrative, Christ's res-urrection. The once cowardly Peter became the rock upon which the Christian Church in Rome was built. He suffered a martyr's death, and the future St. Peter's Basilica was named after him. If stories are meaningful enough to us, they can carry us through the most difficult challenges.

When it comes to persistence, this is a good thing. If we made all our decisions based on the actual odds of success, we'd rarely attempt any-thing risky or achieve anything significant. The reality is, stories can keep us going because of their inaccuracy. Almost any creation of nar-rative is a bit of a lie. Our stories aren't fact-checked documentaries—they allow for narrative interpretation, and they succeed for this very reason. A cold, rationalist view of life, after all, suggests that humans weren't born to do anything other than survive long enough to repro-duce. But when our story says we were born to do something signifi-cant, we're far more likely to persist through dark times and hardship.

So storytelling is a tool we late bloomers can use for good or ill. If, for example, we've interpreted our slower blooming to mean that we're unlucky or unwise or lazy, it's hard to have a positive image of the fu-ture. In this case, our storytelling can lead us to despair and fatalism. Conversely, if we acknowledge that we've made mistakes, faced chal-lenges, and learned from our missteps, we'll feel a much greater sense of agency over our lives. As Kurt Vonnegut wrote in *Mother Night*, "We are what we pretend to be, so we must be careful about what we pretend to be."

Take a moment to reflect on your own story.

That time you were rejected by an employer or laid off—is it fur-ther proof that your career is going nowhere? That you're a failure or a washout, one of those late bloomers who never launched? Or is the layoff one of the best things that ever happened, freeing you to find work that better suits your individual talents?

In writing our stories, the trap for late bloomers is to believe in fate. Fate and destiny are not the same thing, though we often conflate them. As legendary UCLA film professor Howard Suber wrote, "You seek your destiny; you succumb to your fate. Destiny originates within the self; fate comes from outside. Fate is the force that lies beyond individual will and control; it pushes you from behind. Destiny is the attracting force in front of you that acts like a magnet and that you choose to acquire."

We fall back to our fate.

We move forward to our destiny.

Late blooming doesn't come from sourly accepting fate, from submitting to outside forces and abdicating our agency. Blooming is the result of acknowledging our past, then pursuing our destiny through an optimistic personal narrative—real or not—that encourages and inspires. If we're to persist against the forces of culture and in spite of negative self-beliefs, we must be sure we're telling ourselves the right stories.

• • •

The second reason for my certainty in our ability to persist: Our level of persistence isn't fixed. Angela Duckworth, author of the bestselling 2016 book *Grit: The Power of Passion and Perseverance*, is the undisputed expert on grit, another term for perseverance or persistence. In all fairness to her, her definition is a bit more complicated than that. But if you have grit, you can hang in there. Having designed a test that she calls the Grit Scale, she gathered data from a broad range of American adults. The chart below shows how Grit Scale scores varied by age.

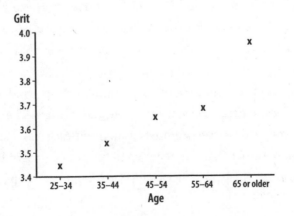

Surprised? Grit, or our ability to persist, increases as we age. As you can see from the graph's horizontal axis, the most persistent adults were in their late sixties or older. The least persistent—well, they were in their twenties. This doesn't mean that if you're in your twenties, you don't have the capability to gut it out or endure. Many twenty-somethings do. It just means that your ability to stick with something important will likely increase as you age.

As this graph shows, persistence, experience, and age go hand in hand. Duckworth believes the data suggest that our level of persistence increases as we determine our life philosophy, learn to rebound from disappointment, and realize how to tell the difference between low-stakes goals that can be abandoned and higher-stakes goals that demand persistence—all emergent traits of late bloomers.

Exactly why do life experiences change our personality? One reason, according to Duckworth, is that we simply learn something we didn't know before. And regardless of what society may think about age and learning, this accumulated knowledge has tremendous value. Over time we learn life lessons, and as we grow older, we're thrust into new circumstances. As Duckworth wrote, "We rise to the occasion. In other words, we change when we need to."

When it comes to persistence, the varied experiences of late blooming appear to be the best teachers.

Let me clarify a couple of points. When I extolled the virtues of quitting in Chapter 6, I wasn't implying that persistence (or grit) isn't necessary at certain points in life. Clearly, to achieve anything of substance, we need to endure. We need to be able to pick ourselves up after we've been knocked down. My point in Chapter 6 was that forced grit without true engagement is ineffective or even detrimental. Forced grit hinders our curiosity and experimentation. Compulsory determination robs us of the time necessary to grow and mature. The idea that there's a timetable for success compels us to mindlessly concoct an illusion of passion, rather than allowing us to unearth our own true mission and purpose. The persistence needed to bloom and keep blooming is a quiet resolve. It's a personal persistence, rather than the bluster of narcissistic confidence or the forced march of youthful achievement.

Also, there's a difference between Roy Baumeister's concept of ego depletion, as discussed in Chapter 6, and Angela Duckworth's Grit Scale results. Ego depletion posits that we have a finite amount of willpower or grit at any given time. As we go through the day focusing, pushing, or restraining ourselves, we use up that finite amount. Duckworth's Grit Scale results show that our overall level of grit—or persistence—can increase as we get older and gain experience. This is welcome news for late bloomers, but we still need to allocate our energy and reserve our grit for things that we're truly passionate about. Regardless of how high our Grit Scale score may be, it still can be squandered.

The clear implication is that we should avoid expending our persistence thoughtlessly to meet every challenge we face. Some challenges simply aren't worth it. And as we learned in Chapter 6, persistence or willpower misspent will exhaust us, even make us ill. Nor does this mean we should sit around waiting for our grit cache to kick in. There are personal qualities that both catalyze and strengthen our persistence: *faith, purpose,* and *patience.*

The good news: All three traits tend to develop as we mature.

. . .

One kind of faith—call it cheap faith— is the simple expectation that tomorrow will be better than today, that we'll have an easier commute or a sunny weekend. Like Suber's description of fate, this type of faith comes without the burden of responsibility. It's the universe's job to make things better, to clear the roads or make the sun shine. Persistence, on the other hand, depends on a different, more accountable type of faith. It depends on the belief that our own efforts shape our future. There's a big difference between hoping that tomorrow will be better and deciding that tomorrow will be better. The faith that persistent people have—and that we as late bloomers need—has nothing to do with chance and everything to do with intent.

Purpose is the next important driver of persistence. Purposeful people are significantly more motivated than others to pursue a meaningful life. In her research, Duckworth found that higher scores on purpose correlate with higher scores on the Grit Scale. Purpose motivates us. It strengthens our ability to persist through the conviction that our pursuit matters. This is not to say that we all need to be saints, but rather that it helps us to see our late-bloomer goals as connected to the broader world.

Finally, there's patience. One of my favorite Silicon Valley late bloomers, and an exemplar of patience in a business culture that exhorts us to "move fast and break things," is Diane Greene. She grew up in Annapolis, Maryland, with a love for the ocean. As a girl, she learned to catch crabs and sell them for five dollars apiece. In college, she majored in engineering but also took up windsurfing—at nineteen she started a world windsurfing competition—as well as competitive sailing. After college she worked for an offshore oil company, but quit when she wasn't allowed to visit the male domain of the ocean-drilling platform. So she went to work for a windsurfing company, and later for Coleman, the camping gear company.

At thirty-three, Greene went back to school and got an advanced degree in computer science. It led to her first job in software. "I was finally ready for a grown-up's job," she says. In 1998, at forty-three, she and her husband and three others founded the software company VMware, which had a method of extracting greater efficiencies out of computer hardware. VMware was a big success, but at fifty-three Greene, then CEO, was fired for being, in part, too unassuming and press shy, the antithesis of the zeitgeist's love of brash young CEOs. But Greene's career wasn't over. In 2010 she became a board director at Google, and until January 2019, was the CEO of Google Cloud.

You might protest my inclusion of Diane Greene, yet another Silicon Valley multimillionaire, as a late bloomer. But I include her because of her self-assessment about not being ready for a "grown-up's

job" until thirty-three. Greene, in fact, sees her first thirty-three years not as a mad chase to early success and fame, in the manner of Jonah Lehrer or Elizabeth Holmes and countless other early-blooming burnouts, but as a call to adventure and a journey of exploration. Her adventures and explorations included catching and selling Maryland crabs for five dollars, starting a world windsurfing competition at nineteen, learning to sail a dinghy competitively, mixing it up with the rough men in the offshore oil business, and tinkering with products at a camping gear company.

Greene's story sounds both sane and wise. She never sat still, but she was not impatient. The paths she followed were her own, and to heck with convention. Her story sounds quirky only in the context of today's crazy Wunderkind Ideal for early success. Her older-style patience expresses itself in how she treats herself and others. While running VMware, her two children were growing up. Greene insisted on getting home for dinner every night. Even in the 1990s, that was considered a rebellious act in the frenzied cauldron of Silicon Valley. Contrast that to early bloomer Elizabeth Holmes of Theranos, whose chief security officer would troll the offices like a secret spy each night at seven thirty p.m., then angrily confront the early departures the next day for not being committed to Theranos. As this book goes to press, Diane Greene's late-blooming, patiently run creation, VMware, was worth $56 billion. Theranos, the wunderkind company, was broke.

Diane Greene's story confirms what neuroscience is only starting to tell us: Success skills like self-regulation, deep focus, and pattern recognition come with time and experience. The moral is that we need to try things. We need to learn.

But we need to have patience.

In *Quiet*, Susan Cain wrote, "The secret to life is to put yourself in the right lighting. For some it's a Broadway spotlight; for others, a lamplit desk. Use your natural powers—of persistence, concentration, insight, and sensitivity—to do work you love and work that matters. Solve problems, make art, think deeply. Figure out what you are meant to contribute to the world and make sure you contribute it."

Great advice. But unless we're incredibly lucky, the only way to find the right lighting is, like Diane Greene, to patiently search for it. And since the willpower needed to patiently try new things and pursue new passions is a limited resource (see Chapter 6), we late bloomers need to be careful with how we "spend" our persistence. This is one of the greatest quandaries of late blooming: How do we decide when to persist and when to quit?

• • •

Scio te ipsum: Know thyself.

We late bloomers are birds of another feather. A different breed of cat. Cut from a different cloth. Use whatever cliché you want, but we late bloomers don't fit the Wunderkind Ideal and the conveyor belt to success. We can't follow the early bloomer model and hope to succeed, at least not in any meaningful, sustainable way. It will burn up our persistence and stunt our exploration. Instead, we have to reflect on our differences, acknowledge our limitations—and gifts—and understand that we're meant to take a different path.

Kimberly Harrington, who published her first book at fifty (see Chapter 8), reflects on learning to embrace her late bloomer self:

> I was always a late bloomer as a kid. I didn't walk until I was almost two. I didn't ride a bike until I was nine. All my friends were riding their bikes without training wheels, but I didn't want mine off yet. I was afraid to crash. Finally, one day I turned to Mom and said, "Take 'em off." She took off the training wheels, and I rode away. I never fell.
>
> Over my life, I've realized that that's me to a T, regardless of my age.
>
> I'll buy into a cultural expectation. Advertising is well known for having the best "30 Under 30" lists or "40 Under 40" or whatever. Those always used to make me feel bad. I'd think: "I'm taking this meandering path. I don't even know

what I'm doing and I'm never going to be on one of these lists." Every industry has some sort of thing where they highlight really young people who are killing it. But then something would happen that would remind me that I've always been a late bloomer. The fact that I had my first book come out the year I turned fifty is, in advertising terms, very on-brand for me as a late bloomer.

How to fight the cultural expectations? Try to look back and recognize what your true nature is. Too often, I think people try to work against their nature. You think it's not cool or it's not culturally what's going on, so you try to be someone you're not. You try to be like your friend or a colleague or someone with a completely different temperament, different drive, and different thought process.

Every time I'm frustrated with things or feeling like a failure, it's because I'm trying to fit into a mold I can never fit into—never in my whole life, not once.

When I do something, I want to feel really sure or really confident. That's just my nature. Then once I do it, I'll really go for it. I might be starting late, but then I'll accelerate. I mean, it's amazing how consistent it is.

So I think it's good to look back and think about what you were like as a kid and what you liked to do and where you found satisfaction. Then return to those things or that method of approaching challenges. If you don't do that, you'll be beating your head against a wall your whole adult life.

Kimberly Harrington's story reminds us that while persistence grows with age, our best use of persistence comes when we discover—or rediscover—a story narrative that fits our truest selves.

For me, this happened during a leadership conference I was attending in 2016. It was a simple assignment, really. The organizers had us write down fifty accomplishments in our life that we were most proud of. Some might be résumé accomplishments, some might be goofy things that we wouldn't dare put on a résumé, such as doing a *New York Times* crossword puzzle in pen. Then there were the achievements we were secretly the proudest of. My secret achievement was almost insane.

It was spring break at Stanford, and half the campus, it seemed, had lit out for skiing vacations. I'd never skied before and lacked the money anyway. But I was in the best shape of my running life. I was running about seventy miles a week.

On this Saturday, I put on my running shoes and headed out Sand Hill Road west of the campus with the idea of running a fourteen-mile loop, then drinking some beer and finding a pickup softball game. But five miles into the run, I had a crazy idea. Maybe I could turn right and head up a steep hill with twisting roads to the Santa Cruz Mountains skyline. I began the thirteen-hundred-foot climb, expecting that my curiosity itch would be scratched, and I would shortly head back down. But at the top, another crazy idea took over. Why not run down the mountain's west side and head for the Pacific Ocean?

I had brought no water or snacks with me. By the time I got to San Gregorio Beach, twenty-six miles from where I had started, I was sugar-bonked and very thirsty. But I had no money. So I did something I'd never done or ever imagined I'd do. I stood outside the San Gregorio general store and begged for money, enough to buy a quart of Gatorade and two Snickers bars. At this point, I should have hitchhiked home. But again, the crazy idea: *Why not just start jogging back, as slow as I need to go?*

On the flatland before I reached the base of the mountain, a vacationing Englishman on a bicycle kept me company as I picked up my pace, the Gatorade no longer sloshing in my stomach. But at the base of the mountain, my temporary friend said goodbye, and now I had to climb another thirteen hundred feet by myself. At the top, in a village called Skylonda, I spent the last of my cadged money on a Coke and another Snickers. I rested long enough to shake out the fizz of the Coke and quaff it. Then back down the mountain to Stanford I went, thinking: *This is insane. But I can't stop now.*

Within two miles of the campus, I was so exhausted that paranoia crept in, along with fits of rage at the jerks in cars I thought were trying to run me over. Then I realized I was running too far into the street. My judgment was rapidly eroding. But somehow I made it back to my dorm. I fetched three Cokes from the eating service, then lugged a chair from my dorm room down to the men's shower. I placed the chair under the showerhead, stripped off my sweat-caked clothes and bloody shoes, and sat under the shower drinking Cokes for a long time. Slowly I felt a profound elation. Oh, man—I had just run fifty-two miles in seven and a half hours, up and down a mountain.

Now, forty-one years later, that insane and noble run was the achievement I chose to put atop my personal list of fifty accomplishments. The drill in the seminar was to try to recognize what drove me on that run. What I learned about this drill was profound, and I regretted that I hadn't absorbed the lesson decades earlier.

What I learned was this: I accomplish the most not when I set out to prove something, but when I set out to discover something.

On that run, I learned that whenever I went around one corner and up the next hill, I was doing it to satisfy my curiosity. The thought process was: *I wonder what would happen if I just kept going for a little longer? If I just ran another mile—patiently, persistently—to take a look? If I begged for money?* What I did not do was plan this run as a competition, a test of my grit, or with any plan at all. The very thought of doing that would have wrecked it. I never would have started. Rather, I just did one little hill at a time, patiently and persistently, and ended up climbing a mountain—twice.

That worked for me.

I learned that the situations where I excel are those where my curiosity takes over. When it does, a sense of exploration also takes over. I get in the zone, and I go for it. I feel pulled, not pushed—pulled by a beautiful power I can't explain. Persistence and patience come to me; I don't need to summon them. That's when I really succeed. It was a great insight into who I am and what drives me. My own blooming occurs when I explore, when I take a step forward, with no particular goal other than to see what's next on the road. In those situations, I feel magically pulled; persistence comes without effort. I don't think most early bloomers think this way. Most of them are driven by goals, to ace their SATs, to get straight A's, to be in the upper percentiles of life. That attitude has always worked for them. The conveyor belt of early achievement handsomely rewarded their competitive attitude.

My run made me realize that I'm a different kind of person. I'm more driven by curiosity, exploration, discovery—and less by goals, competition, and winning. That's the pathway to success I now pursue, whether in business, life, or hobbies. It fuels me, this pursuit of curiosity and exploration. And ultimately, it's more productive because I never burn out on curiosity. The way I burn out is by pursuing rigid goals on rigid timetables, and by trying to be a fierce competitor only for competition's sake. The outside world would call me a slacker for that. But I'm not a slacker. I'm simply not wired like early bloomers.

And since you're reading this book, I suspect you aren't either.

• • •

Blooming has no deadline. Our future story is written in pencil, not carved in stone. It can be changed. There is no fixed chronology to self-determination, no age limit for breakthroughs. Research supports the idea that as we lose some capabilities, we gain others that far outweigh what is lost. Therefore the question we should be asking ourselves is not, What can we accomplish in spite of our nature and life experiences? Instead it should be, What can we accomplish because of them?

If we're not forced to conform to standard timetables for success, we can—and will—bloom on our own schedules. And we can do it with a deeper sense of mission and a greater feeling of contentment. What we accomplish in the marathon of life depends on our persistence, our patience, and an ability to see ourselves as we really are. Our cultural obsession with youthful talent, with early achievement, distracts us from this simple truth.

As late bloomers, we need to understand that we still have power.

It may not feel like the same power we had in our teens or twenties, the kind fed by fantasy, with seemingly endless possibilities all aimed toward some culturally defined vision of success. Our late bloomer power is different. It's the power to renounce what's supposed to happen in life and instead embrace what actually happens in life, with its ups and downs, its twists and turns. It's the power to explore and experience, to be an individual. It's the power that comes with knowing and valuing ourselves.

Each of us faces a very different, very personal journey. Letting go of society's rigid timeline liberates us. It allows us a life—and a career—that unfolds more organically, more authentically. As we face our late-blooming challenges, we never know what the upside may be. Often abject failures are hard-won breakthroughs, difficult endings are fresh starts, and dismal turns of fate are wonderful strokes of luck.

When we take the longer road to success, we develop a clearer sense of where we are, where we want to go, and what new pathways are open to us. Along our different journeys, we find meaning and confidence in our adaptive skills. We try new things. We discover old truths. We conquer our doubts. We stop retreating. We value ourselves enough to take risks—to trust, create, and move forward. No matter what a culture obsessed with early achievement wants us to believe, life can't be perfectly planned. There isn't a single path to self-realization.

We're gifted. We're late bloomers. We have amazing destinies to follow.

The unexpected happened while I was writing *Late Bloomers*. Friends and acquaintances, including some I'd met for the first time at a business or social outing, would ask about my next project. A book on late bloomers, I'd tell them. Some writers prefer to stay mum about future books, afraid of jinxing them or possibly of having their idea stolen. But I've always shared my newest thoughts. People will inevitably say, "Then you should read this book, or talk to this person," and often their advice is valuable. By sharing, I win.

But for *Late Bloomers*, the response was altogether different, charged and emotional. Eyes would light up. People would grab my arm and say, "I'm a late bloomer, too!" It was as if a world of late bloomers existed in a shadow realm, and now someone was opening a window. Almost everyone, I discovered, identifies as a late bloomer and wants you to know it, even people who appear at first glance to be early achievers. In Chapter 4, I wrote about my college roommate, Bob, who made Phi Beta Kappa in his junior year, aced law school, and became a partner at a world-class law firm in just five years. But when I saw him not long ago, Bob insisted he's a late bloomer, too, recounting slights and frustrations from high school.

"What do you suppose people are telling me," I asked my wife, Marji, "when they say, 'I'm a late bloomer, too!'"

"People want to be acknowledged," she said. "Most don't feel acknowledged for who they are, and what they can be. They feel untapped and undiscovered."

Researching *Late Bloomers* has left me thoroughly convinced that

America and many parts of the world face a crisis of untapped and undiscovered human potential. I wonder whether today's angry populism, seen at both ends of the political spectrum, is a misdirected cry of pain from those who see themselves as untapped and undiscovered. Large swaths of people in this country feel unacknowledged, unappreciated, and disrespected. They want us to see their pain but also their potential. This shouldn't happen in an affluent society like ours. But out of ignorant good intent, we've designed a human sorting machine with a conveyor belt to early success that guarantees this unhappy result.

We all have a stake in identifying and promoting late bloomers. We owe it to ourselves and our children, to our friends and their children. Human progress will stop if a majority of us feel untapped and unacknowledged. That's a prescription for social instability, for angry political movements, for destruction. We will all suffer.

But the late bloomer crisis, conversely, makes today the best time for employers, schools, and colleges to step up. The late bloomer market is huge and largely unaddressed. This is a time when employers, schools, and colleges can do extraordinarily well for themselves by doing the right thing for late bloomers.

For employers: The median compensation package at Facebook in 2017 was $240,000. The median first-year salary Google pays, in its efforts to recruit fresh college grads with STEM degrees (in science, technology, engineering, or math) from top colleges is around $175,000 in total compensation per new employee. Can your company compete with that? Of course not. But the hard truth is, if you want to hire early bloomers with the highest tests scores and the most prestigious university degrees, you must. You probably won't because doing so will blow up your payroll costs and wreck your profitability. You therefore will need a different strategy. You will have to play a version of "moneyball," like what the Oakland A's baseball team does, as described in Michael Lewis's bestselling book. The Oakland A's perpetually have the lowest payroll in baseball. When it comes to hiring top talent, the A's can't compete, salarywise, with the New York Yankees, Boston Red Sox, or even the San Francisco Giants. The A's, therefore, must search for untapped and unacknowledged talent. I humbly suggest to employers: So should you.

Fortunately, employers, you're in luck. Late bloomers form the biggest pool of untapped, unacknowledged human talent out there. Seek them out. Show them some love. Help develop their skills. You'll be rewarded with smart, loyal, creative, wise, and persistent employees. Also, consider replacing the shopworn "up-and-out" career path for senior employees with a more productive and humane career arc (see Chapter 3).

For parents: I hope reading *Late Bloomers* will ease your anxiety about the pace of your children's development. You can stop apologizing right now to your friends about their slower development—your children know you do this and resent you for it. Stop thinking you can "solve" their slower development with money alone. Just love them, listen to their frustrations and enthusiasms, and be there for them. Enjoy your children as they are. Relish their curiosity, their dreams, their forays and experiments, their setbacks and heartbreaks, and their breakthroughs. "That's the good stuff," says the Robin Williams character Dr. Sean Maguire in *Good Will Hunting*.

For high schools: The measure of your success is not how many students you sent to Harvard and Caltech this year. The measure of your success is how well the vast majority of your students will mature into independent, happy, and fulfilled adulthood two decades and more later.

For community colleges: You hold some valuable keys for late bloomers. You always have, but your opportunity is greater than it's ever been.

For colleges and universities: If you don't happen to be your state's crown jewel public university, or you aren't ranked in the top fifty colleges in the country, both public and private, then your future is cloudy. But you have a huge addressable market that will ensure your future if you meet the needs of late bloomers. They need you. And you need them.

To religious and spiritual leaders: You've surely seen the pain inflicted on families and individuals by the early-blooming madness. Shared among different faiths in the world is a powerful protest: Humans are divine creations. We all have a supreme destiny: to discover our gifts, however long it takes, to pursue our deepest purposes, and to bloom.

Thank you for reading *Late Bloomers*. Now I'd like to hear your late bloomer story.

Rich Karlgaard
LateBloomer.com

INTRODUCTION

2 **Joanne, fifty-three, is:** Joanne Rowling, better known by her pen name, J. K. Rowling, was born on July 31, 1965. Her story is drawn from, among other sources, Rachel Gillett, "From Welfare to One of the World's Wealthiest Women: The Incredible Rags-to-Riches Story of J. K. Rowling," *Business Insider,* May 18, 2015, https://read .bi/2NkiwF1.

3 **"I had no particular direction":** Ken Fisher was born on November 29, 1950. His story and quotes are sourced from his book *The Ten Roads to Riches* and my multiple conversations with him. Kenneth L. Fisher, *The Ten Roads to Riches: The Ways the Wealthy Got There (and How You Can Too!)* (Hoboken, NJ: John Wiley & Sons, 2017).

6 **"People wouldn't accept me":** Weston's height is listed as five-one at IMDb.com and variously as four-eleven to five-one on other sites. Her tiny stature made it easier for her to fudge her real age—saying she was nineteen, not thirty-two—and so helped her win a $300,000 contract as a scriptwriter for Disney's *Felicity,* a television series about a teenager. Joe Flint, "Riley Weston Fooled Us All About Her Age," *EW,* October 30, 1998.

6 **Every year *Forbes*:** "Presenting the 2018 30 Under 30," *Forbes,* 2018, http://bit.ly/2NEz4Xs. See also *The New Yorker*'s intermittent list, most recently "20 Under 40": *The New Yorker,* June 14 and 21, 2010. *Fortune* publishes an annual list: Robert Hackett, Jeff John Roberts, Lucinda Shen, and Jen Wieczner, "The Ledger: 40 Under 40," *Fortune,* n.d., https://for.tn/2xpFaRo. *Inc.* recently switched from a "35 Under 35" list to a "30 Under 30" list (the trend toward youth continues!): "Rising Stars: Meet the 30 Most Inspiring Young Entrepreneurs of 2018," *Inc.,* n.d., http://bit.ly/2NJsP4A. A few years ago *Time* replaced

its "30 Under 30" list with a "Most Influential Teens" list: "The 30 Most Influential Teens of 2017," *Time*, November 3, 2017, https://ti.me/2x7yBnl.

7 **"full immersion":** For the annual tuition fees of the Atlanta International School and New York's Columbia Grammar School, see Melissa Willets, "11 Unbelievably Expensive Preschools in the U.S.," *Parenting*, n.d., http://bit.ly/2N7FVcq.

7 **"I'm contacted by a lot of parents":** Irena Smith quoted in Georgia Perry, "Silicon Valley's College-Consultant Industry," *Atlantic*, December 9, 2015.

8 **college tuition costs have risen:** "Elite College Prices Now Exceed $70,000 Per Year," *Wealth Management,* March 1, 2017, https://bit.ly/2MsdJMc.

8 **In the 2018 Super Bowl:** "Super Bowl 2018: "How Eagles, Patriots Starters Rated as High School Recruits," CBS Sports, February 1, 2018, https://bit.ly/2CTa0YB. Carson Wentz was five foot eight and 125 pounds as a high school freshman: "Carson Wentz Was 5-8 as High School Freshman and Other Things You Might Not Know About Him," *Morning Call*, April 29, 2016, https://bit.ly/2NFmEic.

9 **"I sent my weird stories":** Janet Evanovich's story derives from her Wikipedia entry; "Janet's Bio," Janet Evanovich, n.d., https://bit.ly/2Qnj9LE; and Debra Nussbaum, "In Person: Imagine Trenton. One Author Did," *New York Times*, November 3, 2002, NJ14.

9 **Billionaire Diane Hendricks:** "Blue Collar Pride: Diane Hendricks' Rise from Teen Mom to Billionaire Entrepreneur," *Forbes*, October 21, 2017, https://bit.ly/2NbI86D.

10 **"I finished in the half":** Scott Kelly, interview by author, 2016.

10 **Mary Barra:** Barra's early job of inspecting hoods and fenders is told in Cal Fussman, "What I've Learned: Mary Barra," *Esquire*, April 26, 2016.

10 **Ursula Burns:** Burns's humble start is chronicled in Nanette Byrnes and Roger O. Crockett, "Ursula Burns: An Historic Succession at Xerox," *Bloomberg Business*, May 28, 2009.

10 **Jeannie Courtney:** Jeannie Courtney, interview by author, 2015.

10 **three student suicides:** Hanna Rosin, "The Silicon Valley Suicides," *Atlantic*, September 19, 2015.

11 **"16 percent reported seriously":** "Suicide Among Youth," Centers for Disease Control, n.d., https://bit.ly/2Bldm12.

11 **depression to be the number one:** As noted in Bruce Dick and B. Jane Ferguson, "Health for the World's Adolescents: A Second Chance in the Second Decade," *Journal of Adolescent Health* 56, no. 1 (2015): 3–6.

11 **depression has doubled:** "Depression and Anxiety Among College Students," JED, n.d., http://bit.ly/2OuMvq6. The study was conducted by the Anxiety Disorders Association of America.

11 **lowest rates of self-reported:** Kevin Eagan et al., *The American Freshman: National Norms Fall 2016* (Los Angeles: Higher Education Research Institute at UCLA, 2016).

11 **campus mental health directors surveyed:** Amy Novotney, "Students Under Pressure," *Monitor on Psychology* 45, no. 8 (2014): 36; Louise A. Douce and Richard P. Keeling, *A Strategic Primer on College Student Mental Health* (Washington, DC: American Council on Education, 2014).

11 **"felt overwhelming anxiety":** Greg Lukianoff and Jonathan Haidt, "The Coddling of the American Mind," *Atlantic*, September 2015.

12 **"I felt a shattering loss":** Carol Fishman Cohen, interview by Susan Salter Reynolds, 2015.

13 **"I spent most days":** Scott Kelly, interview by author, 2016.

14 **Simply put, a late bloomer is:** I wasn't able to find a conclusive definition of a late bloomer that was supported by psychologists or social scientists. The concept appears to be a social construct. My definition comes from an amalgamation of many common definitions, as well as impressions gleaned from interviewing dozens of late bloomers.

14 **"Everyone has a supreme":** Oprah Winfrey, interview at the Stanford Graduate School of Business, April 28, 2014, https://bit.ly/1q0nmlv.

14 **Is there a rigorous, extensive:** I pored over research papers, studies, and abstracts and found virtually no academic or scientific material specifically on late bloomers. Again, I think this is because "late bloomer" is more of a social construct than a cognitive or developmental phase. To research the subject for this book, I looked for traits and characteristics that paralleled, overlapped with, or contributed to the idea of late blooming as recognized in literature, media, and social discourse.

14 **debunking the "myth of average":** Among recent works exploring the complexities of individual development, I recommend Todd Rose,

The End of Average: How We Succeed in a World That Values Sameness (New York: HarperCollins, 2015); L. Todd Rose, Parisa Rouhani, and Kurt W. Fischer, "The Science of the Individual," *Mind, Brain, and Education* 7, no. 3 (2013): 152–58; L. Todd Rose, *Square Peg: My Story and What It Means for Raising Innovators, Visionaries, and Out-of-the-Box Thinkers* (New York: Hachette, 2013); Scott Barry Kaufman, *Ungifted: Intelligence Redefined* (New York: Basic Books, 2013); Scott Barry Kaufman, ed., *The Complexity of Greatness: Beyond Talent or Practice* (New York: Oxford University Press, 2013); Scott Barry Kaufman and Robert J. Sternberg, "Conceptions of Giftedness," in *Handbook of Giftedness in Children* (Boston: Springer, 2008); and Scott Barry Kaufman et al., "Are Cognitive G and Academic Achievement G One and the Same G? An Exploration on the Woodcock-Johnson and Kaufman Tests," *Intelligence* 40, no. 2 (2012): 123–38.

CHAPTER 1: OUR EARLY BLOOMER OBSESSION

17 **Pop-neuroscience writer Jonah Lehrer:** The facts about Lehrer can be found in an extraordinarily long entry in Wikipedia: https://en.wikipedia.org/wiki/Jonah_Lehrer.

18 *Quiet* **author Susan Cain:** Cain coined the term "Extrovert Ideal" in *Quiet: The Power of Introverts in a World That Can't Stop Talking* (New York: Broadway Books, 2013). In more ways than one, Cain's work on introverts inspired this book.

18 *wunderkind* **literally means "wonder child":** Originally a German word, *wunderkind* first appeared in English in 1883. *Wunder* means "wonder," and *Kind* means "child."

18 **Use of the term:** According to Google Books Ngram Viewer, use of the term *wunderkind* skyrocketed between 1960 and 2015: http://bit.ly/2N7GqmO.

18 **Singers like:** Taylor Swift has sold 175 million records and won ten Grammys; Adele has sold 160 million records and won eight Grammys; Rihanna has sold over 200 million records, won nine Grammys, and won an Oscar; and Justin Bieber has sold 140 million records and won one Grammy. Jennifer Lawrence is the second-youngest winner of an Academy Award and regularly makes lists of the highest-paid actors. And what can be said about Donald Glover—he currently has

a hit show on FX, *Atlanta,* and is one of today's most critically acclaimed recording artists under his pseudonym, Childish Gambino. These are just a few examples, but they show the ascendancy of young entertainers.

19 **"Web celebs":** All these "Web celebs" have made a small fortune in endorsements and sponsorship fees. It appears, though, that the Web "influencer" craze has peaked. While there are still young people hustling to capture millions of followers and bag energy drink sponsorships, the overall trend—as well as user growth for many social media sites—has flattened.

19 **how much earlier these athletes:** For decades young football prospects have been plucked from the masses. The interesting point here is that the same thing is now happening for people playing minor sports like lacrosse, swimming, and field hockey. What's next, intramural sports?

20 **general managers:** The analytics craze has dramatically changed the makeup of management in Major League Baseball, spurred by the widespread adoption of statistical platforms like Sabermetrics. Now it's starting to spread to other sports, hockey in particular. Just since this chapter was written, the Toronto Maple Leafs, one of the most storied franchises in the National Hockey League, hired a thirty-one-year-old general manager.

20 **technology is a young person's game:** "PayScale Releases Tech Employers Compared 2016," PayScale, March 2, 2016, https://bit.ly/2p6K4Pw; "Median Age of the Labor Force, by Sex, Race and Ethnicity," Bureau of Labor Statistics, October 24, 2017, https://bit.ly/2xarzOv.

20 *Forbes* **lists ten billionaires in business:** "Meet the Members of the Three-Comma Club," *Forbes,* March 6, 2018, https://bit.ly/2xgC8ic.

20 **Media have latched onto:** All these lists are common. Many of these categories are promoted by Forbes Media. For categories like entertainment, multiple magazines, including *Entertainment Weekly,* publish their own lists. The really interesting ones are in the meatpacking industry: "International Production & Processing Expo Launches Young Leaders '30 Under 30' Program," North American Meat Institute, October 7, 2014, https://bit.ly/2x9Kmts. See also " '40 Under

40' Honorees Recognized at Convention," *Drovers*, February 9, 2015, https://bit.ly/2OiyU5e; and "40 Under 40: Erin Brenneman Brimming with Passion," *Farm Journal's Pork*, April 27, 2016, https://bit.ly/2NHNFRX.

21 **"Most Influential Teens"**: "The 30 Most Influential Teens of 2017," *Time*, November 3, 2017.

21 **"Youth is the new global"**: Simon Doonan, "The Worst of Youth: Why Do We Fetishize and Overpraise the Young?," *Slate*, May 26, 2011.

22 **college preparatory tests**: "Class of 2017 SAT Results," College Board, n.d., https://bit.ly/2QrCUle; Ann Carrns, "Another College Expense: Preparing for the SAT and ACT," *New York Times*, October 28, 2014.

23 **"It's not fun anymore"**: Even youth sports have succumbed to the early-blooming pressure cooker: "Around 70 percent of kids in the United States stop playing organized sports by age 13 'because it's not fun anymore.'" Julianna W. Miner, "Why 70 percent of Kids Quit Sports by Age 13," *Washington Post*, June 1, 2016.

23 **"Our culture no longer supports"**: Ibid.

24 **"continually improving grades"**: Judi Robinovitz, "The 10 Most Important Factors in College Admissions," College Press, n.d., https://bit.ly/2xbM6SM.

26 **parents spend $16 billion**: See, e.g., K. J. Dell'Antonia, "$16 Billion: The Cost of Summer," *New York Times*, June 27, 2012; Vicki Glembocki, "Aren't Kids Supposed to Be Off for the Summer?," *Philadelphia*, May 23, 2013, https://bit.ly/2p2EyNE; and "Parenting in America: Outlook, Worries, Aspirations Are Strongly Linked to Financial Situation," Pew Research Center, December 17, 2015, https://pewrsr.ch/2NaGzG1.

26 **"Local leagues have been nudged"**: Sean Gregory, "How Kid Sports Turned Pro," *Time*, August 24, 2017.

27 **"deliberate practice"**: On Anders Ericsson, see K. Anders Ericsson, Ralf T. Krampe, and Clemens Tesch-Römer. "The Role of Deliberate Practice in the Acquisition of Expert Performance," *Psychological Review* 100, no. 3 (1993): 363; K. Anders Ericsson, "Deliberate Practice and the Acquisition and Maintenance of Expert Performance in Medicine and Related Domains," *Academic Medicine* 79, no. 10 (2004): S70–S81; K. Anders Ericsson, "The Influence of Experience and Deliberate Practice on the Development of Superior Expert Per-

formance," in *The Cambridge Handbook of Expertise and Expert Performance*, ed. K. Anders Ericsson, Neil Charness, Roberft R. Hoffman, and Paul J. Feltovich 38 (New York: Cambridge University Press, 2006); K. Anders Ericsson, "Deliberate Practice and Acquisition of Expert Performance: A General Overview," *Academic Emergency Medicine* 15, no. 11 (2008): 988–994; K. Anders Ericsson, "Attaining Excellence Through Deliberate Practice: Insights from the Study of Expert Performance," in *Teaching and Learning: The Essential Readings*, ed. Charles Deforges and Richard Fox (Oxford: Blackwell, 2002); and Malcolm Gladwell, *Outliers: The Story of Success* (Boston: Little, Brown, 2008).

27 **"He learned to practice by":** Penelope Trunk, "My 11-Year-Old Son Auditioned at Juilliard, and We Both Learned a Lot About How Top Performers Practice," *Business Insider*, May 30, 2017, https://read .bi/2p6Mf5K.

28 **Millions of American children:** I'm using "millions" as an educated guess, but it's not hyperbole. In 2018 the K–12 student population in the United States was 56.6 million. "Fast Facts: Back to School Statistics," National Center for Education Statistics, n.d., https://bit .ly/1DLO7Ux. In 2016, according to the Centers for Disease Control, 6.1 million children between four and seventeen were diagnosed with ADHD. "Attention-Deficit/Hyperactivity Disorder (ADHD)," Centers for Disease Control, March 20, 2018, https://bit.ly/2nphXvC. Sales of Ritalin, the most commonly prescribed ADHD medicine, grew 89 percent from 2003 to 2016, with an estimated $12 to $14 billion of sales in 2016 alone. Ryan D'Agostino, "The Drugging of the American Boy," *Esquire*, March 27, 2014.

28 **"A kid in the United States":** Dr. Leonard Sax, interview by author, 2016.

29 **"The other day, after":** Megan McArdle, "Go Ahead, Let Your Kids Fail," *Bloomberg*, February 20, 2014, https://bloom.bg/2NDZSau. See also Megan McArdle, *The Up Side of Down: Why Failing Well Is the Key to Success* (New York: Penguin, 2015).

29 **"I think society is in crisis":** Carol Dweck, interview by author, 2016.

30 **Rates of teen depression and suicide:** Accurate rates of teen and college-level anxiety and suicide are difficult to pinpoint. This is primarily due to the inaccuracy of self-reporting and a general disparity in the quality of reporting in various sources. One thing that can't

be argued, or ignored, is that teen anxiety and suicide are a serious problem. See Deborah L. McBride, "Young Adolescents as Likely to Die from Suicide as Traffic Accidents," *Journal of Pediatric Nursing* 32 (2016): 83–84; Benoit Denizet-Lewis, "Why Are More American Teenagers Than Ever Suffering from Severe Anxiety?," *New York Times Magazine*, October 11, 2017; Jesse Singal, "For 80 Years, Young Americans Have Been Getting More Anxious and Depressed, and No One Is Quite Sure Why," *Cut*, March 13, 2016, https://bit.ly/2HFyxSZ; Rae Ellen Bichell, "Suicide Rates Climb in US, Especially Among Adolescent Girls," *NPR*, April 22, 2016; Aaron E. Carroll, "Preventing Teen Suicide: What the Evidence Shows," *New York Times*, August 17, 2017; and "Increased Levels of Anxiety and Depression as Teenage Experience Changes over Time," Nuffield Foundation, March 14, 2012, https://bit.ly/1Eo4815.

30 **five to eight times as likely:** Gregg Henriques, "The College Student Mental Health Crisis," *Psychology Today*, February 15, 2014, https://bit.ly/2wkJ1Pc.

30 **depression to be the single:** As noted in Bruce Dick and B. Jane Ferguson, "Health for the World's Adolescents: A Second Chance in the Second Decade," *Journal of Adolescent Health* 56, no. 1 (2015): 3–6.

30 **first experience symptoms at age fourteen:** Ibid.

31 **"The deaths are but the tip":** Bichell, "Suicide Rates Climb."

31 **"It's not an exaggeration":** Jean M. Twenge et al., "It's Beyond My Control: A Cross-Temporal Meta-Analysis of Increasing Externality in Locus of Control, 1960–2002," *Personality and Social Psychology Review* 8 (2004): 308–19; J. Twenge et al., "Birth Cohort Increases in Psychopathology Among Young Americans, 1938–2007: A Cross-Temporal Meta-Analysis of the MMPI," *Clinical Psychology Review* 30 (2010): 145–54. For historical data on intrinsic and extrinsic values, see J. H. Pryor et al., *The American Freshman: Forty-Year Trends, 1966–2006* (Los Angeles: Higher Education Research Institute, 2007).

31 **"being well off financially":** Pryor et al., *The American Freshman*.

32 **millennials appear more risk-averse:** "Think You Know the Next Gen Investor? Think Again," UBS Investor Watch, 1Q 2014, https://bit.ly/2xcc3Rj.

32 **three things associated:** "Millennials in Adulthood: Detached from Institutions, Networked with Friends," Pew Research Center, March 7, 2014, https://pewrsr.ch/2MHYSgN.

32 **lived at a different address:** Richard Fry, "For First Time in Modern Era, Living with Parents Edges Out Other Living Arrangements for 18- to 34-Year-Olds," Pew Research Center, May 24, 2016, https://pewrsr.ch/25jN9ga; Richard Fry, "More Millennials Living with Family Despite Improved Job Market," Pew Research Center, July 29, 2015, https://pewrsr.ch/1VNfQLa.

33 **home for an extended stay:** Richard Fry, "It's Becoming More Common for Young Adults to Live at Home—and for Longer Stretches," Pew Research Center, May 5, 2017, https://pewrsr.ch/2pOttBM.

33 **"It's somewhat terrifying":** Christine Hassler, *20 Something Manifesto: Quarter-Lifers Speak Out About Who They Are, What They Want, and How to Get It* (Novato, CA: New World Library, 2008); Robin Marantz Henig, "What Is It About 20-Somethings?," *New York Times Magazine*, August 18, 2010.

33 **"I feel this awful pressure":** Meg, a graduate of the University of Wisconsin, interview by author, 2017.

34 **visual platforms like Facebook:** "#StatusofMind," Royal Society for Public health, n.d., https://bit.ly/2t1OI68.

35 **the median employee:** "PayScale Releases Tech Employers Compared 2016."

35 **"people over forty-five basically die":** Noam Scheiber, "The Brutal Ageism of Tech: Years of Experience, Plenty of Talent, Completely Obsolete," *New Republic*, March 23, 2014, https://bit.ly/2pSIeS2.

35 **"When Matarasso first opened shop":** Ibid.

35 **Robert Withers, a consultant:** Ibid.

35 **"that older people can't work that fast":** Sarah McBride, "Special Report: Silicon Valley's Dirty Secret—Age Bias," Reuters, November 17, 2012, https://reut.rs/2pbXf1P.

36 **92 percent of adults:** Kenneth Terrell, "Age Discrimination Goes Online," *AARP Bulletin,* December 2017, https://bit.ly/2nJFrgv; David Neumark, Ian Burn, and Patrick Button, "Age Discrimination and Hiring of Older Workers," Federal Reserve Bank of San Francisco, February 27, 2017, https://bit.ly/2MvCSG5.

36 **one-fifth cited age:** Kelly O. Scott, "Age Discrimination Claims Remain Popular," Ervin Cohen & Jessup, May 16, 2013, https://bit.ly/2p4u68v.

36 **age is cited in 26 percent:** "Diversity in High Tech," U.S. Equal Employment Opportunity Commission, n.d., https://bit.ly/1TsiNzi.

36 **The unemployment rate:** Jennifer Schramm, "Unemployment Rate for Those Ages 55+ Increases in December," AARP, January 5, 2018, https://bit.ly/2Qs0Zs4.

36 **challenges of long-term unemployment:** Sara E. Rix, "Long-Term Unemployment: Great Risks and Consequences for Older Workers," AARP Public Policy Institute, February 12, 2015, http://bit.ly/2xjQlfl.

36 **thirty-six weeks compared:** Mark Miller, "Older American Workers Are Still Struggling to Find Jobs," *Fortune*, September 8, 2016.

36 **older job seekers who do find:** Rix, "Long-Term Unemployment."

37 **prospects for women over fifty:** Alexander Monge-Naranjo and Faisal Sohail, "Age and Gender Differences in Long-Term Unemployment: Before and After the Great Recession" (Economic Synopses, no. 26, 2015).

37 **age discrimination in the hiring:** David Neumark, Ian Burn, and Patrick Button, "Is It Harder for Older Workers to Find Jobs? New and Improved Evidence from a Field Experiment" (working paper no. 21669, National Bureau of Economic Research, 2015).

37 **"Older workers are involuntarily":** Maria Heidkamp, Nicole Corre, and Carl E. Van Horn, "The New Unemployables," Center on Aging and Work at Boston College, October 5, 2012, https://bit .ly/2NDFOoA. The fact is, the job market is difficult for both older women and older men. See "Millions of Men Are Missing from the Job Market," editorial, *New York Times*, October 16, 2016; Lydia DePillis, "Losing a Job Is Always Terrible. For Workers over 50, It's Worse," *Washington Post*, March 30, 2015; Miller, "Older American Workers Are Still Struggling to Find Jobs"; Ashton Applewhite, "You're How Old? We'll Be in Touch," *New York Times,* September 3, 2016.

38 **"It's a hard thing to describe":** Michael Moynihan, "Jonah Lehrer's Deceptions," *Tablet*, July 30, 2012.

39 **aroused suspicion of plagiarism:** Joe Coscarelli, "Jonah Lehrer's Self-Plagiarism Issues Are Snowballing," *New York*, June 20, 2012.

39 **"Books are still the slow food":** Jennifer Senior, "Review: Jonah Lehrer's 'A Book About Love' Is Another Unoriginal Sin," *New York Times,* July 6, 2016.

40 **"You know, I do think":** Scott Mendel quoted in Neda Ulaby, "'The Lies Are Over': A Journalist Unravels," NPR, July 31, 2012.

42 **countless examples of late bloomers:** A Google search will turn up countless examples of famous late bloomers. These are just a few examples.

CHAPTER 2: THE CRUEL FALLACY OF
HUMAN MEASUREMENT

45 **In 1975 a precocious Bill Gates:** Bill Gates's life, including his high school, college, and early Microsoft days, have been well documented. I highly recommend Stephen Manes, *Gates: How Microsoft's Mogul Reinvented an Industry and Made Himself the Richest Man in America* (New York: Touchstone, 1994). In April 1992 and September 1992, I spent several hours interviewing Gates for *Upside* magazine and *Forbes ASAP*. In October 1993 I spent five days traveling with Gates. We met at the Four Seasons Hotel in Washington and I accompanied him during a business trip for which he was promoting Office 4.0, the new version of Microsoft's business software suite. The journey included stops in Boston, New York, Chicago, and Oakland. We flew commercial on Delta Shuttle and United, and I spent many hours in conversation with Gates, on planes, in limos, and in hotel conference rooms. The result was my article "Five Days with Bill Gates," *Forbes ASAP*, February 28, 1994. In the 1990s Gates was at the top of his game as a software CEO. I found him to be extremely quick, high energy, animated, brash, funny, and also wickedly sarcastic and cutting. His comments about Microsoft being an IQ-driven company, "better than Oracle, as good as Goldman Sachs," occurred multiple times during these discussions. "IQ" as a yardstick came up in most of our discussions. I should add that the public face of Bill Gates today is quite different: his image as a circumspect global philanthropist is a stark change from his mercurial personality in the 1990s.

46 **a German-born Swiss patent application examiner:** By far the best book about the history of IQ tests and the SAT, and how one led to the other, is Nicholas Lemann, *The Big Test: The Secret History of the American Meritocracy* (New York: Farrar, Straus & Giroux, 1999).

47 **Alfred Binet:** Ibid.

48 **"Lewis Terman thought of the IQ test":** Ibid.

49 **Carl Brigham:** Ibid.

54 **Terman Study of the Gifted:** Lewis M. Terman and Melita H. Oden, *The Gifted Child Grows Up: Twenty-Five Years' Follow-Up of a Superior Group* (Stanford, CA: Stanford University Press, 1947).

55 **Just 80,000 students took the SAT:** Lemann, *Big Test.*

55 **"the more any quantitative social indicator":** Jerry Z. Muller, *The Tyranny of Metrics* (Princeton, NJ: Princeton University Press, 2018).

58 **Logic-based puzzles and mathematical word:** Maya Kossoff, "41 of Google's Toughest Interview Questions," *Inc.*, n.d., http://bit.ly /2CRBrC4.

58 **they've continued to survive—and even flourish:** Annie Murphy Paul, *The Cult of Personality Testing: How Personality Tests Are Leading Us to Miseducate Our Children, Mismanage Our Companies, and Misunderstand Ourselves* (New York: Simon & Schuster, 2010).

59 **"In the past, man was first":** Frederick Winslow Taylor, *The Principles of Scientific Management* (New York: Harper, 1914).

60 **firmly entrenched in education:** Maduakolam Ireh, "Scientific Management Still Endures in Education," *ERIC*, June 2016, https://eric .ed.gov/?id=ED566616. See also Shawn Gude, "The Industrial Classroom," *Jacobin*, April 21, 2013, http://bit.ly/2NQSOqT.

61 **"Our schools still follow":** Todd Rose, *The End of Average: How We Succeed in a World That Values Sameness* (New York: HarperCollins, 2015).

61 **the historian Raymond Callahan:** Raymond E. Callahan, *Education and the Cult of Efficiency* (Chicago: University of Chicago Press, 1964).

62 **we all learn in different ways:** Rose, *End of Average*; Scott Barry Kaufman, *Ungifted: Intelligence Redefined* (New York: Basic Books, 2013).

64 **"felt that hiring only the best":** Brad Stone, *The Everything Store: Jeff Bezos and the Age of Amazon* (New York: Random House, 2013).

64 **claims there is a mismatch:** Rich Karlgaard, "Atoms Versus Bits: Where to Find Innovation," *Forbes*, January 23, 2013.

64 **"bits" companies:** Nicholas P. Negroponte, "Products and Services for Computer Networks," *Scientific American* 265, no. 3 (1991): 106–15.

65 **"The old brick-and-mortar economy":** Mark Penn and Andrew Stein, "Back to the Center, Democrats," *New York Times*, July 6, 2017.

66 **"technology that could take":** John Carreyrou, *Bad Blood: Secrets and Lies in a Silicon Valley Startup* (New York: Knopf, 2018). See also John Carreyrou, "Hot Startup Theranos Has Struggled with Its Blood-Test Technology," *Wall Street Journal,* October 21, 2015.

67 **"What I really want out of life":** From a letter Holmes wrote to her father at age nine. "The World's Youngest Self-Made Female Billionaire," CBS News, April 16, 2015.

69 **University graduation rates:** Janelle Jones, John Schmitt, and Valerie Wilson, "50 Years After the Kerner Commission," Economic Policy Institute, February 26, 2018, http://bit.ly/2pivww9.

69 **Michael Jordon and Magic Johnson:** Michael Jordan owns approximately 90 percent of the NBA team the Charlotte Hornets. Magic Johnson heads a group that bought Major League Baseball's Los Angeles Dodgers from Frank McCourt for $2 billion.

69 **most recent *Forbes* list:** "Forbes Releases 2018 List of America's Richest Self-Made Women, a Ranking of the Successful Women Entrepreneurs in the Country," *Forbes,* July 11, 2018, https://bit.ly/2NI4zje.

69 **Apple CEO:** Tim Cook, "Tim Cook Speaks Up," *Bloomberg,* October 30, 2014.

69 **attitudes toward diversity:** Gary R. Hicks and Tien-Tsung Lee, "Public Attitudes Toward Gays and Lesbians: Trends and Predictors," *Journal of Homosexuality* 51, no. 2 (2006): 57–77; Andrew Markus, "Attitudes to Multiculturalism and Cultural Diversity," in *Multiculturalism and Integration: A Harmonious Relationship*, ed. James Jupp and Michael Clyne (Canberra: ANU E Press, 2011). See also "4. Attitudes Toward Increasing Diversity in the U.S.," Pew Research Center, February 16, 2017, https://pewrsr.ch/2p6nkza; and Hannah Fingerhut, "Most Americans Express Positive Views of Country's Growing Racial and Ethnic Diversity," Pew Research Center, June 14, 2018, https://pewrsr.ch/2p4LgTr.

71 **After a troubled childhood:** J. D. Vance, *Hillbilly Elegy: A Memoir of a Family and Culture in Crisis* (New York: HarperCollins, 2016).

72 **"I expect that more than *one-third*":** Larry Summers, "Men Without Work," RSS Archive, September 26, 2016, http://bit.ly/2CRCIsQ.

72 **"America's invisible crisis":** Nicholas Eberstadt, *Men Without Work: America's Invisible Crisis* (West Conshohocken, PA: Templeton Press, 2016).

72 **"the U.S. should invest in"**: "Artificial Intelligence, Automation, and the Economy," Executive Office of the President, December 20, 2016, http://bit.ly/2xmVJOD.

73 **"White House: Robots May Take"**: Andrea Riquier, "White House: Robots May Take Half of Our Jobs, and We Should Embrace It," MarketWatch, December 31, 2016, https://on.mktw.net/2xcV6q0.

73 **"rules-based"**: David H. Autor, Frank Levy, and Richard J. Murnane, "Upstairs, Downstairs: Computers and Skills on Two Floors of a Large Bank," *ILR Review* 55, no. 3 (2002): 432–47.

CHAPTER 3: A KINDER CLOCK FOR HUMAN DEVELOPMENT

76 **At fifteen, Ashley:** "Ashley" (not her real name) told her story in January 23, 2016, at the Camelback Inn in Scottsdale, Arizona. The occasion, which I attended, was the retirement party of Spring Ridge Academy founder Jeannie Courtney.

81 **Emerging research suggests:** Since the advent of functional magnetic resource imaging (fMRI) technology, the study of childhood, adolescent, and adult cognitive development has exploded, with numerous studies on the development of the prefrontal cortex, executive function, the limbic system, white matter, and myelin. To learn more about adolescent cognitive development, see Laurence Steinberg, "Cognitive and Affective Development in Adolescence," *Trends in Cognitive Sciences* 9, no. 2 (2005): 69–74; Beatriz Luna et al., "Maturation of Widely Distributed Brain Function Subserves Cognitive Development," *Neuroimage* 13, no. 5 (2001): 786–93; Sarah-Jayne Blakemore and Suparna Choudhury, "Development of the Adolescent Brain: Implications for Executive Function and Social Cognition," *Journal of Child Psychology and Psychiatry* 47, nos. 3–4 (2006): 296–312; B. J. Casey, Jay N. Giedd, and Kathleen M. Thomas, "Structural and Functional Brain Development and Its Relation to Cognitive Development," *Biological Psychology* 54, nos. 1–3 (2000): 241–57; James J. Gross, "Emotion Regulation in Adulthood: Timing Is Everything," *Current Directions in Psychological Science* 10, no. 6 (2001): 214–19; Zoltan Nagy, Helena Westerberg, and Torkel Klingberg, "Maturation of White Matter Is Associated with the Development of Cognitive Functions During Childhood," *Journal of Cognitive Neuroscience* 16, no. 7 (2004): 1227–

33; Tomáš Paus, "Mapping Brain Maturation and Cognitive Development During Adolescence," *Trends in Cognitive Sciences* 9, no. 2 (2005): 60–68; Catalina J. Hooper et al., "Adolescents' Performance on the Iowa Gambling Task: Implications for the Development of Decision Making and Ventromedial Prefrontal Cortex," *Developmental Psychology* 40, no. 6 (2004): 1148; Sara B. Johnson, Robert W. Blum, and Jay N. Giedd, "Adolescent Maturity and the Brain: The Promise and Pitfalls of Neuroscience Research in Adolescent Health Policy," *Journal of Adolescent Health* 45, no. 3 (2009): 216–21; Nitin Gogtay et al., "Dynamic Mapping of Human Cortical Development During Childhood Through Early Adulthood," *Proceedings of the National Academy of Sciences* 101, no. 21 (2004): 8174–79; David Moshman, "Cognitive Development Beyond Childhood," DigitalCommons@ University of Nebraska–Lincoln, 1998; Sarah-Jayne Blakemore et al., "Adolescent Development of the Neural Circuitry for Thinking About Intentions," *Social Cognitive and Affective Neuroscience* 2, no. 2 (2007): 130–39. For a little lighter reading, see Carl Zimmer, "You're an Adult. Your Brain, Not So Much," *New York Times*, December 21, 2016.

81 **Cognitive researchers have used:** Joaquín M. Fuster, "Frontal Lobe and Cognitive Development," *Journal of Neurocytology* 31, nos. 3–5 (2002): 373–85; Jay N. Giedd, "The Teen Brain: Insights from Neuroimaging," *Journal of Adolescent Health* 42, no. 4 (2008): 335–43; Jay N. Giedd, "Structural Magnetic Resonance Imaging of the Adolescent Brain," *Annals of the New York Academy of Sciences* 1021, no. 1 (2004): 77–85; Jay N. Giedd et al., "Brain Development During Childhood and Adolescence: A Longitudinal MRI Study," *Nature Neuroscience* 2, no. 10 (1999): 861.

84 **today's twenty-five-year-olds:** Laurence Steinberg, "The Case for Delayed Adulthood," *New York Times*, September 19, 2014.

85 **"emerging adulthood":** Jeffrey Jensen Arnett, *Emerging Adulthood: The Winding Road from the Late Teens Through the Twenties* (New York: Oxford University Press, 2004); Jeffrey Jensen Arnett, "Emerging Adulthood: A Theory of Development from the Late Teens Through the Twenties," *American Psychologist* 55, no. 5 (2000): 469; Jeffrey Jensen Arnett, "Emerging Adulthood: What Is It, and What Is It Good For?," *Child Development Perspectives* 1, no. 2 (2007): 68–73;

Jeffrey Jensen Arnett, *Adolescence and Emerging Adulthood* (Boston: Pearson, 2014). See also Robin Marantz Henig, "What Is It About 20-Somethings?," *New York Times Magazine*, August 18, 2010.

86 **new synapses continue to proliferate:** New York University neuroscientist Elkhonon Goldberg, interview by author, July 2018.

87 **"The skills I developed working":** Aubrey Dustin quoted in Celia R. Baker, "How Taking a 'Gap Year' Between High School and College Can Improve Your Life," *Deseret News*, November 4, 2013.

87 **taking a break between college:** Phil Knight, *Shoe Dog* (New York: Scribner's, 2016).

88 **"If you leave now":** Kyle DeNuccio, "Independence Days: My Perfect Imperfect Gap Year," *New York Times*, April 8, 2017.

88 **"They had higher performance outcomes":** Andrew J. Martin, "Should Students Have a Gap Year? Motivation and Performance Factors Relevant to Time Out After Completing School," *Journal of Educational Psychology* 102, no. 3 (2010): 561.

89 **gap year increased their maturity:** Nina Hoe, *American Gap Association National Alumni Survey Report* (Temple University Institute for Survey Research, 2015), http://bit.ly/2NLNx47.

89 **"Taking a gap year is a great opportunity":** Kate Simpson. "Dropping Out or Signing Up? The Professionalisation of Youth Travel," *Antipode* 37, no. 3 (2005): 447-69.

90 **no fewer than 160 colleges and universities:** Hoe, *American Gap Association National Alumni Survey Report*.

90 **Malia, took a gap year:** Valerie Strauss, "Why Harvard 'Encourages' Students to Take a Gap Year. Just like Malia Obama Is Doing," *Washington Post*, May 1, 2016.

90 **"Getting a skilled trade job":** Mark Mills, interview by author, February 2018.

91 **"At any given age, you're getting":** Joshua K. Hartshorne and Laura T. Germine, "When Does Cognitive Functioning Peak? The Asynchronous Rise and Fall of Different Cognitive Abilities Across the Life Span," *Psychological Science* 26, no. 4 (2015): 433–43; Alvin Powell, "Smarter by the Minute, Sort Of," *Harvard Gazette*, March 19, 2015, http://bit.ly/2NaCf9W; Anne Trafton, "The Rise and Fall of Cognitive Skills," *MIT News*, March 6, 2015, http://bit.ly/2CPin7s.

91 **K. Warner Schaie:** K. Warner Schaie, Sherry L. Willis, and Grace I. L. Caskie, "The Seattle Longitudinal Study: Relationship Between

Personality and Cognition," *Aging Neuropsychology and Cognition* 11, nos. 2–3 (2004): 304–24; K. Warner Schaie, "The Seattle Longitudinal Studies of Adult Intelligence," *Current Directions in Psychological Science* 2, no. 6 (1993): 171–75. See also K. Warner Schaie, ed., *Longitudinal Studies of Adult Psychological Development* (New York: Guilford Press, 1983); K. Warner Schaie, *Intellectual Development in Adulthood: The Seattle Longitudinal Study* (New York: Cambridge University Press, 1996); K. Warner Schaie, *Developmental Influences on Adult Intelligence: The Seattle Longitudinal Study* (New York: Oxford University Press, 2005); K. Warner Schaie, "Intellectual Development in Adulthood," in *Handbook of the Psychology of Aging*, ed. James E. Birren, Klaus Warner Schaie, Ronald P. Abeles, Margaret Gatz, and Timothy A. Salthouse, 4th ed. (1996); and K. Warner Schaie, "The Course of Adult Intellectual Development," *American Psychologist* 49, no. 4 (1994): 304.

92 **"How you live your life":** Richard Seven, "Study on Aging Still Going Strong Some 50 Years Later," *Seattle Times*, November 24, 2008.

92 **"It seems that the middle-aged mind":** Melissa Lee Phillips, "The Mind at Midlife," *Monitor on Psychology* 42 (2011): 38–41.

92 **"There is an enduring potential":** Ibid.

93 **two types of intelligence:** Caroline N. Harada, Marissa C. Natelson Love, and Kristen L. Triebel, "Normal Cognitive Aging," *Clinics in Geriatric Medicine* 29, no. 4 (2013): 737–52. See also Cecilia Thorsen, Jan-Eric Gustafsson, and Christina Cliffordson, "The Influence of Fluid and Crystallized Intelligence on the Development of Knowledge and Skills," *British Journal of Educational Psychology* 84, no. 4 (2014): 556–70; Andrea Christoforou et al., "GWAS-Based Pathway Analysis Differentiates Between Fluid and Crystallized Intelligence," *Genes, Brain and Behavior* 13, no. 7 (2014): 663–74.

93 **the best way for older adults to compensate:** Phillip Ackerman and Margaret E. Beier, "Trait Complexes, Cognitive Investment, and Domain Knowledge," in *Psychology of Abilities, Competencies, and Expertise,* ed. Robert J. Sternberg and Elena L. Grigorenko (New York: Cambridge University Press, 2003).

94 **"Liver transplants are like":** Mayo Clinic liver transplant specialist Dr. Charles. B. Rosen, interview by author, 2013.

94 **constantly forming neural networks:** Dr. Elkhonon Goldberg, interview by author, July 2018.

95   **What about our creativity:** Nicolas Gauvrit et al., "Human Behavioral Complexity Peaks at Age 25," *PLOS Computational Biology* 13, no. 4 (2017): e1005408.

95   **"random item generation":** Ibid.

95   **"salience network":** Elkhonon Goldberg, *Creativity: The Human Brain in the Age of Innovation* (New York: Oxford University Press, 2018). I confirmed Dr. Goldberg's thinking on "creative yield" increasing as we age in our July 2018 conversation.

96   **"Age is, of course, a fever chill":** Dirac's poem is in Benjamin F. Jones, "Age and Great Invention," *Review of Economics and Statistics* 92, no. 1 (2010).

96   **average age of discovery:** Benjamin F. Jones and Bruce A. Weinberg, "Age Dynamics in Scientific Creativity," *Proceedings of the National Academy of Sciences* 108, no. 47 (2011): 18910–14. See also Benjamin Jones, E. J. Reedy, and Bruce A. Weinberg, "Age and Scientific Genius" (working paper no. 19866, National Bureau of Economic Research, 2014), http://www.nber.org/papers/w19866.

96   **peak innovation age is:** Pagan Kennedy, "To Be a Genius, Think Like a 94-Year-Old," *New York Times*, April 7, 2017.

96   **average age of U.S. patent applicants:** Ibid.

97   **"so cheap, lightweight and safe":** Ibid.

97   **average age of entrepreneurship:** Robert W. Fairlie et al., "The Kauffman Index 2015: Startup Activity| National Trends," May 2015, doi .org/10.2139/ssrn.2613479.

97   **Erik Erikson:** Erikson is well known for his eight-stage theory of psychological development, issued in 1959. Stage seven, ages forty to sixty-five, is known as "Generativity vs. Stagnation" and is a time when "people experience a need to create or nurture things that will outlast them, often having mentees or creating positive changes that will benefit other people." Saul McLeod, "Erik Erikson's Stages of Psychosocial Development," *Simply Psychology,* 2018, http://bit.ly /2Multx9.

CHAPTER 4: WORTH THE WAIT: THE SIX STRENGTHS OF
LATE BLOOMERS

106 **All healthy children have curiosity in buckets:** "At no time in life is curiosity more powerful than in early childhood," writes the eminent child psychiatrist Dr. Bruce D. Perry. "Why Young Children Are Curious," *Scholastic*, n.d., http://bit.ly/2xgGAxo.

107 **"curiosity, a passion":** "The 100 Best Companies to Work For," *Fortune*, 2017, https://for.tn/2QoKrl3.

107 **"overlooked key":** Michael Hvisdos and Janet Gerhard, "Hiring for Curiosity, the Overlooked Key to Business Innovation," Recruiter, October 3, 2017, http://bit.ly/2xnqyCK.

107 **"People should consider it":** Don Peppers, "Why Curiosity Is a Prerequisite for Innovation," *Inc.*, September 21, 2016, http://bit.ly /2Mkdnke.

108 **"curiosity is a cognitive process":** "The Neuroscience Behind Curiosity and Motivation," *Cube*, April 21, 2015, http://bit.ly/2pj5yZJ.

108 **"an important role in maintaining":** Sakaki Michiko, Ayano Yagi, and Kou Murayama, "Curiosity in Old Age: A Possible Key to Achieving Adaptive Aging," *Neuroscience and Biobehavioral Reviews* 88 (May 2018): 106–16.

109 **With empathy, we feel another's pain:** Jeffrey Weiner, "Managing Compassionately," *LinkedIn Pulse*, October 15, 2012, http://bit .ly/2xwmoaT.

109 **Among college students:** Sasha Zarins and Sara Konrath, "Changes over Time in Compassion-Related Variables in the United States," in *The Oxford Handbook of Compassion Science*, ed. Emma M. Seppälä et al. (New York: Oxford University Press, 2016); Sara H. Konrath, Edward H. O'Brien, and Courtney Hsing, "Changes in Dispositional Empathy in American College Students over Time: A Meta-Analysis," *Personality and Social Psychology Review* 15, no. 2 (2011): 180–98.

109 **They show greater reflective thinking:** Mihaly Csikszentmihalyi and Kevin Rathunde, "The Psychology of Wisdom: An Evolutionary Interpretation," in *Wisdom: Its Nature, Origins, and Development*, ed. Robert J. Sternberg (Cambridge: Cambridge University Press, 1990); V. P. Clayton and J. E. Birren, "The Development of Wisdom Across the Life Span: A Reexamination of an Ancient Topic," in *Life-Span Development and Behavior*, ed. P. B. Baltes and O. G. Brim, Jr. (San

Diego: Academic Press, 1980); Monika Ardelt, "Antecedents and Effects of Wisdom in Old Age: A Longitudinal Perspective on Aging Well," *Research on Aging* 22, no. 4 (2000): 360–94.

109 **"reduction in self-centeredness":** Monika Ardelt, "Empirical Assessment of a Three-Dimensional Wisdom Scale," *Research on Aging* 25, no. 3 (2003): 275–324.

109 **"having a wide horizon":** Phyllis Korkki, "The Science of Older and Wiser," *New York Times*, March 12, 2014.

109 **eight-man American rowing team:** Daniel J. Brown, interview by Susan Salter Reynolds, 2015.

111 **Compassionate leaders appear to be stronger:** Shimul Melwani, Jennifer S. Mueller, and Jennifer R. Overbeck, "Looking Down: The Influence of Contempt and Compassion on Emergent Leadership Categorizations," *Journal of Applied Psychology* 97, no. 6 (2012): 1171.

111 **improves employee retention:** Hershey H. Friedman and Miriam Gerstein, "Leading with Compassion: The Key to Changing the Organizational Culture and Achieving Success," *Psychosociological Issues in Human Resource Management* 5, no. 1 (2017); M. Gemma Cherry et al., "Emotional Intelligence in Medical Education: A Critical Review," *Medical Education* 48, no. 5 (2014): 468–78; Matthew J. Williams et al., "Examining the Factor Structures of the Five Facet Mindfulness Questionnaire and the Self-Compassion Scale," *Psychological Assessment* 26, no. 2 (2014): 407; Clara Strauss et al., "What Is Compassion and How Can We Measure It? A Review of Definitions and Measures," *Clinical Psychology Review* 47 (2016): 15–27.

111 **reduction in sick leave:** J. Williams, G. Mark, and Willem Kuyken, "Mindfulness-Based Cognitive Therapy: A Promising New Approach to Preventing Depressive Relapse," *British Journal of Psychiatry* 200, no. 5 (2012): 359–60.

111 **"farsighted, tolerant, humane":** Rajendra Sisodia, David Wolfe, and Jagdish N. Sheth, *Firms of Endearment: How World-Class Companies Profit from Passion and Purpose* (Upper Saddle River, NJ: Wharton, 2007).

111 **"achieve significantly higher levels":** Kim Cameron et al., "Effects of Positive Practices on Organizational Effectiveness," *Journal of Applied Behavioral Science* 47, no. 3 (2011): 266–308.

1380, en route to Philadelphia, on April 17, 2018. As starting points, I recommend Eli Rosenberg, "She Landed a Southwest Plane After an Engine Exploded. She Wasn't Supposed to Be Flying That Day," *Washington Post*, May 10, 2018.

116 **WNMU was unranked:** "MidAmerica Nazarene University: Overview," *U.S. News & World Report*, http://bit.ly/2OpH0c4. Its acceptance rate is cited in "MidAmerica Nazarene University: Ranking Indicators," http://bit.ly/2CQV5Ie. For WSNM's rankings, see "Western New Mexico University: Rankings," http://bit.ly/2OkRvgS.

116 **"ziggurat":** Tom Wolfe, *The Right Stuff* (New York: Random House, 2005).

117 **"nerves of steel":** Samantha Schmidt, " 'Nerves of Steel': She Calmly Landed the Southwest Flight, Just as You'd Expect of a Former Fighter Pilot," *Washington Post*, April 18, 2018.

117 **"happiness becomes less":** Heidi Grant Halvorson, "How Happiness Changes with Age," *Atlantic*, May 28, 2013.

117 **excitement and elation:** Cassie Mogilner, Sepandar D. Kamvar, and Jennifer Aaker, "The Shifting Meaning of Happiness," *Social Psychological and Personality Science* 2, no. 4 (2011): 395–402.

118 **optimal performance quickly degrades:** Robert Sanders, "Researchers Find Out Why Some Stress Is Good for You," *Berkeley News*, April 16, 2013, http://bit.ly/2pkaBcm. See also Elizabeth D. Kirby et al., "Acute Stress Enhances Adult Rat Hippocampal Neurogenesis and Activation of Newborn Neurons Via Secreted Astrocytic FGF2," *eLife*, April 16, 2013, http://bit.ly/2pi8NjT.

118 **we're better problem solvers:** Travis Bradberry, "How Successful People Stay Calm," *Forbes*, February 6, 2014, http://bit.ly/2x8XWMK.

118 **under stress, people gravitate:** Brent Gleeson, *Taking Point: A Navy SEAL's 10 Fail-Safe Principles for Leading Through Change* (New York: Touchstone, 2018).

118 **By conventional standards:** Coach Bill Walsh, several interviews by author, 1992–94. We would meet at his Stanford office to discuss his column on innovative management for *Forbes ASAP*. During one meeting he told me about the football short-passing insight derived from watching a high school basketball team conducting a full-court press drill during practice.

119 **"early to mid-30s":** Elkhonon Goldberg, *Creativity: The Human Brain in the Age of Innovation* (New York: Oxford University Press, 2018).

111 **"compassion is good for"**: Emma Seppälä, *The Happiness Track: How to Apply the Science of Happiness to Accelerate Your Success* (New York: HarperCollins, 2017).

112 **"but then the lid came off"**: *This Emotional Life: My Transformation from High School Dropout to Surgeon* (documentary), PBS, aired January 4, 2011.

112 **Rick Ankiel, by contrast, had a charmed life:** On the story of the St. Louis Cardinals pitcher and his sudden loss of directional control, I especially liked the late Charles Krauthammer's "The Return of the Natural," *Washington Post*, August 17, 2007, not least because Krauthammer tragically lost his own youthful prowess when he broke his neck in a diving accident, resulting in quadriplegia.

113 **Janet Schneider was born into a blue-collar family:** Janet Evanovich's story derives from her website, Evanovich.com; "Janet's Bio," Janet Evanovich, n.d., https://bit.ly/2Qnj9LE; and Debra Nussbaum, "In Person: Imagine Trenton. One Author Did," *New York Times*, November 3, 2002.

113 **A Taiwanese teenager failed:** "Family and Friends Praise Ang Lee's Quiet Dedication," *Taipei Times*, March 7, 2006.

114 **"resilience is that ineffable quality"**: "All About Resilience," *Psychology Today*, n.d., http://bit.ly/2D6hY0M.

114 **"an ongoing process of responding"**: Dr. Morton Shaevitz, *Cuida Health Blog*, January 23, 2018, http://bit.ly/2xvyilD.

115 **"There is a naturally learnable set"**: Adam Grant quoted in Tara Parker-Pope, "How to Build Resilience in Midlife," *New York Times*, July 25, 2017.

115 **students who acknowledged the adversity:** Joshua D. Margolis and Paul G. Stoltz, "How to Bounce Back from Adversity," *Harvard Business Review* 88, nos. 1–2 (2010): 86–92.

115 **tend to be self-centered:** Henry Bodkin, "Teenagers Are Hard Wired to Be Selfish, Say Scientists," *Telegraph*, October 6, 2016, http://bit.ly/2CQVh08.

115 **"brittle"**: Carol Dweck, interview by author, August 2016.

116 **This Tammie Jo grew up on a ranch:** The amazing story of Southwest Airlines pilot Captain Tammie Jo Shults was widely reported following the catastrophic engine failure and depressurization of Flight

122 **quantify and define wisdom:** Vivian Clayton quoted in Stephen S. Hall, "The Older-and-Wiser Hypothesis," *New York Times Magazine*, May 6, 2007; Phyllis Korkki, "The Science of Older and Wiser," *New York Times*, March 12, 2014.

123 **"an interest in wisdom":** Paul B. Baltes and Ursula M. Staudinger, "The Search for a Psychology of Wisdom," *Current Directions in Psychological Science* 2, no. 3 (1993): 75–81; Paul B. Baltes, Jacqui Smith, and Ursula M. Staudinger, "Wisdom and Successful Aging," in *Nebraska Symposium on Motivation*, ed. T. Sonderegger (Lincoln: University of Nebraska Press, 1992); Ursula M. Staudinger, Jacqui Smith, and Paul B. Baltes, "Wisdom-Related Knowledge in a Life Review Task: Age Differences and the Role of Professional Specialization," *Psychology and Aging* 7, no. 2 (1992): 271; Hall, "Older-and-Wiser Hypothesis"; Korkki, "Science of Older and Wiser."

123 **"Great executives know how":** Julie Sweet, interview by author, March 2018.

123 **wisdom emerges through:** Monika Ardelt, "Wisdom and Life Satisfaction in Old Age," *Journals of Gerontology Series B: Psychological Sciences and Social Sciences* 52, no. 1 (1997): P15–P27; Ardelt, "Antecedents and Effects of Wisdom in Old Age"; Francesca G. E. Happé, Ellen Winner, and Hiram Brownell, "The Getting of Wisdom: Theory of Mind in Old Age," *Developmental Psychology* 34, no. 2 (1998): 358; Ursula M. Staudinger, "Older and Wiser? Integrating Results on the Relationship Between Age and Wisdom-Related Performance," *International Journal of Behavioral Development* 23, no. 3 (1999): 641–64.

123 **"what doesn't go down":** Ursula Staudinger quoted in Anil Ananthaswamy, "The Wisdom of the Aging Brain," *Nautilus*, May 12, 2016, http://bit.ly/2xrFlvy.

124 **"cognitive templates":** Goldberg, *Creativity*. See also Barbara Strauch, *The Secret Life of the Grown-Up Brain: The Surprising Talents of the Middle-Aged Mind* (New York: Penguin, 2010).

124 **"social expertise":** Thomas M. Hess and Corinne Auman, "Aging and Social Expertise: The Impact of Trait-Diagnostic Information on Impressions of Others," *Psychology and Aging* 16, no. 3 (2001): 497; Christina M. Leclerc and Thomas M. Hess, "Age Differences in the Bases for Social Judgments: Tests of a Social Expertise Perspective," *Experimental Aging Research* 33, no. 1 (2007): 95–120; Thomas M. Hess, Nicole L. Osowski, and Christina M. Leclerc, "Age and

Experience Influences on the Complexity of Social Inferences," *Psychology and Aging* 20, no. 3 (2005): 447; Thomas M. Hess, Daniel C. Rosenberg, and Sandra J. Waters, "Motivation and Representational Processes in Adulthood: The Effects of Social Accountability and Information Relevance," *Psychology and Aging* 16, no. 4 (2001): 629.

124 **"It's stunning how well":** Strauch, *The Secret Life of the Grown-Up Brain*. See also Trey Hedden and John D. E. Gabrieli, "Insights into the Ageing Mind: A View from Cognitive Neuroscience," *Nature Reviews Neuroscience* 5, no. 2 (2004): 87.

125 **"greater sensitivity to fine-grained":** Michael Ramscar et al., "The Myth of Cognitive Decline: Non-Linear Dynamics of Lifelong Learning," *Topics in Cognitive Science* 6, no. 1 (2014): 5–42.

125 **a specific neurocircuitry of wisdom:** Ananthaswamy, "The Wisdom of the Aging Brain." See also Dilip V. Jeste and James C. Harris, "Wisdom—a Neuroscience Perspective," *JAMA* 304, no. 14 (2010): 1602–3; Colin A. Depp and Dilip V. Jeste, "Definitions and Predictors of Successful Aging: A Comprehensive Review of Larger Quantitative Studies," *American Journal of Geriatric Psychiatry* 14, no. 1 (2006): 6–20; Thomas W. Meeks and Dilip V. Jeste, "Neurobiology of Wisdom: A Literature Overview," *Archives of General Psychiatry* 66, no. 4 (2009): 355–65; Dilip V. Jeste et al., "Expert Consensus on Characteristics of Wisdom: A Delphi Method Study," *Gerontologist* 50, no. 5 (2010): 668–80; Dilip V. Jeste and Andrew J. Oswald, "Individual and Societal Wisdom: Explaining the Paradox of Human Aging and High Well-Being," *Psychiatry: Interpersonal and Biological Processes* 77, no. 4 (2014): 317–30.

126 **Hemispheric Asymmetry Reduction:** Ananthaswamy, "The Wisdom of the Aging Brain." See also Roberto Cabeza, "Hemispheric Asymmetry Reduction in Older Adults: The HAROLD Model," *Psychology and Aging* 17, no. 1 (2002): 85.

126 **older adults tend to use both:** Simon W. Davis et al., "Frequency-Specific Neuromodulation of Local and Distant Connectivity in Aging and Episodic Memory Function," *Human Brain Mapping* 38, no. 12 (2017): 5987–6004; Patricia A. Reuter-Lorenz, Louise Stanczak, and Andrea C. Miller, "Neural Recruitment and Cognitive Aging: Two Hemispheres Are Better Than One, Especially as You Age," *Psychological Science* 10, no. 6 (1999): 494–500; Patricia A. Reuter-Lorenz et al., "Age Differences in the Frontal Lateralization of Verbal

and Spatial Working Memory Revealed by PET," *Journal of Cognitive Neuroscience* 12, no. 1 (2000): 174–87; Kenneth Hugdahl, "Lateralization of Cognitive Processes in the Brain," *Acta Psychologica* 105, nos. 2–3 (2000): 211–35; Roberto Cabeza et al., "Task-Independent and Task-Specific Age Effects on Brain Activity During Working Memory, Visual Attention and Episodic Retrieval," *Cerebral Cortex* 14, no. 4 (2004): 364–75; Patricia A. Reuter-Lorenz, "New Visions of the Aging Mind and Brain," *Trends in Cognitive Sciences* 6, no. 9 (2002): 394–400.

126 **best-performing older adults:** Roberto Cabeza et al., "Aging Gracefully: Compensatory Brain Activity in High-Performing Older Adults," *Neuroimage* 17, no. 3 (2002): 1394–402.

126: **"brain integration":** Strauch, *The Secret Life of the Grown-Up Brain.* See also George Bartzokis et al., "Age-Related Changes in Frontal and Temporal Lobe Volumes in Men: A Magnetic Resonance Imaging Study," *Archives of General Psychiatry* 58, no. 5 (2001): 461–65.

127: **nothing to do with the early-blooming:** Ardelt, "Antecedents and Effects of Wisdom in Old Age."

CHAPTER 5: CREATE YOUR OWN HEALTHY CULTURE

129 **"I was raised in a system":** Erik Wahl, interview by author, 2016. I came to know him during a Vistage conference in 2014 and was astonished by the emotional power of his onstage performance.

133 **Our parents play a key role:** Few people are as important as our parents in shaping our beliefs, personalities, and aspirations—and therefore our futures. There's nearly an endless amount of research on this topic, but start with E. Mavis Hetherington, Martha Cox, and Roger Cox, "Effects of Divorce on Parents and Children," in *Nontraditional Families: Parenting and Child Development,* ed. Michael E. Lamb (Hillsdale, NJ: Erlbaum, 1982); Joan Kaufman and Edward Zigler, "Do Abused Children Become Abusive Parents?," *American Journal of Orthopsychiatry* 57, no. 2 (1987): 186–92; ALSPAC Study Team, "ALSPAC—the Avon Longitudinal Study of Parents and Children," *Paediatric and Perinatal Epidemiology* 15, no. 1 (2001): 74–87; Kathleen V. Hoover-Dempsey and Howard M. Sandler, "Parental Involvement in Children's Education: Why Does It Make a Difference?," *Teachers College Record* 97, no. 2 (1995): 310–31; Gillian Pugh, Erica

De'Ath, and Celia Smith, *Confident Parents, Confident Children: Policy and Practice in Parent Education and Support* (Washington, DC: National Children's Bureau, 1994); Concha Delgado-Gaitan, *Literacy for Empowerment: The Role of Parents in Children's Education* (London: Routledge, 1990); Sylvia Palmer and Larry Cochran, "Parents as Agents of Career Development," *Journal of Counseling Psychology* 35, no. 1 (1988): 71; Ashton D. Trice and Linda Knapp, "Relationship of Children's Career Aspirations to Parents' Occupations," *Journal of Genetic Psychology* 153, no. 3 (1992): 355–57; Richard A. Young and John D. Friesen, "The Intentions of Parents in Influencing the Career Development of Their Children," *Career Development Quarterly* 40, no. 3 (1992): 198–206; and Ramona Paloş and Loredana Drobot, "The Impact of Family Influence on the Career Choice of Adolescents," *Procedia—Social and Behavioral Sciences* 2, no. 2 (2010): 3407–11.

133 **"For my family and my friends":** Robert Zemeckis, interview published by the Academy of Achievement: A Museum of Living History, June 29, 1996.

134 **They influence our achievement:** Jill Antonishak, Erin L. Sutfin, and N. Dickon Reppucci, "Community Influence on Adolescent Development," in *Handbook of Adolescent Behavioral Problems: Evidence-Based Approaches to Prevention and Treatment,* ed. Thomas P. Gullotta and Gerald R. Adams (Boston: Springer, 2005); Cristina L. Reitz-Krueger et al., "Community Influence on Adolescent Development," in *Handbook of Adolescent Behavioral Problems: Evidence-Based Approaches to Prevention and Treatment,* ed. Thomas P. Gullotta, Robert W. Plant, and Melanie A. Evans (Boston: Springer, 2015); Margo Gardner and Laurence Steinberg, "Peer Influence on Risk Taking, Risk Preference, and Risky Decision Making in Adolescence and Adulthood: An Experimental Study," *Developmental Psychology* 41, no. 4 (2005): 625; Jeanne Brooks-Gunn et al., "Do Neighborhoods Influence Child and Adolescent Development?," *American Journal of Sociology* 99, no. 2 (1993): 353–95; Tamara F. Mangleburg, Patricia M. Doney, and Terry Bristol, "Shopping with Friends and Teens' Susceptibility to Peer Influence," *Journal of Retailing* 80, no. 2 (2004): 101–16; Karl E. Bauman and Susan T. Ennett, "On the Importance of Peer Influence for Adolescent Drug Use: Commonly Neglected Considerations," *Addiction* 91, no. 2 (1996): 185–98; Jason Chein et al., "Peers

Increase Adolescent Risk Taking by Enhancing Activity in the Brain's Reward Circuitry," *Developmental Science* 14, no. 2 (2011): F1–F10.

134 **peer pressure doesn't end with our teenage years:** Laurence Steinberg and Kathryn C. Monahan, "Age Differences in Resistance to Peer Influence," *Developmental Psychology* 43, no. 6 (2007): 1531; Gardner and Steinberg, "Peer Influence on Risk Taking."

135 **"People talk about hard work":** J. D. Vance, *Hillbilly Elegy: A Memoir of a Family and Culture in Crisis* (New York: HarperCollins, 2016).

135 **Childhood poverty is correlated:** It's very difficult to zero in on accurate numbers for the health effects of poverty. But when it comes to both the immediate and long-term negative effects poverty has on children, the research is overwhelming. See Greg J. Duncan and Jeanne Brooks-Gunn, "Family Poverty, Welfare Reform, and Child Development," *Child Development* 71, no. 1 (2000): 188–96; Gary W. Evans, "The Environment of Childhood Poverty," *American Psychologist* 59, no. 2 (2004): 77; Rebecca M. Ryan, Rebecca C. Fauth, and Jeanne Brooks-Gunn, "Childhood Poverty: Implications for School Readiness and Early Childhood Education," in *Handbook of Research on the Education of Young Children*, ed. Bernard Spodek and Olivia N. Saracho, 2nd ed. (Hillsdale, NJ: Erlbaum, 2007); Greg J. Duncan et al., "How Much Does Childhood Poverty Affect the Life Chances of Children?," *American Sociological Review* 63, no. 3 (1998): 406–23; Gary W. Evans and Pilyoung Kim, "Childhood Poverty and Health: Cumulative Risk Exposure and Stress Dysregulation," *Psychological Science* 18, no. 11 (2007): 953–57; Valentina Nikulina, Cathy Spatz Widom, and Sally Czaja, "The Role of Childhood Neglect and Childhood Poverty in Predicting Mental Health, Academic Achievement and Crime in Adulthood," *American Journal of Community Psychology* 48, nos. 3–4 (2011): 309–21; J. Lawrence Aber et al., "The Effects of Poverty on Child Health and Development," *Annual Review of Public Health* 18, no. 1 (1997): 463–83; Daniel T. Lichter, Michael J. Shanahan, and Erica L. Gardner, "Helping Others? The Effects of Childhood Poverty and Family Instability on Prosocial Behavior," *Youth and Society* 34, no. 1 (2002): 89–119; Natalie Slopen et al., "Poverty, Food Insecurity, and the Behavior for Childhood Internalizing and Externalizing Disorders," *Journal of the American Academy of Child and Adolescent Psychiatry* 49, no. 5 (2010): 444–52; Clancy Blair and

C. Cybele Raver, "Child Development in the Context of Adversity: Experiential Canalization of Brain and Behavior," *American Psychologist* 67, no. 4 (2012): 309; Martha J. Farah et al., "Childhood Poverty: Specific Associations with Neurocognitive Development," *Brain Research* 1110, no. 1 (2006): 166–74; and Katherine A. Magnuson and Elizabeth Votruba-Drzal, *Enduring Influences of Childhood Poverty* (Madison: University of Wisconsin, Institute for Research on Poverty, 2008).

136 **the wealth gap between rich and poor:** Rakesh Kochhar and Anthony Cilluffo, "How Wealth Inequality Has Changed in the U.S. Since the Great Recession, by Race, Ethnicity and Income," Pew Research Center, November 1, 2017, https://pewrsr.ch/2NXW6IS.

136 **"Pressure from peers might cause":** Shilagh Mirgain quoted in "Dealing with Peer Pressure When You're an Adult," *UW Health*, September 21, 2015, http://bit.ly/2OnPfpq.

138 **"the highest cultural grouping":** Samuel P. Huntington, "The Clash of Civilizations?," *Foreign Affairs* 72, no. 3 (Summer 1993): 22–49.

138 **The society we live in provides:** Hazel R. Markus and Shinobu Kitayama, "Culture and the Self: Implications for Cognition, Emotion, and Motivation," *Psychological Review* 98, no. 2 (1991): 224; Robert M. Bond et al., "A 61-Million-Person Experiment in Social Influence and Political Mobilization," *Nature* 489, no. 7415 (2012): 295; Teun A. Van Dijk, *Society and Discourse: How Social Contexts Influence Text and Talk* (New York: Cambridge University Press, 2009); Cristina Bicchieri, *The Grammar of Society: The Nature and Dynamics of Social Norms* (New York: Cambridge University Press, 2005); Michael Marmot et al., *Fair Society, Healthy Lives: The Marmot Review* (London: Institute of Health Equality, 2010); Peter Aggleton and Richard Parker, *Culture, Society and Sexuality: A Reader* (London: Routledge, 2002).

138 **we spend nearly eleven hours per day:** John Koblin, "How Much Do We Love TV? Let Us Count the Ways," *New York Times*, June 30, 2016.

138 **the mass media:** The literature on the power and effects of media on us is overwhelming. Here is a small sample: Craig A. Anderson et al., "The Influence of Media Violence on Youth," *Psychological Science in the Public Interest* 4, no. 3 (2003): 81–110; L. Rowell Huesmann, "Psychological Processes Promoting the Relation Between Exposure

to Media Violence and Aggressive Behavior by the Viewer," *Journal of Social Issues* 42, no. 3 (1986): 125–39; Albert Bandura, "Social Cognitive Theory of Mass Communication," in *Media Effects: Advances in Theory and Research,* ed. Jennings Bryant and Mary Beth Oliver, 3rd ed. (New York: Routledge, 2009); Cynthia-Lou Coleman, "The Influence of Mass Media and Interpersonal Communication on Societal and Personal Risk Judgments," *Communication Research* 20, no. 4 (1993): 611–28; Kristen E. Van Vonderen and William Kinnally, "Media Effects on Body Image: Examining Media Exposure in the Broader Context of Internal and Other Social Factors," *American Communication Journal* 14, no. 2 (2012): 41–57; Rebecca Coleman, "The Becoming of Bodies: Girls, Media Effects, and Body Image," *Feminist Media Studies* 8, no. 2 (2008): 163–79; Shelly Grabe, L. Monique Ward, and Janet Shibley Hyde, "The Role of the Media in Body Image Concerns Among Women: A Meta-Analysis of Experimental and Correlational Studies," *Psychological Bulletin* 134, no. 3 (2008): 460; Patti M. Valkenburg, Jochen Peter, and Joseph B. Walther, "Media Effects: Theory and Research," *Annual Review of Psychology* 67 (2016): 315–38; Christopher P. Barlett, Christopher L. Vowels, and Donald A. Saucier, "Meta-Analyses of the Effects of Media Images on Men's Body-Image Concerns," *Journal of Social and Clinical Psychology* 27, no. 3 (2008): 279–310; Brad J. Bushman and L. Rowell Huesmann, "Short-Term and Long-Term Effects of Violent Media on Aggression in Children and Adults," *Archives of Pediatrics and Adolescent Medicine* 160, no. 4 (2006): 348–52; and Yuko Yamamiya et al., "Women's Exposure to Thin-and-Beautiful Media Images: Body Image Effects of Media-Ideal Internalization and Impact-Reduction Interventions," *Body Image* 2, no. 1 (2005): 74–80.

138 **average American high school student:** Again, these numbers are hard to pin down. The reality is, how much TV we watch—or how much we use any form of media or technology—varies as we adopt new habits and new devices. Suffice it to say that when it comes to TV, we watch a lot.

139 **"by reinforcing existing values":** Joan E. Grusec and Paul David Hastings, eds., *Handbook of Socialization: Theory and Research* (New York: Guilford, 2014).

140 **"cultivation":** James Shanahan and Michael Morgan, *Television and Its Viewers: Cultivation Theory and Research* (New York: Cambridge

University Press, 1999); W. James Potter, "Cultivation Theory and Research: A Conceptual Critique," *Human Communication Research* 19, no. 4 (1993): 564–601; W. James Potter, "A Critical Analysis of Cultivation Theory," *Journal of Communication* 64, no. 6 (2014): 1015–36; Michael Morgan, James Shanahan, and Nancy Signorielli, "Growing Up with Television: Cultivation Processes," *Media Effects: Advances in Theory and Research* 3 (2009): 34–49.

141 **Social norms are a society's unstated rules:** Rachel I. McDonald and Christian S. Crandall, "Social Norms and Social Influence," *Current Opinion in Behavioral Sciences* 3 (2015): 147–51; Robert B. Cialdini, Carl A. Kallgren, and Raymond R. Reno, "A Focus Theory of Normative Conduct: A Theoretical Refinement and Reevaluation of the Role of Norms in Human Behavior," in *Advances in Experimental Social Psychology*, ed. Mark P. Zanna, vol. 24 (San Diego, CA: Academic Press, 1991); Carl A. Kallgren, Raymond R. Reno, and Robert B. Cialdini, "A Focus Theory of Normative Conduct: When Norms Do and Do Not Affect Behavior," *Personality and Social Psychology Bulletin* 26, no. 8 (2000): 1002–12; Maria Knight Lapinski and Rajiv N. Rimal, "An Explication of Social Norms," *Communication Theory* 15, no. 2 (2005): 127–47; Ernst Fehr and Urs Fischbacher, "Social Norms and Human Cooperation," *Trends in Cognitive Sciences* 8, no. 4 (2004): 185–90; Robert B. Cialdini and Melanie R. Trost, "Social Influence: Social Norms, Conformity and Compliance," in *The Handbook of Social Psychology*, ed. D. T. Gilbert, S. T. Fiske, and G. Lindzey, vol. 2 (New York: McGraw-Hill, 1998).

142 **Imagine that you've been asked:** Solomon E. Asch and H. Guetzkow, "Effects of Group Pressure upon the Modification and Distortion of Judgments," in *Groups, Leadership, and Men: Research in Human Relations*, ed. Harold Steere Guetzkow (Pittsburgh: Carnegie Press, 1951); Solomon E. Asch, "Group Forces in the Modification and Distortion of Judgments," *Social Psychology* 10 (1952): 450–501.

143 **A number of subsequent studies:** Rod Bond and Peter B. Smith, "Culture and Conformity: A Meta-Analysis of Studies Using Asch's (1952b, 1956) Line Judgment Task," *Psychological Bulletin* 119, no. 1 (1996): 111–37. A caveat: Many other subsequent studies were unable to reproduce Asch's results, to the point that some researchers suggested that the "Asch effect" was a product of the conformist 1950s.

144 **most of us are clueless:** Jessica M. Nolan et al., "Normative Social Influence Is Underdetected," *Personality and Social Psychology Bulletin* 34, no. 7 (2008): 913–23; Wesley P. Schultz, Azar M. Khazian, and Adam C. Zaleski, "Using Normative Social Influence to Promote Conservation Among Hotel Guests," *Social Influence* 3, no. 1 (2008): 4–23; Rishee K. Jain et al., "Can Social Influence Drive Energy Savings? Detecting the Impact of Social Influence on the Energy Consumption Behavior of Networked Users Exposed to Normative Eco-Feedback," *Energy and Buildings* 66 (2013): 119–27.

144 **"Given the ubiquity and strength":** Robert Cialdini quoted in Nolan et al., "Normative Social Influence Is Underdetected."

144 **Normative thinking creates the belief:** Todd Rose, *The End of Average: How We Succeed in a World That Values Sameness* (New York: HarperCollins, 2015).

146 **"Call it a clan, call it a network":** Jane Howard, *Margaret Mead: A Life* (New York: Ballantine Books, 1989).

146 **physiological effects of deviation:** Gregory S. Berns et al., "Neurobiological Correlates of Social Conformity and Independence During Mental Rotation," *Biological Psychiatry* 58, no. 3 (2005): 245–53. See also Mirre Stallen, Ale Smidts, and Alan Sanfey, "Peer Influence: Neural Mechanisms Underlying In-Group Conformity," *Frontiers in Human Neuroscience* 7 (2013): 50; Mirre Stallen and Alan G. Sanfey, "The Neuroscience of Social Conformity: Implications for Fundamental and Applied Research," *Frontiers in Neuroscience* 9 (2015): 337; Juan F. Domínguez D, Sreyneth A. Taing, and Pascal Molenberghs, "Why Do Some Find It Hard to Disagree? An fMRI Study," *Frontiers in Human Neuroscience* 9 (2016): 718.

CHAPTER 6: QUIT! SUBVERSIVE ADVICE FOR
LATE BLOOMERS

149 **books extol the benefits of determination:** Charles Duhigg, *The Power of Habit: Why We Do What We Do in Life and Business* (New York: Random House, 2013); Jocko Willink and Leif Babin, *Discipline Equals Freedom* (New York: St. Martin's Press, 2017); Kelly McGonigal, *The Willpower Instinct: How Self-Control Works, Why It Matters, and What You Can Do to Get More of It* (New York: Penguin, 2011);

William H. McRaven, *Make Your Bed: Little Things That Can Change Your Life . . . and Maybe the World* (New York: Grand Central Publishing, 2017); Jordan B. Peterson, *12 Rules for Life: An Antidote to Chaos* (Toronto: Random House Canada, 2018).

149 **"Even before I was seventeen":** Daniel J. Brown, interview by *Late Bloomers* contributor Susan Salter Reynolds, 2015.

152 **"exhibit[ed] clear interest in the chocolates":** Hans Villarica, "The Chocolate-and-Radish Experiment That Birthed the Modern Conception of Willpower," *Atlantic*, April 9, 2012. See also R. F. Baumeister et al., "Ego Depletion: Is the Active Self a Limited Resource?," *Journal of Personality and Social Psychology* 74, no. 5 (1998): 1252–65; R. F. Baumeister et al., "The Strength Model of Self-Control," *Current Directions in Psychological Science* 16 (2007): 351–55; M. Muraven and R. F. Baumeister, "Self-Regulation and Depletion of Limited Resources: Does Self-Control Resemble a Muscle?" *Psychological Bulletin* 126, no. 2 (2000): 247–59; D. Tice et al., "Restoring the Self: Positive Affect Helps Improve Self-Regulation Following Ego Depletion," *Journal of Experimental Social Psychology* 43, no. 3 (2007): 379–84.

153 **The rider (the ego) is generally in charge:** Sigmund Freud, *The Ego and the Id: Standard Edition,* ed. James Strachey (1923; New York: W. W. Norton, 1960).

154 **"Over his career, he trained thirty-one":** Kenny Moore, *Bowerman and the Men of Oregon: The Story of Oregon's Legendary Coach and Nike's Cofounder* (Emmaus, PA: Rodale, 2006).

155 **"Bowerman began exhorting":** Ibid.

157 **a woman who'd just made partner:** William Burnett and David John Evans, *Designing Your Life: How to Build a Well-Lived, Joyful Life* (New York: Knopf, 2016).

157 **quitting is actually a healthy thing:** Carsten Wrosch et al., "Giving Up on Unattainable Goals: Benefits for Health?," *Personality and Social Psychology Bulletin* 33, no. 2 (2007): 251–65.

158 **Andy Grove and his company, Intel:** For the story of how Intel decided to quit its original line of business, memory chips, see Andrew Grove, *Only the Paranoid Survive* (New York: Doubleday, 1996).

158 **"I asked Gordon [Moore], you know":** Laura Sydell, "Digital Pioneer Andrew Grove Led Intel's Shift From Chips to Microprocessors," NPR, March 22, 2016, https://n.pr/2MvQCAm.

160 **Sunk cost is the money, time:** Hal R. Arkes and Catherine Blumer, "The Psychology of Sunk Cost," in *Judgment and Decision Making: An Interdisciplinary Reader*, ed. Terry Connolly, Hal R. Arkes, and Kenneth R. Hammond, 2nd ed. (New York: Cambridge University Press, 2000).

160 **The sunk-cost fallacy is:** Daniel Friedman et al., "Searching for the Sunk Cost Fallacy," *Experimental Economics* 10, no. 1 (2007): 79–104.

160 **opportunity cost:** John W. Payne, James R. Bettman, and Mary Frances Luce, "When Time Is Money: Decision Behavior Under Opportunity-Cost Time Pressure," *Organizational Behavior and Human Decision Processes* 66, no. 2 (1996): 131–52; Robert Kurzban et al., "An Opportunity Cost Model of Subjective Effort and Task Performance," *Behavioral and Brain Sciences* 36, no. 6 (2013): 661–79.

160 **That's how beholden we are to the sunk-cost fallacy:** Interesting to note—and good for late bloomers—older adults are possibly less subject to the sunk-cost fallacy than younger adults: "Older adults were less likely than younger adults to commit the sunk-cost fallacy." JoNell Strough et al., "Are Older Adults Less Subject to the Sunk-Cost Fallacy Than Younger Adults?," *Psychological Science* 19, no. 7 (2008): 650–52.

160 **"Assume that you have spent":** Hal R. Arkes and Peter Ayton, "The Sunk Cost and Concorde Effects: Are Humans Less Rational Than Lower Animals?," *Psychological Bulletin* 125, no. 5 (1999): 591.

161 **"cognitive dissonance":** Dan Ariely in Stephen J. Dubner, "The Upside of Quitting," *Freakonomics* (podcast), http://bit.ly/2x8fxoY. See also Dan Ariely, *Predictably Irrational* (New York: HarperCollins, 2008).

162 **"smart quitters":** Seth Godin, *The Dip: A Little Book That Teaches You When to Quit (and When to Stick)* (New York: Penguin, 2007).

163 **"If I were to say one":** Steven Levitt in Stephen J. Dubner, "The Upside of Quitting," *Freakonomics* (podcast), http://bit.ly/2x8fxoY.

164 **"I've pretty much quit everything":** Levitt in ibid.

164 **"The first thing is you've got":** Arkes in ibid.

CHAPTER 7: THE SUPERPOWER THAT IS SELF-DOUBT

167 **From an evolutionary standpoint, doubt:** Ellen Hendriksen, "Why Everyone Is Insecure (and Why That's Okay)," *Scientific American,* April 12, 2018, http://bit.ly/2D3sdmv.

167 **Self-doubt, therefore, means:** Anthony D. Hermann, Geoffrey J. Leonardelli, and Robert M. Arkin, "Self-Doubt and Self-Esteem: A Threat from Within," *Personality and Social Psychology Bulletin* 28, no. 3 (2002): 395–408.

168 **self-handicapping:** Matthew D. Braslow et al., "Self-Doubt," *Social and Personality Psychology Compass* 6, no. 6 (2012): 470–82. See also Sean M. McCrea, Edward R. Hirt, and Bridgett J. Milner, "She Works Hard for the Money: Valuing Effort Underlies Gender Differences in Behavioral Self-Handicapping," *Journal of Experimental Social Psychology* 44, no. 2 (2008): 292–311; Leah R. Spalding and Curtis D. Hardin, "Unconscious Unease and Self-Handicapping: Behavioral Consequences of Individual Differences in Implicit and Explicit Self-Esteem," *Psychological Science* 10, no. 6 (1999): 535–39.

168 **"other enhancement":** Ibid. See also James A. Shepperd and Robert M. Arkin, "Behavioral Other-Enhancement: Strategically Obscuring the Link Between Performance and Evaluation," *Journal of Personality and Social Psychology* 60, no. 1 (1991): 79.

169 **"stereotype threat":** Ibid. See also Ryan P. Brown and Robert A. Josephs, "A Burden of Proof: Stereotype Relevance and Gender Differences in Math Performance," *Journal of Personality and Social Psychology* 76, no. 2 (1999): 246.

169 **aren't the only psychological approaches:** In facing self-doubt, many people also resort to strategies like overachievement and impostor phenomenon. But the three strategies mentioned in this chapter—self-handicapping, other enhancement, and stereotype threat—seem to be the most widespread for late bloomers. Overachievement, in particular, seems to be an early bloomer strategy.

170 **the smartest and most accomplished physicists:** Joseph C. Hermanowicz, "Scientists and Self-Doubt Across Strata of Academic Science," *Research in Higher Education* 46, no. 3 (2005): 309–26.

170 **"When you get a series of two or three":** Ibid.

171 **"I say to myself, 'I don't know how to act'":** Meryl Streep, interview by Oprah Winfrey, "Oprah Talks to Meryl Streep, Nicole Kidman and Julianne Moore," *O: The Oprah Magazine,* January 2003.

171 **"I have written eleven books":** Maya Angelou quoted in Carl Richards, "Learning to Deal with the Impostor Syndrome," *New York Times*, October 26, 2015.

171 **self-doubt benefits performance:** Tim Woodman et al., "Self-Confidence and Performance: A Little Self-Doubt Helps," *Psychology of Sport and Exercise* 11, no. 6 (2010): 467–70; Deborah L. Feltz and Jared M. Wood, "Can Self-Doubt Be Beneficial to Performance? Exploring the Concept of Preparatory Efficacy," *Open Sports Sciences Journal* 2 (2009): 65–70; Alison Ede, Philip J. Sullivan, and Deborah L. Feltz, "Self-Doubt: Uncertainty as a Motivating Factor on Effort in an Exercise Endurance Task," *Psychology of Sport and Exercise* 28 (2017): 31–36.

173 **In the field of psychology, Albert Bandura is a giant:** Steven J. Haggbloom et al., "The 100 Most Eminent Psychologists of the 20th Century," *Review of General Psychology* 6, no. 2 (2002): 139. See also "Eminent Psychologists of the 20th Century," *Monitor on Psychology* 33, no. 7 (2002): 29.

173 **"the students had to take charge":** M. G. Lindzey and W. M. Runyan, eds., *A History of Psychology in Autobiography*, vol. 9 (American Psychological Association, 2007).

173 **"the content of most textbooks is":** Ibid.

174 **"One morning, I was wasting time":** Ibid.

174 **His 1977 paper:** Albert Bandura, "Self-Efficacy: Toward a Unifying Theory of Behavioral Change," *Psychological Review* 84, no. 2 (1977): 191.

174 **dozens of studies have examined the importance of self-efficacy:** Albert Bandura, "Perceived Self-Efficacy in Cognitive Development and Functioning," *Educational Psychologist* 28, no. 2 (1993): 117–48; Albert Bandura, "Self-Efficacy Mechanism in Human Agency," *American Psychologist* 37, no. 2 (1982): 122; Barry J. Zimmerman, "Self-Efficacy: An Essential Motive to Learn," *Contemporary Educational Psychology* 25, no. 1 (2000): 82–91; Alexander D. Stajkovic and Fred Luthans, "Social Cognitive Theory and Self-Efficacy: Implications for Motivation Theory and Practice," *Motivation and Work Behavior* 126 (2003): 140; Dale H. Schunk, "Self-Efficacy and Academic Motivation," *Educational Psychologist* 26, nos. 3–4 (1991): 207–31; Marilyn E. Gist and Terence R. Mitchell, "Self-Efficacy: A Theoretical Analysis of Its Determinants and Malleability," *Academy of Management Review*

17, no. 2 (1992): 183–211; Frank Pajares, "Self-Efficacy Beliefs in Academic Settings," *Review of Educational Research* 66, no. 4 (1996): 543–78; Icek Ajzen, "Perceived Behavioral Control, Self-Efficacy, Locus of Control, and the Theory of Planned Behavior," *Journal of Applied Social Psychology* 32, no. 4 (2002): 665–83; Karen D. Multon, Steven D. Brown, and Robert W. Lent, "Relation of Self-Efficacy Beliefs to Academic Outcomes: A Meta-Analytic Investigation," *Journal of Counseling Psychology* 38, no. 1 (1991): 30; Barry J. Zimmerman, Albert Bandura, and Manuel Martinez-Pons, "Self-Motivation for Academic Attainment: The Role of Self-Efficacy Beliefs and Personal Goal Setting," *American Educational Research Journal* 29, no. 3 (1992): 663–76; Alexander D. Stajkovic and Fred Luthans, "Self-Efficacy and Work-Related Performance: A Meta-Analysis," *Psychological Bulletin* 124, no. 2 (1998): 240; Ralf Schwarzer, ed., *Self-Efficacy: Thought Control of Action* (New York: Routledge, 2014); Maureen R. Weiss, Diane M. Wiese, and Kimberley A. Klint, "Head over Heels with Success: The Relationship Between Self-Efficacy and Performance in Competitive Youth Gymnastics," *Journal of Sport and Exercise Psychology* 11, no. 4 (1989): 444–51.

175 **denied the two primary sources:** V. S. Ramachandran, *Encyclopedia of Human Behavior* (San Diego, CA: Academic Press, 1994), 4:71–81.

176 **call this little voice self-talk:** James Hardy, "Speaking Clearly: A Critical Review of the Self-Talk Literature," *Psychology of Sport and Exercise* 7, no. 1 (2006): 81–97.

177 **motivational self-talk significantly improved:** Antonis Hatzigeorgiadis et al., "Investigating the Functions of Self-Talk: The Effects of Motivational Self-Talk on Self-Efficacy and Performance in Young Tennis Players," *Sport Psychologist* 22, no. 4 (2008): 458–71; Antonis Hatzigeorgiadis, Yannis Theodorakis, and Nikos Zourbanos, "Self-Talk in the Swimming Pool: The Effects of Self-Talk on Thought Content and Performance on Water-Polo Tasks," *Journal of Applied Sport Psychology* 16, no. 2 (2004): 138–50.

177 **The power of self-talk has been conclusively:** Shahzad Tahmasebi Boroujeni and Mehdi Shahbazi, "The Effect of Instructional and Motivational Self-Talk on Performance of Basketball's Motor Skill," *Procedia—Social and Behavioral Sciences* 15 (2011): 3113–17; Judy L. Van Raalte et al., "Cork! The Effects of Positive and Negative Self-Talk on Dart Throwing Performance," *Journal of Sport Behavior* 18, no. 1

(1995): 50; Jennifer Cumming et al., "Examining the Direction of Imagery and Self-Talk on Dart-Throwing Performance and Self-Efficacy," *Sport Psychologist* 20, no. 3 (2006): 257–74; Antonis Hatzigeorgiadis et al., "Self-Talk and Sports Performance: A Meta-Analysis," *Perspectives on Psychological Science* 6, no. 4 (2011): 348–56; Judy L. Van Raalte et al., "The Relationship Between Observable Self-Talk and Competitive Junior Tennis Players' Match Performances," *Journal of Sport and Exercise Psychology* 16, no. 4 (1994): 400–15; Christopher P. Neck et al., " 'I Think I Can; I Think I Can': A Self-Leadership Perspective Toward Enhancing Entrepreneur Thought Patterns, Self-Efficacy, and Performance," *Journal of Managerial Psychology* 14, no. 6 (1999): 477–501; Antonis Hatzigeorgiadis et al., "Investigating the Functions of Self-Talk: The Effects of Motivational Self-Talk on Self-Efficacy and Performance in Young Tennis Players," *Sport Psychologist* 22, no. 4 (2008): 458–71; Eleni Zetou et al., "The Effect of Self-Talk in Learning the Volleyball Service Skill and Self-Efficacy Improvement," *Journal of Sport and Human Exercise* 7, no. 4 (2012): 794-805; Chris P. Neck and Charles C. Manz, "Thought Self-Leadership: The Influence of Self-Talk and Mental Imagery on Performance," *Journal of Organizational Behavior* 13, no. 7 (1992): 681–99; Robert Weinberg, Robert Grove, and Allen Jackson, "Strategies for Building Self-Efficacy in Tennis Players: A Comparative Analysis of Australian and American Coaches," *Sport Psychologist* 6, no. 1 (1992): 3–13; Daniel Gould et al., "An Exploratory Examination of Strategies Used by Elite Coaches to Enhance Self-Efficacy in Athletes," *Journal of Sport and Exercise Psychology* 11, no. 2 (1989): 128–40.

179 *Why am I so scared?*: Elizabeth Bernstein, " 'Self Talk': When Talking to Yourself, the Way You Do It Makes a Difference," *Wall Street Journal*, May 5, 2014; Kristin Wong, "The Benefits of Talking to Yourself," *New York Times*, June 8, 2017. See also Ethan Kross et al., "Self-Talk as a Regulatory Mechanism: How You Do It Matters," *Journal of Personality and Social Psychology* 106, no. 2 (2014): 304.

179 **"it allows them to give themselves objective"**: Bernstein, " 'Self Talk.' "

180 **"Persuasive boosts in perceived"**: Bandura, "Self-Efficacy: Toward a Unifying Theory of Behavioral Change"; Bandura, "Self-Efficacy Mechanism in Human Agency."

180 **according to Bandura:** Ramachandran, *Encyclopedia of Human Behavior*.

180 **"framing"**: Amy C. Edmondson, "Framing for Learning: Lessons in Successful Technology Implementation," *California Management Review* 45, no. 2 (2003): 34–54. See also Amos Tversky and Daniel Kahneman, "The Framing of Decisions and the Psychology of Choice," *Science* 211, no. 4481 (1981): 453–58.

181 **we can use cognitive frames to shape**: Robert M. Entman, "Framing: Toward Clarification of a Fractured Paradigm," *Journal of Communication* 43, no. 4 (1993): 51–58; Robert D. Benford and David A. Snow, "Framing Processes and Social Movements: An Overview and Assessment," *Annual Review of Sociology* 26, no. 1 (2000): 611–39; George Lakoff, "Simple Framing," *Rockridge Institute* 14 (2006).

181 **framing anxiety as excitement**: Alison Wood Brooks, "Get Excited: Reappraising Pre-Performance Anxiety as Excitement," *Journal of Experimental Psychology: General* 143, no. 3 (2014): 1144.

181 **we can change our frames**: Maxie C. Maultsby, Jr., *Rational Behavior Therapy* (Appleton, WI: Rational, 1990).

182 **two contrasting alternatives**: Carol S. Dweck and Ellen L. Leggett, "A Social-Cognitive Approach to Motivation and Personality," *Psychological Review* 95, no. 2 (1988): 256.

183 **effectively reframing challenges**: Amy C. Edmondson, *Teaming: How Organizations Learn, Innovate, and Compete in the Knowledge Economy* (Hoboken, NJ: John Wiley & Sons, 2012); Amy C. Edmondson, Richard M. Bohmer, and Gary P. Pisano, "Disrupted Routines: Team Learning and New Technology Implementation in Hospitals," *Administrative Science Quarterly* 46, no. 4 (2001): 685–716; Chris Argyris and Donald A. Schön, "Organizational Learning: A Theory of Action Perspective," *Reis*, nos. 77–78 (1997): 345–48.

185 **increased self-compassion**: Laura K. Barnard and John F. Curry, "Self-Compassion: Conceptualizations, Correlates, and Interventions," *Review of General Psychology* 15, no. 4 (2011): 289.

185 **"In general, these studies suggest"**: Mark R. Leary et al., "Self-Compassion and Reactions to Unpleasant Self-Relevant Events: The Implications of Treating Oneself Kindly," *Journal of Personality and Social Psychology* 92, no. 5 (2007): 887.

185 **closely associated with emotional resilience**: Laura K. Barnard and John F. Curry, "Self-Compassion: Conceptualizations, Correlates, and Interventions," *Review of General Psychology* 15, no. 4 (2011): 289.

185 **correlated with measures of emotional well-being:** Kristin D. Neff, Stephanie S. Rude, and Kristin L. Kirkpatrick, "An Examination of Self-Compassion in Relation to Positive Psychological Functioning and Personality Traits," *Journal of Research in Personality* 41, no. 4 (2007): 908–16; Filip Raes, "The Effect of Self-Compassion on the Development of Depression Symptoms in a Non-Clinical Sample," *Mindfulness* 2, no. 1 (2011): 33–36.

186 **self-compassion enhances motivation:** Juliana G. Breines and Serena Chen, "Self-Compassion Increases Self-Improvement Motivation," *Personality and Social Psychology Bulletin* 38, no. 9 (2012): 1133–43; Jeannetta G. Williams, Shannon K. Stark, and Erica E. Foster, "Start Today or the Very Last Day? The Relationships Among Self-Compassion, Motivation, and Procrastination," *American Journal of Psychological Research* 4, no. 1 (2008).

186 **"When you're in the trenches":** Kristin Neff, "The Space Between Self-Esteem and Self-Compassion: Kristin Neff at TEDx Centennial-ParkWomen," *YouTube,* February 6, 2013, http://bit.ly/2xyNLRV.

186 **"Self-compassion is treating yourself":** Kristin Wong, "Why Self-Compassion Beats Self-Confidence," *New York Times*, December 28, 2017.

188 **Global consultancies like McKinsey & Company:** Robert I. Sutton, "Why Good Bosses Tune In to Their People," *McKinsey Quarterly*, August 2010, https://mck.co/2MONArc; Antonio Feser, Nicolai Nielsen, and Michael Rennie, "What's Missing in Leadership Development?," *McKinsey Quarterly*, August 2017, https://mck.co/2PPw08f; Bernadette Dillon and Juliet Bourke, "The Six Signature Traits of Inclusive Leadership: Thriving in a Diverse New World," DeLoitte Insights, April 14, 2016, http://bit.ly/2OC9a3Y.

CHAPTER 8: SLOW TO GROW? REPOT YOURSELF
IN A BETTER GARDEN

190 **"crab pot syndrome":** Carliss D. Miller, "A Phenomenological Analysis of the Crabs in the Barrel Syndrome," *Academy of Management Proceedings* 2015, no. 1 (2015); Carliss D. Miller, "The Crabs in a Barrel Syndrome: Structural Influence on Competitive Behavior," *Academy of Management Proceedings* 2014, no. 1. (2014).

190 **"Status has more or less":** Tom Wolfe quoted in David A. Price, "Where Tom Wolfe Got His Status Obsession," *Nieman Storyboard*, July 5, 2016, http://bit.ly/2xbQdh6.

191 **"Are you an extrovert or":** Todd Rose, *The End of Average: How We Succeed in a World That Values Sameness* (New York: HarperCollins, 2015).

193 **decrease in geographic mobility:** Richard Fry, "Americans Are Moving at Historically Low Rates, in Part Because Millennials Are Staying Put," Pew Research Center, February 13, 2017, https://pewrsr .ch/2DdAXX2.

194 **"Could I have written a book":** Kimberly Harrington, interview by author, 2018.

195 **less emphasis on person-to-job fit:** Daniel M. Cable and Timothy A. Judge, "Person-Organization Fit, Job Choice Decisions, and Organizational Entry," *Organizational Behavior and Human Decision Processes* 67, no. 3 (1996): 294–311.

196 **some people are naturally hardy:** Susan Cain, *Quiet: The Power of Introverts in a World That Can't Stop Talking* (New York: Broadway Books, 2013).

196 **"high-reactive" babies:** Jerome Kagan, *Galen's Prophecy: Temperament in Human Nature* (New York: Basic Books, 1998).

196 **more likely to suffer from depression:** David Dobbs, "The Science of Success," *Atlantic*, December 2009, http://bit.ly/2pc8tmS. For Belsky's work, see Jay Belsky et al., "Vulnerability Genes or Plasticity Genes?," *Molecular Psychiatry* 14, no. 8 (2009): 746; Michael Pluess and Jay Belsky, "Differential Susceptibility to Rearing Experience: The Case of Childcare," *Journal of Child Psychology and Psychiatry* 50, no. 4 (2009): 396–404; Michael Pluess and Jay Belsky, "Differential Susceptibility to Parenting and Quality Child Care," *Developmental Psychology* 46, no. 2 (2010): 379; and Jay Belsky and Michael Pluess, "Beyond Diathesis Stress: Differential Susceptibility to Environmental Influences," *Psychological Bulletin* 135, no. 6 (2009): 885.

198 **Quentin Hardy, a former colleague:** Hardy was Forbes Media's San Francisco bureau chief in the early 2000s.

200 **"The real work of Saddleback":** Rick Warren, interview by author, 2004.

200 **people who can identify more closely:** Hal E. Hershfield et al., "Increasing Saving Behavior Through Age-Progressed Renderings of the

Future Self," *Journal of Marketing Research* 48 (2011): S23–S37; Hal Ersner Hershfield et al., "Don't Stop Thinking About Tomorrow: Individual Differences in Future Self-Continuity Account for Saving," *Judgment and Decision Making* 4, no. 4 (2009): 280; Hal Ersner Hershfield, G. Elliott Wimmer, and Brian Knutson, "Saving for the Future Self: Neural Measures of Future Self-Continuity Predict Temporal Discounting," *Social Cognitive and Affective Neuroscience* 4, no. 1 (2008): 85–92; Hal E. Hershfield, "Future Self-Continuity: How Conceptions of the Future Self Transform Intertemporal Choice," *Annals of the New York Academy of Sciences* 1235, no. 1 (2011): 30–43; Hal E. Hershfield, Taya R. Cohen, and Leigh Thompson, "Short Horizons and Tempting Situations: Lack of Continuity to Our Future Selves Leads to Unethical Decision Making and Behavior," *Organizational Behavior and Human Decision Processes* 117, no. 2 (2012): 298–310; Jean-Louis Van Gelder et al., "Friends with My Future Self: Longitudinal Vividness Intervention Reduces Delinquency," *Criminology* 53, no. 2 (2015): 158–79.

200 **achieving an important goal:** Peter M. Gollwitzer, "When Intentions Go Public: Does Social Reality Widen the Intention-Behavior Gap?," *Psychological Science* 20, no. 5 (2009): 612–18.

201 **An ex-marine:** "Frederick W. Smith," FedEx, n.d., http://bit.ly /2QsDfUH.

201 **Richard Branson's companies:** Branson and Virgin are refreshingly candid about Virgin businesses that failed and were abandoned. Jack Preston, "Six Memorable Virgin Fails," Virgin, January 18, 2016, http://bit.ly/2MsUH8H.

201 **Diane Greene, who co-founded:** D. Connor, "Diane Greene, the Humble Executive," *Network World*, December 26, 2005, http://bit.ly /2CSlMlX.

202 **Amazon founder and CEO Jeff Bezos:** Denise Lee Yohn, "Company Culture Doesn't Need to Be 'Warm and Fuzzy' to Be Effective," *Quartz@Work*, March 13, 2018, http://bit.ly/2MsDJHs.

202 **goal commitment is the key:** There are literally dozens (if not hundreds) of studies on various aspects of goal commitment, ranging from individual to team goal commitment, to its effects on achievement and on finances. Here's just a small sampling: Edwin A. Locke, Gary P. Latham, and Miriam Erez, "The Determinants of Goal Commitment," *Academy of Management Review* 13, no. 1 (1988): 23–39;

John R. Hollenbeck and Howard J. Klein, "Goal Commitment and the Goal-Setting Process: Problems, Prospects, and Proposals for Future Research," *Journal of Applied Psychology* 72, no. 2 (1987): 212; Howard J. Klein et al., "Goal Commitment and the Goal-Setting Process: Conceptual Clarification and Empirical Synthesis," *Journal of Applied Psychology* 84, no. 6 (1999): 885; John R. Hollenbeck et al., "Investigation of the Construct Validity of a Self-Report Measure of Goal Commitment," *Journal of Applied Psychology* 74, no. 6 (1989): 951; Howard J. Klein and Jay S. Kim, "A Field Study of the Influence of Situational Constraints, Leader-Member Exchange, and Goal Commitment on Performance," *Academy of Management Journal* 41, no. 1 (1998): 88–95; Vincent K. Chong and Kar Ming Chong, "Budget Goal Commitment and Informational Effects of Budget Participation on Performance: A Structural Equation Modeling Approach," *Behavioral Research in Accounting* 14, no. 1 (2002): 65–86; Jerry C. Wofford, Vicki L. Goodwin, and Steven Premack, "Meta-Analysis of the Antecedents of Personal Goal Level and of the Antecedents and Consequences of Goal Commitment," *Journal of Management* 18, no. 3 (1992): 595–615; Howard J. Klein and Paul W. Mulvey, "Two Investigations of the Relationships Among Group Goals, Goal Commitment, Cohesion, and Performance," *Organizational Behavior and Human Decision Processes* 61, no. 1 (1995): 44–53; Caroline Aubé and Vincent Rousseau, "Team Goal Commitment and Team Effectiveness: The Role of Task Interdependence and Supportive Behaviors," *Group Dynamics: Theory, Research, and Practice* 9, no. 3 (2005): 189; and Gabriele Oettingen et al., "Mental Contrasting and Goal Commitment: The Mediating Role of Energization," *Personality and Social Psychology Bulletin* 35, no. 5 (2009): 608–22.

203 **"We have to modify our identities":** Rebecca Webber, "Reinvent Yourself," *Psychology Today,* May 2014.

203 **"Even at sixty":** Ravenna Helson, "A Longitudinal Study of Creative Personality in Women," *Creativity Research Journal* 12, no. 2 (1999): 89–101.

CHAPTER 9: LATE BLOOMERS: THE LONG RUN

204 **Geraldine Weiss knows:** "How to Invest Like . . . Geraldine Weiss, the Queen of Blue Chip Dividends," *Telegraph,* September 18, 2017.

208 **stories can change the way we think:** Jonathan Gottschall, *The Storytelling Animal: How Stories Make Us Human* (Boston: Houghton Mifflin Harcourt, 2012); Jonathan Gottschall, "Why Fiction Is Good for You," *Boston Globe*, April 29, 2012.

209 **Theodore Sarbin:** Theodore R. Sarbin, "The Narrative as Root Metaphor for Psychology," in T. R. Sarbin, ed., *Narrative Psychology: The Storied Nature of Human Conduct* (New York: Praeger, 1986); Theodore R. Sarbin, "The Narrative Quality of Action," *Theoretical and Philosophical Psychology* 10, no. 2 (1990): 49–65; Theodore R. Sarbin, "The Poetics of Identity," *Theory and Psychology* 7, no. 1 (1997): 67–82; Joseph De Rivera and Theodore R. Sarbin, eds., *Believed-In Imaginings: The Narrative Construction of Reality* (Washington, DC: American Psychological Association, 1998); Theodore R. Sarbin, "Embodiment and the Narrative Structure of Emotional Life," *Narrative Inquiry* 11, no. 1 (2001): 217–25.

209 **Jerome Bruner:** Jerome S. Bruner, *Acts of Meaning* (Cambridge, MA: Harvard University Press, 1990); Jerome S. Bruner, *Actual Minds, Possible Worlds* (Cambridge, MA: Harvard University Press, 2009).

209 **Dan McAdams:** Dan P. McAdams, *Power, Intimacy, and the Life Story: Personological Inquiries into Identity* (New York: Guilford Press, 1988); Dan P. McAdams and E. D. de St. Aubin, "A Theory of Generativity and Its Assessment Through Self-Report, Behavioral Acts, and Narrative Themes in Autobiography," *Journal of Personality and Social Psychology* 62, no. 6 (1992): 1003; Dan P. McAdams, *The Stories We Live By: Personal Myths and the Making of the Self* (New York: Guilford Press, 1993); Dan P. McAdams, "Personality, Modernity, and the Storied Self: A Contemporary Framework for Studying Persons," *Psychological Inquiry* 7, no. 4 (1996): 295–321; Dan P. McAdams, "The Psychology of Life Stories," *Review of General Psychology* 5, no. 2 (2001): 100; Dan P. McAdams, "Personal Narratives and the Life Story," in *Handbook of Personality: Theory and Research*, ed. Oliver P. John, Richard W. Robins, and Lawrence A. Pervin, 3rd ed. (New York: Guilford Press, 2008): 242–62; Dan P. McAdams, "The Psychological Self as Actor, Agent, and Author," *Perspectives on Psychological Science* 8, no. 3 (2013): 272–95.

209 **correlated with a breakdown in story:** Sigmund Freud, *The Interpretation of Dreams: The Complete and Definitive Text*, trans. and ed. James Strachey (New York: Basic Books, 2010); Sigmund Freud, *The*

Standard Edition of the Complete Psychological Works of Sigmund Freud, trans. and ed. James Strachey (London: Hogarth Press, 1953). See also Donald P. Spence, "Narrative Truth and Theoretical Truth," *Psychoanalytic Quarterly* 51, no. 1 (1982): 43–69.

210 **characteristics like "aggressive":** Michael Murray, "Narrative Psychology and Narrative Analysis," in *Qualitative Research in Psychology: Expanding Perspectives in Methodology and Design,* ed. Paul M. Camic, Jean E. Rhodes, and Lucy Yardley (Washington, DC: American Psychological Association, 2003).

210 **Paul Ricoeur, a French philosopher:** Paul Ricoeur, "Life in Quest of Narrative," in *On Paul Ricoeur: Narrative and Interpretation* (London: Routledge, 1991). See also Michele L. Crossley, *Introducing Narrative Psychology: Self, Trauma, and the Construction of Meaning* (Philadelphia: Open University Press, 2000); and Michele L. Crossley, "Narrative Psychology, Trauma and the Study of Self/Identity," *Theory and Psychology* 10, no. 4 (2000): 527–46.

210 **Dozens of studies:** James W. Pennebaker and Janel D. Seagal, "Forming a Story: The Health Benefits of Narrative," *Journal of Clinical Psychology* 55, no. 10 (1999): 1243–54.

211 **a story doesn't have to be true:** Keith Oatley, *Such Stuff as Dreams: The Psychology of Fiction* (Hoboken, NJ: John Wiley & Sons, 2011); Raymond A. Mar and Keith Oatley, "The Function of Fiction Is the Abstraction and Simulation of Social Experience," *Perspectives on Psychological Science* 3, no. 3 (2008): 173–92; Keith Oatley, "A Taxonomy of the Emotions of Literary Response and a Theory of Identification in Fictional Narrative," *Poetics* 23, no. 1 (1994): 53–74; Keith Oatley, "Why Fiction May Be Twice as True as Fact: Fiction as Cognitive and Emotional Simulation," *Review of General Psychology* 3, no. 2 (1999): 101; Raymond A. Mar, "The Neuropsychology of Narrative: Story Comprehension, Story Production and Their Interrelation," *Neuropsychologia* 42, no. 10 (2004): 1414–34; Raymond A. Mar, "The Neural Bases of Social Cognition and Story Comprehension," *Annual Review of Psychology* 62 (2011): 103–34.

212 **"You seek your destiny":** Howard Suber, *The Power of Film* (Michael Wiese Productions, 2006).

213 **Our level of persistence isn't fixed:** Angela L. Duckworth, *Grit: The Power of Passion and Perseverance* (New York: Scribner's, 2016); Angela L. Duckworth et al., "Grit: Perseverance and Passion for Long-

Term Goals," *Journal of Personality and Social Psychology* 92, no. 6 (2007): 1087.

214 **One reason:** Ibid.

214 **"We rise to the occasion":** Ibid.

216 **Purposeful people are significantly more motivated:** Ibid.

216 **"I was finally ready for":** D. Connor, "Diane Greene, the Humble Executive," *Network World*, December 26, 2005, http://bit.ly/2NIAqk6.

217 **"The secret to life is to put":** Susan Cain, *Quiet: The Power of Introverts in a World That Can't Stop Talking* (New York: Broadway Books, 2013).

218 **"I was always a late bloomer as a kid":** Kimberly Harrington, interview by author, 2018.

EPILOGUE

226 **The median compensation package at Facebook:** Rob Price, "The Median Salary at Facebook Is More than $240,000 per Year," *Business Insider*, April 17, 2018.

226 **Google pays:** Estimate is the author's, based on $120,000 base salary, $30,000 bonus, and the first year of a four-year vesting of stock options.

· Acknowledgments

The idea for *Late Bloomers*, baking in my head for decades, finally came to life in 2014 when I wrote down my history of slow blooming from roughly ages twelve to twenty-seven. I wrote it over a Memorial Day weekend, and it came to about six thousand words, or about 7 percent of what you hold in your hands. How does one go from such a ragged start to a book?

Answer: with a lot of help and encouragement. At the top of the list is Jeff Leeson, whom I think of as this book's managing editor and coauthor. I had worked with Jeff before on a corporate culture book called *The Soft Edge*. His contributions were enormously valuable in helping organize a bundle of thoughts into a structured narrative and digging up research that would support *The Soft Edge* thesis about why some companies were able to thrive for decades.

For *Late Bloomers*, Jeff was even more involved and helpful. While I'm by nature a conceptual thinker and collector of stories and anecdotes, Jeff is an architect. He has a disciplined sense of what works and doesn't in a manuscript, what's too loose or tight, what drives the narrative and what derails it, and where research is needed to lend authority to a point. I could have steered *Late Bloomers* into blind alleys right and left, but Jeff kept it going. He and his wife, Rachel, now run a high-level publishing consulting service out of Minneapolis called Benson-Collister. If you need the very best professional service of that kind, look them up.

Super agent Todd Shuster of Aevitas Creative, within a month of receiving our proposal, was able to get eight offers for *Late Bloomers*.

That was an astonishing display of Todd's stature in the book world. His colleagues Chelsey Heller and Justin Brouckaert are similarly amazing. Roger Scholl, who edits the Crown Currency imprint at Penguin Random House provided the winning offer, along with an incredible level of enthusiasm and tactical advice. I want to salute the entire Currency team devoted to the success of *Late Bloomers*: Tina Constable, Ayelet Gruenspecht, Nicole McArdle, Megan Perritt, Campbell Wharton, Erin Little, and Jayme Boucher. Mark Fortier of Fortier Public Relations is a superstar, as is teammate Lauren Kuhn. Nancy Rosa and Lior Taylor were invaluable in the launch of *Late Bloomers*, as were Ken Gillett and his fine team at Target Marketing. Writers Michael S. Malone (my coauthor on a 2015 book called *Team Genius*), Susan Salter Reynolds, and Nic Albert made valuable contributions along the way. Additionally, Elizabeth Gravitt provided essential research and fact-checking support.

I would like to thank my colleagues at Forbes Media where I have been employed for twenty-seven years. In particular, Steve Forbes for his early and ongoing interest in this book, Forbes CEO Mike Federle, Forbes Asia CEO Will Adamopoulos, Randall Lane, Moira Forbes, Mark Howard, Mike Perlis, Sherry Philips, Jessica Sibley, Tom Davis, and Janett Haas. Additionally I'd like to thank Shari Rosen and Julia Mart of Interconnect-Events, Jo Ann Jenkins, Jonathan Stevens, Ramsey Laine Alwin and Staci Alexander of AARP, Bob Daugherty and Ray Powers of the Forbes School of Business and Technology, Greg Tehven of Fargo TEDx, Stanford University's Tom Byers, and friends Mark and Donnamarie Mills and Bob and Deborah Schueren for their early support, close reads, and invaluable advice. Same goes for old friends Dr. Bruce Perry and Dr. Jeffrey Prater.

Keppler Speakers has represented me since 2016 and I would like to thank the entire gang, including Ronda Estridge, Gary McManis, John Truran, Jay Callahan, Jay Conklin, Chris Clifford, Nathan Thompson, Joel Gheesling, Jeff Gilley, Alison Goehring, Kelly Skibbie, Jared Schaubert, Theo Moll, Joel Murphy, Warren Jones, Patrick Snead, Randy Ehman, and Jim and Debbie Keppler. Also a shout-out to Tony

D'Amelio, Mike Humphrey, David Lavin, Danny Stern, Mark French, Christine Farrell, Katrina Smith, and other agents who've helped build my speaking career.

Several trusting souls allowed themselves to be interviewed for *Late Bloomers*, including Leonard Sax, Jean Courtney, Scott Kelly, Carol Dweck, Stuart Smith, Vera Koo, Kimberly Harrington, Jerry Bowyer, Pontish Yeramyan, Ken Fisher, Tess Reynolds, Daniel James Brown, Carol Cohen Fishman, Dr. Richard Karl, Joe Rainey, Elkhonon Goldberg, Beth Kawasaki, Erik Wahl, Adriane Brown, and dozens of others. Not all interviewees made it into the book, so I doubly thank those generous people.

I would be remiss if I didn't mention a handful of books that inspired *Late Bloomers*, including *Quiet* by Susan Cain, *The End of Average* by Todd Rose, *The End of Work* by John Tamny, *Ungifted* by Scott Barry Kaufman, *Shoe Dog* by Phil Knight, *Grit* by Angela Duckworth, *Boys Adrift* and *Girls on the Edge* by Leonard Sax, *Mindset* by Carol Dweck, *The Obstacle Is the Way* by Ryan Holiday, *Emerging Adulthood* by Jeffrey Arnett, *Originals* by Adam Grant, *The Alchemist* by Paul Coelho, *Hillbilly Elegy* by J. D. Vance, *Creativity* by Elkhonon Goldberg, *Drive* by Dan Pink, and *The Big Test* by Nicholas Lemann. Great works, all.

My wife, Marji, a late-blooming ballet dancer and watercolorist, is a deep well of cogent editorial advice and inspiration, along with our children, Katie and Peter, and my accomplished siblings, Mary Karlgaard Burnton and Joe Karlgaard. As I was slogging through my slow-blooming years in junior and senior high school, my mother, Pat, was my most devoted supporter. And finally an acknowledgment of my late father, Dick, and sister, Liz, who are not here to read *Late Bloomers*. Wish you were.

ABOUT THE AUTHOR

Rich Karlgaard is the publisher and futurist at Forbes Media, where he has worked for twenty-seven years and writes about technology, the economy, business, and human development. His previous books include *Life 2.0*, *The Soft Edge*, and *Team Genius* (cowritten with Michael S. Malone). Karlgaard is a cofounder of *Upside* magazine, Garage Technology Partners, and Silicon Valley's premier public business forum, the 7,500-member Churchill Club. For the latter, he won a Northern California Ernst & Young Entrepreneur of the Year Award. Karlgaard lives in Silicon Valley, but travels extensively around the world on business.